T0301991

INCLUSIVE LEADERSHIP

This book reflects on the models of leadership espoused by ancient Indic traditions, in particular the Advaita Vedanta tradition. Focusing primarily on the Rajarshi—'the philosopher king'—the essays in this volume showcase how using these models in contemporary society could lead to the creation of self-aware and empathic leaders and an inclusive society.

The book explores examples of the Brahmarshi, or the wise scholar; Rajarshi, or the wise ruler; and Devarshi, or the visionary, to bring together all the ideal virtues of inclusive leadership in the current cultural and political space. The essays in the volume adopt a critical sociological, philosophical and management lens to analyse Indic traditions and dharmic concepts. The volume uses concepts such as dharma, karma and yoga, along with organisational psychology, technology, and management, to arrive at the concept of transcendental leadership. It theorises new definitions of the Rajarshi ideal, which can be used towards public service, social transformation and self-discovery.

The volume will be useful for scholars and academics interested in Indic philosophies of leadership and governance, sociology, and social and political inclusivity. It will also be useful for readers in public administration, business and management.

Swami Bodhananda is a well-known Management Guru, Chairman of the Sambodh Foundation, India; Bodhananda Research Foundation for Management & Leadership Studies, India; The Sambodh Society, Inc., USA; and The Sambodh Center for Human Excellence, Michigan, USA.

Tilak Agerwala has recently retired as Vice President of Data Centric Systems for IBM Research. He is currently an IBM Emeritus and an Adjunct Professor with the National Institute of Advanced Studies, Indian Institute of Science Campus, Bangalore, India.

Sangeetha Menon is Professor and Head of the Consciousness Studies Programme at the National Institute of Advanced Studies, Indian Institute of Science Campus, Bangalore, India.

'The book presents an altogether new idea on the subject of leadership. Swami Bodhananda has proposed that the "Rajarshi" model of leadership will be a leadership of virtues in action. A leader in this model will be democratic, committed and without greed for personal gratification. The personality of such a leader is characterized by sense control, humility and self-knowledge. He works for common good. He does ordinary things in extraordinary ways. He functions in an optimal manner, drawing from his resources of intelligence (IQ), emotions (EQ) and consciousness (CQ). He acts happily rather than doing actions for happiness. In an increasingly complex world, flooded with an overload of information and data, a Rajarshi wins without defeating. His strategy consists of conciliation, mediation, negotiation, persuasion and consensus. He is an exemplary leader as Krishna says in the Bhagavat Gita (3.21). A reader of this book will feel inspired to reflect deeply on how to participate in the development process for the benefit of all.'

Surendra S Yadav, Professor, Department of Management Studies, IIT Delhi, and Editor-in-Chief, *Journal of Advances in Management Research*, UK

'In a fast and ever-changing world, "numbers" are getting to matter more than "members". Leaders are getting more painfully myopic and startlingly untrustworthy. This shortsightedness is leading to rapid deterioration of human values of "Love and Recognition". The book, through all its chapters, addresses the inclusive model of leadership that focuses on interplay between Humans, Machines and Environment as a global family. There can be no better foundation than the philosophical foundation of Advaita Vedanta as meta-theory enunciated by Swami Bodhananda. The transcendental leadership model, which is the need for sustainable tomorrow, is clearly enunciated as self-less action leadership, with consensual decision-making process for the economic, social, and environmental factors. This emphasizes on moving beyond a singular focus on Profit, to a multiple focus on Profits, People, and Planet. This is a must-read book for those wanting to transform themselves to tomorrow's leaders'.

M Krishna is a business leader with over 20 years' experience on the Executive Boards of diverse global multinationals like Eaton India, Dresser Valves, Concentric Pumps, Invensys, and Master Fluids. He is credited with over 3 successful green field projects in India and China.

'As written in Chapter 2 of this book by Swami Bodhananda, Rajarshi is happily active, not active for happiness. This is the definition of a quintessential great leader that the world thirsts for. Throughout this book each element of the Rajarshi model of leadership is explained in theory and practice by an accomplished group of scholars, managers and leaders. The world we live in is constantly changing with ever-increasing and compounding challenges. The book recognizes this and expounds on how the Rajarshi model of leadership can deal with these challenges. This is a must reading for all aspiring and committed managers and leaders in private and public organizations, not only in India but throughout the world.'

Dr. Gopal Singh, Executive, Eaton Corporation (retired) and Board Member, Singh Family Foundation and JSM Trust

INCLUSIVE LEADERSHIP

Perspectives from Tradition and Modernity

Edited by Swami Bodhananda, Tilak Agerwala and Sangeetha Menon

Routledge
Taylor & Francis Group

LONDON AND NEW YORK

First published 2020 by Routledge

2 Park Square, Milton Park, Abingdon, Oxon OX14 4RN

605 Third Avenue, New York, NY 10017

Routledge is an imprint of the Taylor & Francis Group, an informa business

First issued in paperback 2021

Publisher's Note
The publisher has gone to great lengths to ensure the quality of this reprint but points out that some imperfections in the original copies may be apparent.

British Library Cataloguing-in-Publication Data
A catalogue record for this book is available from the British Library

Library of Congress Cataloging-in-Publication Data
A catalog record for this book has been requested

ISBN: 978-1-138-71655-1 (hbk)
ISBN: 978-1-03-217697-0 (pbk)
DOI: 10.4324/9780367808273

Typeset in Sabon
by Apex CoVantage, LLC

CONTENTS

CONTENTS

CONTRIBUTORS

Tilak Agerwala is an IBM Emeritus, Adjunct Associate Professor, PACE University, New York; Adjunct Professor at the National Institute for Advanced Studies, Bangalore; and Member, TKMA Consulting. His interests are applying data-driven approaches and advanced computing technologies to world-class science and engineering and the workforce of the future, including education and leadership development. In his IBM career, spanning 35 years, Tilak held executive positions in research, strategy, advanced development, marketing, and business development. Tilak was part of and led teams that developed and brought to the market technologies and systems for high-performance computing.

Anuradha Balaram has developed an expertise in writing economic policy briefs, appraising public projects and implementing government projects after 30 years as a member of the Indian Economic Service. After seeking voluntary retirement, she devotes her time on ensuring that children get the right values. She has a team of 80 people all over India who are determined to ensure that children and the youth of India discover their immense potential through free and responsible choices. Schoolchildren today do not have time to reflect on who they are and what they want to do in life. It has been heartening to see seeds of transformation in the mindset of the children of over 4,200 schools that are part of this programme all over the country. A member of the Board of Governors, IIM Indore, she lectures on a variety of contemporary economic issues and on the assimilation of values.

Swami Bodhananda is a well-known management guru and a pioneer in leadership studies. He is the Spiritual Director and Chairman/President of Sambodh institutions in India and the USA, such as The Sambodh Society, Inc., USA and Sambodh Foundation India. He is the Founder Chairman of the Bodhananda Research Foundation for Management & Leadership Studies, a pioneer research establishment on management studies. In Michigan, USA, he heads and guides a unique institution devoted to interfaith dialogue, healing systems and Vedanta: The Sambodh Centre for Human Excellence. He teaches Advaita Vedanta, Yogasutras, Bhagavad Gita, Upanishads, and scores of other texts of the Vedanta and Indian philosophical traditions. He is the author of many popular titles, like *Gita and Management* (1994) and *Indian Management and Leadership (2007)*.

B.P. Mathur is a former member of the Indian Audit & Accounts service (IA&AS) and has held the post of Deputy Comptroller & Auditor General, Additional Secretary and Financial Adviser, Ministry of Steel & Mines, Joint Secretary and Additional Financial Adviser, Ministry of Defence and Accountant General, Maharashtra. He has also served as an Adviser with the Government of Afghanistan. In a brief stint as Director of the National Institute of Financial Management, he also was a visiting faculty member of the Bajaj Institute of Management, Bombay and Punjab University, Chandigarh. He holds a PhD and DLitt degree in economics from the University of Allahabad. He has written several books and a large number of articles on governance, public finance and economics-related issues, besides two novels in Hindi. He is currently engaged as a spiritual seeker, author and social activist.

Sangeetha Menon is Professor and Head of the NIAS Consciousness Studies Programme and the Dean of School of Humanities at the National Institute of Advanced Studies, in the Indian Institute of Science campus, Bangalore. Her major area of research is in the philosophy of psychology and her expertise lies in Indian philosophy, consciousness studies, philosophy of psychology, and the philosophy and psychology of self. She works with colleagues and collaborators in India and across the world in creating and encouraging a first-person centred approach to understanding consciousness and cognitive capabilities that favours experiential well-being. Dr. Menon's professional qualifications include degrees in biology and philosophy. Her recent works include *Brain, Self and Consciousness: Explaining the Conspiracy of Experience* (2014); *Interdisciplinary Perspectives on Consciousness and the Self* (2014); and *Self, Culture and Consciousness: Interdisciplinary Convergences on Knowing and Being* (2018).

R. Narayanan is a mathematician who has contributed to software development in the domains of molecular biophysics and space mechanics. He headed the Software Quality Assurance Division of the Indian Space Research Organization's Trivandrum Centre. Later, as Vice President of Tata Consultancy Services, he headed the company's Global Learning & Development efforts. Having held significant positions in IEEE (Kerala), Computer Society of India (Trivandrum) and Program Committee of the Conference on Software Engineering Education and Training, he has also published several technical and popular papers, and has coauthored *Management and Mahabharata (2017)* with Swami Bodhananda.

Deepti Navaratna is a Bangalore-based neuroscientist and musician. She is currently serving as the Executive Director of the Indira Gandhi National Centre for the Arts, Bengaluru. As an accomplished South Indian classical musician, Deepti has presented her work at the Symphony Space and Asia Society, New York; Museum of Fine Arts, Boston; Yale School of Music, New Haven; and Harvard Arts Museum, Cambridge, among others. She has contributed to many national and international journals and has participated in a number of conferences and seminars.

Radhakrishnan Pillai is the Director of the SPM Foundation and Founder Director of Atma Darshan, a spiritual tourism company. With a PhD in philosophy, he has 25 years of combined working and business experience as a well-known management speaker, trainer, author, and consultant and has also hosted a radio show, 'Ask Chanakya', on the Moksha Channel of Worldspace satellite radio. He has represented India in various national and international conferences, including the World Congress of Philosophy in Athens, Greece; Academy of Management in San Antonio, Texas, USA; and the Indian Philosophical Congress. He chaired a session at Afro-Asian Philosophical Congress and taught in Germany (Heidelberg and Cologne Universities), Dubai, Muscat, Singapore, Indonesia, and the UK (Oxford and Cambridge).

Srividya Ramasubramanian is a Professor of Communications, Affiliated Professor of Women's & Gender Studies, and former Associate Dean for Climate & Inclusion at Texas A&M University. She is the cofounder of Media Rise (a nonprofit for meaningful media for social change), Director of Aggie Agora Difficult Dialogues on Campus Race Relations, and Convener of the campuswide Inclusive Pedagogy Workshop Series. Ramasubramanian's research focuses on media and identity (especially race, ethnicity, religion, gender, and sexuality), media literacy, stereotyping processes, intercultural and intergroup communication, and social justice. Apart from top communication journals, her work has been featured in popular outlets such as the *Huffington Post*, National Public Radio, *Dallas Morning News*, and *India Today*. She has delivered several public talks and keynotes around the world, including at TEDx-Lee College and in the UK, Singapore, the Netherlands, Australia, Germany, India, and China.

Shriram Sarvotham holds a PhD degree in electrical engineering from Rice University, Houston, and presently works at Apple Inc. as an Algorithms Scientist in the HID team in Cupertino, California. An ardent yoga practitioner since 1986, he began teaching yoga in India in 1991 and in the USA since 2002, and he holds the highest accreditation with the Yoga Alliance as an experienced yoga teacher. Awarded for his outstanding contributions to yoga teaching, he was the faculty member at three yoga studios and regularly presents lectures at yoga conferences (such as Yoga Alliance Leadership; Conference, Texas Yoga Conference, and more) and at medical conferences on holistic health (such as the Annual Conference of Texas Medical Association).

GLOSSARY

abhyudaya   worldly achievement
adharma   what is wrong
ahimsa   nonviolence
ajatasatru   enemy-less
ananta   endlessly
antaranga sadhana   internal practices
antaryami   indwelling self
anumanam   inference
anvikshiki   enquiry
aparigraha   non-hoarding, nonpossession
apat dharma   duty of self-protection
apunya   result of wrong action
Ardhanarishvara   Shiva and Shakti in one body
arohana   ascending sequence of notes
astheya   non-stealing
atma ajnana   self-forgetfulness or self-ignorance
atma nishta   the contemplative subject
atma sampadana   self-knowledge
audhaseenya   maintaining neutrality
avarnas   envelopments
avarohana   descending sequence of notes
Avidya ignorance
brahmacharya   living the highest version of our self
brahmavidya   knowledge of Brahman
buddhi   the intellect
citta vrtti nirodha   mind control by watching
danda   punishment
dharamrajya   state based on righteousness
dharana   focus
dharma virudha kama   desire opposed to dharma
dharma   righteous living, what is right
dharmasankat   conflicting situation

dhyana tranquility
drisya prapancham the tripartite, objective world
dukha unhappiness
grand samashti universal intelligence
gunas natural traits
Indrajaal Indra's net
indriyajaya control over the senses
Indriya nigraha sense control
indriyas and *devatas* senses and presiding deities
Iswara bhakti devotion to God
Iswara pranidhana surrender to God
jivanmukta living liberated
jnana self-knowledge
kala time
karmayoga nonreaction to the fruits of action
kama worldly pleasures
karana cause
karmaphala fruits of actions
karta agents of action
karuna compassion
Karya effect
Kashi present-day Varanasi
Lasya feminine dance
loka samgraha common good
maitre friendliness
manodharma conscience
mantra dristas seers of mantra, or mystic meanings, connections and
    interactions
manushyavati bhumi arthah the result of human effort applied to natural
    resources
Maya Power of God
Mithya appearance
mitras allies
moksha enlightenment
mudita appreciation
naishkarmya actionlessness or actionless action
nishkama karma self-giving work
nivruthi withdrawal
parameshti pure consciousness
parampara an unbroken flow of wisdom, insight, values, and beliefs
prabhava prosperity
praja sukham citizens' well-being
Pramada error
pramana means of knowledge

prana   energy or breath
Prasada   blessings
pratyaksha pramanam   experiential learning through sense organs
Pravritti   activity
pravruthi   activity
preyas   pleasure
preyo marga   path of pleasure
punya   good work
aarth   wealth
putra moha   attachment to son
rajarshi   sage king or philosopher king
Rajarshitvam   Being a sage king
rishi   seer
Rishitvam   being a sage
sabdabodham   understanding meaning of words
sahajananda   natural bliss
samadhi   mental equilibrium
samanvaya darsana   an integrating vision
samatvam yoga ucyate yoga   is equanimity of mind
sampradayas   sects
Samsara   sensuous life
samsara cakra   cycle of birth and death
samtosha   contentment
Sanatana   eternal
Sannyas   renunciation
sastra   system of knowledge
satya   truthfulness
satyam   truth
sewa   service
shivam   goodness
Shivoham   I am Shiva
shreyas   the path of good
soucha   cleanliness
sravana   reflective listening
sreyo marga   spiritual path
sthitaprajna   who without forgetting his or her spiritual plenitude interacts
   with the world, exploring and expressing latent spiritual potentialities
sukha   happiness
sundaram   beauty
Svadharma   work according to one's nature and training
swadhyaya   self-inspired study
talaivi   heroine
Tandava   Shiva's dance
tapas   austerity, willingness to step out of our comfort zone

Tatvamasi   you are what you seek, happiness
tyag   renunciation
upama   learning through similes and metaphors
upeksha   forgiveness
Varnasrama   division of society and stages of life
vasudhaiva kutumbakam   world as one family
Vidya   knowledge
vinaya   humility
visayas   objects
vishaya nishta   hedonistic pleasure
vriddha   elder
vyashti   unique individuals
yajaman   owner
Yoga   integration of body, mind and spirit

1

INCLUSIVE LEADERSHIP

An introduction

Swami Bodhananda, Tilak Agerwala
and Sangeetha Menon

Distinct from the classical approaches to understanding the mind from a single disciplinary point of view, contemporary approaches in science, philosophy and psychology adopt an interdisciplinary approach. This concept of 'leadership' is central in understanding the human mind, since it brings in the nature of social interactions as well as the contours of the self and identity that one forms through interactions and social living. Further, in present times, the challenge in leadership studies is to account for the possibilities that are extended by attitudes and approaches of the leader in terms of considering multiple factors in decision making and team building. Thus, inclusivity is central.

Significant perspectives on inclusivity and inclusive approaches in leadership can be traced back to Kautilya's philosophy. The 'rajarshi' model of leadership for contemporary world was enunciated by Kautilya, the prime minister of Chandragupta Maurya, (321–297 BC), the first known emperor in the Indian subcontinent, who ruled a vast swath of land from his capital at Pataliputra, present-day Bihar. The word 'raja' signifies power and the word 'rishi' denotes wisdom. 'Rajarshi', a compound of these two words, denotes a 'wise king' or a 'thoughtful leader'. This reminds one of Plato's idea of a 'philosopher king' or the Confucian concept of a 'virtuous leader'. Kautilya was a stellar political thinker of ancient India, with the single-mindedness of a Machiavelli, the strategic thinking of a Sun Tsu and the public spirit of a Confucius all rolled into one. He stipulated *praja sukham* (citizens' well-being) as the goal of the state and defined national wealth as *manushyavati bhumi arthah* (a result of human effort applied to natural resources).

The concept of Rajarshi in juxtaposition with the idea of 'inclusive leadership' offers a space to understand group and individual psychology of social interactions both from traditional and modern perspectives. The chapters in this book excavate ancient Indian wisdom for ideas and concepts for modern leadership practices. Hence the title of this volume, *Inclusive Leadership: Perspectives from Tradition and Modernity*.

1

The goal of focusing on the Rajarshi model in the context of inclusive leadership is to contribute constructively towards the development of a comprehensive management and leadership model for emerging India, the largest democracy and the third-largest Asian economy, which is expected to grow to be the second- or third-largest economy in the world by 2050. The challenge for India is to achieve within the framework of democracy, pluralism and political freedom what China has achieved through ruthless, authoritarian one-party rule. India could be a shining example for freedom and prosperity for the rest of the world if this feat can be pulled off in the foreseeable future. India's success in economic development will be hailed as the success of democracy, rule of law and freedom. And the Indian model of development could be replicated in developing countries with democratic values; here lies the importance of this exercise in model building.

What emerge from the chapters are five foundational principles which can undergird modern leadership. First, individuals are essentially spiritual beings with an indivisible self at their core, hence, personal integrity and moral and ethical behaviour in public conduct alone can ensure general well-being. Second, progress of humanity will not be complete without incorporating feminine perspectives in the decision-making process. Third, the process of decision-making should also involve multiple voices and the interests of all stakeholders, including the marginalized sections of society. Fourth, environmental considerations are critical in leadership decisions and policy choices. Finally, leadership in future would be a combination of computer power and human intelligence. These five principles lead to a system of dispersed, decentralized and nested leadership where the leader will not be a person, but a presence; not a face, but a space; not an authority figure, but a facilitating coach; not a source of power, but a point of inspiration; not a commissar, but a yogi.

The philosophical foundation of inclusive leadership envisaged in this book is advaita vedanta as enunciated by Swami Bodhananda in his article which introduces advaita vedanta as a metatheory. Advaita is the quintessential wisdom of India, a philosophy that propounds consciousness as the source of individual awareness and the manifested world. The oneness that advaita proposes has vertical and horizontal dimensions. Vertically it sees individuals as a combination of body, mind and consciousness and horizontally individuals are inalienably related to family, community, culture, environment, and the whole evolutionary process. He disputes the notion of matter–consciousness divide and propounds a seamless reality in which matter and consciousness are presented as two expressions of the same phenomenon. Swami Bodhananda questions the prevalent notion that advaita vedanta is otherworldly and establishes with textual references and epistemological instances cited from the vedanta and by its well-known practitioners that this system of Indian philosophy advocates common good through reflective action and detached engagement in the world. Such an inclusive psychology is analysed by Sangeetha Menon in the context of the philosophical and management underpinnings of desire, human action, agency, and common good in her chapter describing the manner in which the model of 'transcendental leadership' has been developed by Swami Bodhananda. This analysis is intended to give an alternate approach to understand the fundamental notion and experience of well-being in comparison to the other models in vogue.

The chapter by R. Narayanan takes up the leads from Swami Bodhananda's arguments and explains the core concept of Rajarshi model of ancient Indian wisdom as cognisance of unlimited individual potential energy and its conversion to kinetic energy through dedicated work in order to promote public good. With the help of systems thinking, a holistic perspective and deep strategy to the idea of inclusive leadership is suggested in this chapter. The chapter on leadership principles from yoga by Shriram Sarvotham connects Aristotelian concepts of 'ethos, logos and pathos' to the *ashtanga yoga* concept focusing on the leader as a person who brings value to the practice of leadership. A perfect harmony of values, reason and compassion makes the leader ethically rooted, rationally clear headed and emotionally balanced and empathetic. This inspires the call for a 'change of heart', recalling Gandhi as the panacea for the crises in contemporary leadership challenges.

Continuing the excavation into Indian wisdom tradition, the chapter by Radhakrishna Pillai, focuses exclusively on Kautilya's description in Arthashastra of an ideal king. *Indriya jaya* (sense control) is the key to mastery of self and the art of leadership. The king should be trained in the 'oughts' and 'ought nots' of leadership. Self-control means overcoming weaknesses and excesses like lust, anger, pride, arrogance, and foolhardiness. Twenty-one reasons are enumerated for the downfall of a leader. Personal duplicity and unethical business practices of chief executives of big corporations and banks which led to the economic meltdown in 2008 is reminded in the chapter, appealing readers to rethink and go back to the practice of traditional concepts of morality and ethics in personal and public life.

From the sphere of philosophy, moral imperatives and prescriptive ethics, a section of chapters in this book turn the discussion to sociopolitical, cultural and economic issues and critical analysis for leadership insights. The lead in such a perspective is made by the chapter by B.P. Mathur. Analysing the works of economists like Joseph Stiglitz, Jeffrey Sachs and Thomas Piketty, he pointedly critiques modern economic thought and practices, the mindless materialistic pursuit of profit, money and wealth that leads to soulless consumerism, environmental degradation and dangerous levels of income inequalities. He highlights the failure of both socialist and free market systems and looks for the 'right economic model'. This chapter depicts a protest on the tendency to equate free-market globalization and the Indian concept of *vasudhaiva kutumbakam* (world as one family). Free market leads to competition, rivalry and conflict, whereas world as one family is about love, harmony, cooperation, and mutual support based on self-imposed control, equitable sharing of resources and taking care of every member of the society. This chapter offers a response to the modern paradox of 'afflictions of affluence' in focusing on morally integrated individuals organized in an ethically bounded economy led by spiritually inspired leaders. Such a response is grounded by the author with extensive literature from the Mahabharata and Arthashastra.

The chapter by Anuradha Balaram, with an in-depth survey of the past and contemporary administrative practices in India poses a rhetorical question on the glaring gap between constitutional ideals and their practice in daily lives. Balaram reasons out that there is a lack of an enlightened administration based on sound spiritual and moral value system. With an extensive survey of India's cultural landscape, Deepti Navaratna in her chapter writes with anguish about the lack of entrepreneurial leadership in monetizing and marketing by leveraging on the vast and varied cultural assets of the ancient civilization. Culture cannot survive on pittance received as donations from voluntary organizations or grants allotted by government agencies. Culture is an inexhaustible resource, though unfortunately, it is rarely considered as an agent of the present, but a relic of the past. However, with the combined efforts of all stakeholders, enlightened connoisseurs, research scholars, government, nonprofits, international agencies, artists, tourists, and curators under the leadership of smart entrepreneurs, it is possible to package and market culture based on a sound business model. Indian classical music and dance, traditional arts and crafts, iconography, temple rituals, martial arts, Sanskrit language, yoga, Ayurveda, and such cultural symbols, values, beliefs, and practices are soft products which have vast international appeal. Digitisation, globalisation and intercultural syncretism must harness to predict consumer behavior. The author calls it 'glocal' entrepreneurship. In the process of marketing culture all will be enriched, emphasizes Deepti Navaratna who herself is a neuroscientist-turned-artist and cultural administrator.

The chapter by Srividya Ramasubramanian on 'Feminism and inclusive leadership' offers a feminist approach to understanding leadership. In a scathing critique of the patriarchy and male-dominated leadership, the author suggests that there is not much emphasis laid on emotional literacy, distribution of power and social justice. Equating patriarchy with neoliberal capitalist mindset, the chapter argues that hierarchies, division of labour and organisational structures are created so that stereotypical conceptions of gender, race and social class are reinforced. The author does not support radical feminism but believes that feminist leadership is an inclusive leadership ethic which can be embraced and practiced by all genders. Expanding the category of the feminine the argument given is that people of all genders can be feminist leaders. It is all a matter of how power is distributed, whether in terms of inclusive, participatory, collaborative, horizontal, or relational modes. Discarding the Western feminist movements perhaps for being elitist and contravening the principles of equity and inclusion, the chapter advocates the eastern form of spiritual feminism which is anchored in overcoming dualities including feminine and masculine by integrating them to generate non-dualistic synergies.

The chapter by Tilak Agerwala addresses the rapid growth in computing capability and its negative and positive impact on human progress and survival. In this age of exponential growth of data, most of which are unstructured, our ability to extract meaningful information, patterns and trends requires use of advanced computing technologies. Without computers our limited brain will be lost in a deluge of overwhelming data. In a prophetic statement, the author concludes that the leader of the future will be a system of humans and computers that interact in natural ways, learn from each other, and are collectively more effective than either humans or computers acting alone. Computers analyse data and make recommendations and humans set visions, goals and values. Computerised data analysis has wide applications in public policy making, business decision making and talent management. Three challenges of the digital universe are loss of privacy, cyber security and the loss of control on decision-making through increased automation. Furthermore, the logic by which deep learning algorithms arrive at certain decisions is beyond human comprehension and data used to train machine learning systems might have built-in biases. Therefore, it is cautioned that leaders must be aware of the ethical issues associated with big data, analytics and machine learning. However, the author does not subscribe to the fear expressed in some influential quarters that unchecked machine intelligence can overpower and enslave humans. According to the author, machines with no self-referral identity may not have selfish purposes and fear-based need to dominate and exploit. On the other hand, such fear about machine dominance could be a case of humans projecting their own dishonesty, selfishness and cruelty on machines. The real danger is the possibility of elite power blocks of humans harnessing and misusing machine power to dominate and enslave other disadvantaged peoples for their selfish ends.

In the final chapter of this book, Sangeetha Menon offers a review of the model suggested by Swami Bodhananda, namely, 'transcendental leadership'. Focusing on the leadership model developed in the philosophical and management works of Swami Bodhananda, the author recapitulates a theory of teamwork through active engagement with transformative powers embedded in it. Transcendental leadership as suggested by Swami Bodhananda is founded on the principles of being-in-the-moment and selfless action with the actualization of a higher purpose as the goal. And from the point of view of this model any action has the potential to realise the highest and deepest point of life purpose and existence. Employing concepts of dharma, karma and yoga from traditional Indian sources and contemporary challenges in leadership studies, Swami Bodhananda promulgates a style of leadership where hierarchies and divisions coalesce to highlight the hidden potential in each individual to take initiatives, think creatively and go beyond the given. The leadership paradigm suggested by Swami Bodhananda is to find groundedness in the unbroken tradition for contemporary Indian thought and for organizational and leadership values. Decision-making is the greatest leadership challenge and is a function of knowledge, values and purpose, according to Swami Bodhananda.

The integral nature of Indian philosophy can contribute significantly to measure the challenges in understanding the nature of inclusive leadership and the human self, where science and evolutionary biology have failed humanity. The concept of 'transcendental leadership' is an attempt to go beyond the binaries of reason and emotion, intellect and intuition, the one who leads and one who follows, the present and the future, and in essence the schism that is thought to be existent between the highest life purpose and the joy in living the same every moment. Thus, the final chapter offers the significant perspective of the book, which is considering inclusivity as transcendence.

The ten chapters on inclusive and Rajarshi models of leadership can be summarised as an attempt to offer the interplay of three dominant partnerships: between humans and machines, gender identity and societal frameworks, and humans and environment. And in such a scenario, both the notion and experience of leadership will be dispersed, fluid, ethically moderated, spiritually rooted, and collaborative, thriving in and promoting an ecosystem of diversity.

2

VEDANTA AND THE RAJARSHI MODEL OF LEADERSHIP

Swami Bodhananda

No system of philosophy is complete and fulfilled unless and until it is embodied in human action and becomes a creation of beauty, harmony and utility. Action involves subject–object divide and their interactions, resulting in a spiral of higher-order structures, values and experiences. Vedanta as a system of thought and spiritual experience is not immune to this principle. Vedanta fulfils itself in the realisation of *jivanmukta*, a living, liberated, embodied individual, a person of universal consciousness and steady wisdom, a *sthitaprajna* (Gita Ch: 54–72) who without forgetting his or her spiritual plenitude interacts with the world, exploring and expressing latent spiritual potentialities.

Introduction

The Vedic textual name for the jivanmukta is rishi, one who is wise and detached. The jivanmukta is not an isolated state of spiritual bliss, but is part of enlarging circles of organizations, like family, community, humanity, and environment. All those associations place responsibilities on the jivanmukta, as family head, community leader, corporate executive, country's president, humanity's conscience, and environment's friend. The Sanskrit word for a leader, who exercises power and whose decisions affect others, is raja. Thus, the jivanmukta or rishi, by virtue of dispensing responsibilities and enjoying privileges, automatically becomes raja and rishi that is Rajarshi, sage king or philosopher king. Rajarshi is the ideal of Indian leadership.

There are three models of the rishi concept: Brahmarshi, wise scholar; Rajarshi, wise ruler; and Devarshi, wise visionary. Vasishta, the advisor of Dasaratha was a Brahmarshi; Janaka, the king of Videha, a Rajarshi; and Narada, the globetrotting messenger of Vishnu, a Devarshi. The modern rishi has to incorporate all these capabilities—knowledge, vision and decisiveness—while executing leadership functions. Vasishta was humble, Janaka detached and Narada committed. The modern leader has to be humble, detached and committed.

As India and its 1.2 billion people are becoming more aspirational, they look into their past for inspiration and clues for decisive action which would enable them to march into the future with self-confidence, determination and purpose. None can forget the past while designing the future. At the same time, India cannot act in isolation, as we live in a networked, interdependent world in which everyone's decision affects the other. India has to carry the world with it, either as leader, or at least as one of the four or five leading nations, or continue to be led by foreign powers and their ideas as before. The land of Vyasa, Buddha, Chanakya, Ashoka, Shankara, Akbar, Vivekananda, Tagore, and Gandhi would not be satisfied playing second fiddle to any other nation or imitating alien ideologies. Hence, the Rajarshi model of leadership—a model that India had developed over a long period of time and which had been tried and tested and proved efficacious by its successful practitioners—would become more relevant and useful in contemporary times.

Leadership is conceiving a vision

Leadership entails the conception of a vision, communicating and persuading others to share the same, putting together an organization of skilled people to imagine it in concrete terms and postulate strategies and tactics to accomplish it in terms of definable goals and measurable outcomes within a specific time frame and in a fluid sociopolitical context, despite various constraints and scarcity of resources. In short, leadership makes things happen and inspires skilled people to work hard aligning their self-interest with public good. Leadership is all about long-term vision, success, power, and common good.

Life unfolds in terms of choices and choice making is a leadership task. For individuals living in a complex body–mind–ego structure, embedded in a complicated system of culture and nature, which in turn is a blip in an evolving cosmos, every decision is a make-or-break event, consciously and unconsciously, calibrating millions and trillions of pieces of information whose roots go back to the Big Bang itself. Modern leaders have their fingers on the nuclear button which can, if activated, destroy the planet 25 times over. Corporate and individual decisions leading to mass consumption can pollute the planet and cause irretrievable levels of climate change. Again, in the name of religion and sectarian ideologies, millions can be put to death through organized orgies of violence. Hence, decision-making becomes a global responsibility and a rare privilege. Leaders become almost like gods with powers to save or savage the world. The ideal of common good is critical and paramount in such a scenario. Leaders should not behave like the Bhasmasura of the Puranas who caused his own destruction by the powers he had acquired through hard work, but impetuously employed in a moment's uncontrolled passion.

Classical and Neo-Vedanta

Vedanta is the finest flowering of Indic/Vedic civilisation and Rajarshi is the embodiment of that civilisation and its time-tested ethos. Vedanta is a system of *brahmavidya* (knowledge) and yoga *sastra* (practice) which leads to full realisation of human potential in interaction with the world, while pursuing worthy goals and creating win–win solutions to common problems. Vedanta teaches the secret of happiness, health and the art of living in awareness. The knowledge of Vedanta is based on a corpus of revelations enshrined in the Upanishads (13 in number), codified in the Brahma Sutras (555 sutras), and practically explained for daily life in the Bhagavad Gita (700 verses). The commentaries on these basic texts constitute schools of thought and their practitioners become different *sampradayas* (sects).

There are three main sampradayas: Advaita, propounded by Adi Shanka-racharya; Vishishtadvaita, as interpreted by Ramanujacharya; and Dvaita, as seen by Madhvacharya. Advaita establishes oneness of existence and posits the phenomenal world of subjects and objects as a shadow play of consciousness. Vishishtadvaita claims that the world of material objects as well as individual souls is real, both being the gross body of the *antaryami* (indwelling self) which is Isvara/Brahman. Dvaita teaches that Isvara, the world of multiple objects and souls are real and mutually different and Isvara is the absolute sovereign. These three modes explain the reality that truth is one though the wise speak of it in different ways. Buddha's theory of impermanence and dependent origination is another way of presenting the same truth.

Over a period of time, in interaction with modern science and Western culture, a transdenominational Vedanta has evolved in India conceived and initiated by reformist thinkers and social activists (of the 18th, 19th and 20th centuries) like Raja Rammohan Roy, Dayananda Saraswati, Swami Vivekananda, Bankim Chandra Chatterjee, Maharshi Aurobindo, Bhaga-van Ramana, Bal Gangadhar Tilak, Rabindranath Tagore, B.R. Ambedkar, Narayana Guru, Mahatma Gandhi et al. They made bold interpretations of the Vedanta within the bounds of Astika Vedic (dharma) traditions (those traditions that believe in the authority of the Veda), keeping in mind the requirements of modern society. The salient features of Neo Vedanta are: a) social responsibility and purposeful action; b) ideal of a casteless, classless, equitable society; c) respect for all religions; d) acceptance of science and technology and secular institutions as the engine of progress; e) personal practice/experience and logical enquiry, along with reflection on Vedic revelation as the means of pursuing true knowledge; f) nation as a unit of collective action; g) civilisational integrity, cultural diversity and national unity; h) individual freedom moderated by sense of common good; i) individual as the ultimate source and purpose of value; and j) unity of Brahman, world and the individual.

Some of the statements of the Vedas that capture this spirit of the Neo-Vedanta are: a) *Prajnanam Brahma* (truth is consciousness); b) *Tat Tvam Asi* (we are essentially consciousness); c) *Ayam atma Brahma* (consciousness is the witnessing light of mental and material events); d) *Aham Brahmasmi* (I am the changeless consciousness that supports all changing experiences); and e) *Sarvam khalu idam Brahma* (the mental and material worlds are a play of consciousness). This new interpretational emphasis on action was in answer to colonialist criticism that Vedic/Indic philosophy was otherworldly. The great Indologist and Sanskrit scholar Prof. Max Muller has captured this widely shared colonialist interpretation of Vedanta in the following statement:

> I quite admit that as a popular philosophy, the Vedanta would have its dangers, that it would fail to call out and strengthen the manly qualities required for the practical side of life, and that it might raise the human mind to a height from which the most essential virtues of social and political life might dwindle away into mere phantoms. . . . After all it is not everybody who is called upon to take an active part in life, whether in defending or ruling a country, in amassing wealth, or in breaking stones; and for fitting men to lead contemplative and quiet lives, I know no better preparation than the Vedanta.
>
> (Mueller, 1899: 193)

The greatest exponents of Vedanta, especially of its Advaitic interpretation, Adi Sankaracharya and its later proponent Swami Vivekananda, were renunciants, travelling, debating, teaching, commenting on texts, debunking archaic customs, reforming social practices, building institutions, and training teachers. Similarly, Gautama Buddha, the exponent of impermanence and contentless consciousness, spent his enlightened life on the road teaching the message of nirvana. Sage kings like Janaka and Aswapati ruled powerful kingdoms while steeped in Vedanta wisdom. The Bhagavad Gita, the foremost text on Vedanta, teaches detached engagement in the performance of duties to win and enjoy the world. Therefore, 'get up and fight' was the clarion call of Krishna to Arjuna. Also, the Gita assures 'success, prosperity, progress and peace' to such a fighter (Ch: 18:76). On the contrary, those who refuse to engage in action were condemned by Krishna to live an inglorious, guilt-ridden, wretched life of indignity and immorality.

Concept of action and agency

A series of arguments advanced by Vedanta to show the relativity of human action have led to a misperception that has been dogging Vedanta and the entire Indic tradition since the time of the sramanas and the Buddha. If there is a choice between action and contemplation, which is purely theoretical, a life of contemplation was considered superior to that of action. Ironically, the choice is not between action and contemplation, but between reflective action and reactive action. Action is natural and necessary for sheer physical survival. The truth is that conscious, purposeful action is in human predicament. All other sentient beings, including plants, act or respond to inner and outer stimuli impulsively. Once the stimulus is pacified, there is repose or sleep. Humans act for security, power, pleasure, control and such other imagined goods. The more one acts, more action is engendered, leading the agent to a never-ending circle of action and reaction.

Vedanta distinguishes between action for survival and action for ego fulfilment. Ego is a product of unhappiness born of ignorance or lack of contemplative awareness. The ancient Greek wise man Socrates warned that an unanalysed life is not worth living. Indian sage Yajnavalkya cautioned that a life lived without self-knowledge will be wretched and contemptible. Ego is a fictitious entity and its fulfilment is a chimera. Ego fulfilment is confused with happiness and all egoistic pursuits like that for power, domination, name and fame, approval and appreciation, glory, pelf and pleasure were expected to accrue happiness. On the contrary, Vedanta claims that happiness is the nature of the self and is realised in contemplative states.

So, the Vedanta proposes: a) to work for survival and creature comforts and b) meditate for mental peace and happiness. Since an unhappy and disturbed person cannot work efficiently and an inactive, lazy person cannot meditate deeply, the Bhagavad Gita suggests contemplative action or detached action or action as an offering to Brahman or motivated by common good. Work itself becomes mental discipline and a conducive setting for surrender, devotion and meditation. This state is called actionlessness which is mistaken for inactivity and lack of ethical sensitivity devoid of social and political commitment.

Evolution of human action

In the hunter–gatherer and farming matriarchal communities, human action was moderated by seasons and life cycles, hence, action was in alignment with nature and oneself. The producer enjoyed the process of production and consumed the product; work and consumption were not self-alienating. Action was creation and recreation. But in the feudalist and industrialist societies in which means of production were controlled by a few patriarchal chieftains, action became work, a commodity alienated from the agent, which was to be extracted by force or coercion. This transformation of action into work and work into labour is the history of man's downfall.

For a hunter or a farmer, hunting or sowing was contemplative action. In a matriarchal nurturing community, all actions were self-fulfilling. In a feudalist or industrial society, work became mechanical, self-insulting labour. The worker yearned for distractions, leisure and entertainments outside work, while these goods became unapproachable for the worker and considered as the exclusive privilege of the leisure class. The worker, maintained on subsistence level, was made to do back-breaking work, the alternative to it being death or destitution. The brick and mortar factories, division of labour and specialisation, time measured by the clock, monetisation of exchange of produce, mechanisation, free trade, and the new God—capital, new-world, market economy—all created a worker class distinct and in contrast to a leisure class yielding a new dilemma to act or to meditate.

India faced this dilemma even during the Vedic period due to the excesses of the brahmin class in cahoots with the powerful kshatriya class oppressing the producer vaishya class and worker sudra class for their expensive rituals like aswamedha, meant to expand kshatriya power and brahmin influence. There was a powerful reaction and backlash against karma and rituals and a large number of sramanas (intellectuals) from all classes abandoned villages and their mindless rituals and migrated to the forests and mountains to lead contemplative lives, while brahmins went on with their usual rituals. These two lifestyles continued to be the central theme of philosophical discussion throughout Indian history. The Upanishads mention the conflict of *sreyo marga* and *preyo marga* (Katha Upanishad) or the path of *vidya* and *avidya* (Isavasya Upanishad); dharma sastras as the path of *pravritti* and nivritti (Manusmriti); and the Bhagavad Gita as the path of *jnana* and *yoga* (Ch: 3–3).

The Bhagavad Gita introduces the conflict between path of action and that of contemplation through a series of questions by the protagonist Arjuna – questions like karma versus *jnana* (intellect), karma yoga versus karma *sannyasa* (giving up of action), and bhakti versus *dhyana*. Krishna sees no conflict between karma, yoga and jnana. Karma, as Krishna defines it, is purposeful action, yoga is detached purposeful action and jnana is joyful, detached and purposeful action. Karma taken to the next level is karma yoga which fulfils in jnana yoga or *naishkarmya* (actionlessness or actionless action). One who remains as the actionless centre while performing all actions, inspires all actions as the actionless centre and sees inaction as a form of negative action, knows the secret of action and fulfils the purpose of all actions.[1]

The Gita ideal of contemplative action

The Bhagavad Gita advocates contemplative action as the ultimate experience of self-realisation, reconciling action and contemplation in the ideal of karma yoga or *nishkama* karma, which is the basic philosophy of the Rajarshi model of leadership. In the process, the Gita lifts karma from the narrow definition of ritualism (Gita Ch: 2–42, 45, 46) and expands its meaning to include all actions meant for the well-being of individuals and society. In fact, Krishna reconciles all four spiritual paths – karma, bhakti, yoga, and jnana – in *svadharma*. Performing svadharma skillfully and efficiently, that

12

is, action according to one's temperament and training, is karma (ibid., 2: 49); *svakarmana tam abhyarchya*, or bhakti (ibid., 18:46), doing those karmas as worshipful offering to Isvara or for the purpose of *loka samgraha* (common good); accepting the fruits of one's work as Isvara *prasada* (blessings), or putting in simple words without reaction is *samatvam yoga ucyate* or yoga (ibid., 2–48); and performing all actions joyfully without egoistic identification is jnana (ibid., 5–8, 9, 14).

The Bhagavad Gita provides many reasons why action is embedded in human constitution. According to the Gita, to act is natural and inactivity is unnatural and forced on the self because of deformed desires and false consciousness. The reasons for action are the following:

- No one can remain inactive.
- All are programmed to act impelled by inborn natural desires.
- Desire without purposeful action leads to inner conflicts and hypocrisy.
- Disciplined wakeful action to fulfil natural desires leads to wisdom.
- Self-giving actions lead to freedom and happiness.
- Self aggrandising actions lead to bondage and suffering.
- Self-knowledge gives rise to self-giving actions and self-ignorance causes self-aggrandising actions.
- Purpose of action is to understand its limitations and overcome mental entanglements.
- Actions and their outcomes do not add up to happiness.
- Happiness is the nature of self and the fruit of self-knowledge.

In this context, a quote from Yoga Vasistha, a Vedanta treatise, purportedly meant to lift Prince Rama from his melancholic thoughts and prepare him to take up royal responsibilities, believed to have been taught by the royal guru Vasistha, would be relevant: 'with the mind established in desirelessness, the body can do what needs to be done; inactivity is not good for body or mind; let me do my duties without sense of "I" and "mine"'. Gandhi said, 'my actions speak louder than my written or spoken words'. Narayana Guru, the south Indian dalit spiritual leader, Sanskrit scholar, poet, and Vedanta master told his legions of followers 'to organise, educate, start enterprises, and work for a prosperous, classless society'. Swami Vivekananda's mission was *atmano mokshartham/jagat hitaya cha*—to attain enlightenment through selfless work meant for common good.

Vedanta is not a philosophy of inaction

India produced great works of art, literature, linguistics, philosophy, medicine, architecture, science, mathematics, engineering, astronomy, metallurgy, and built great civilisational nation-states that commanded 35 percent global wealth and which were the envy of the world until the 11th century.

Hence, condemning Vedanta as the philosophy of inaction and other world-liness is childish and portrays one's ignorance of history and incapacity to understand subtle philosophy. But, in a sense, the detractors of Indic civilisa-tion and its epitome philosophy, the Vedanta, are right in pointing out the defects in the presentation of Vedanta and its application in practical lives of individuals and Indian society, and in the process of nation building. India has been the only continental-sized civilisation in the world that was under foreign domination for more than 1,000 years. The Indian ideal of Rajarshi seems to be a weak synthesis or uneasy balance of rishi and raja that withered easily under stress and external attacks, reminding one of the story of partnership between the lump of clay and the dry leaf. Both went on a pilgrimage to Kashi (present-day Varanasi). On the way when it rained, the dry leaf protected the clay from dissolving by covering it and when the wind blew the clay protected the dry leaf from being blown away by sitting on its top. But when the wind blew and the torrential rain fell simultane-ously, their partnership dissolved – the clay melted and the leaf was blown away. Similarly, when the pressure built stressfully on the Rajarshi, the rishi ran to the mountains and the Raja clueless perished on the battlefield. The hapless producers and supporting classes switched sides where the bread was buttered. The Indian ship was adrift in high seas since then, in spite of 'the soul of a nation long suppressed finds utterance' (Nehru 1947) in 1947. The failure of India as a nation was the severest test for the efficacy of the Rajarshi model of leadership. Western scholars dubbed India variously as a 'functioning anarchy', as a 'soft state', and India's economic performance, as 'the Hindu rate of growth'. The total rout of the Indian army units by the Chinese in the 1962 border conflict was the nadir of India's humiliation.

What is the Rajarshi model?

With time, bemoaned Krishna, the teaching of yoga got lost, causing the downfall of India.[2] The mutual failure of brahmins and kshatriyas in their respective duties of guiding and protecting the nation, mainly due to endoga-mous caste practices and the rigidity of birth-based varna system and the consequent drying up of fresh talents of thinkers and administrators from a wider pool of human resource and the lethargy, lust, greed, and arrogance of the ruling class contributed to India's downfall. 'Lust, greed and the vain passions of the ruling class and the loss of discernment and judgement of the thinking class', says Sankara in the introduction to his Bhagavad Gita commentary, were the reasons for the loss of Vedantic knowledge;[3] the same reasons that caused the fall of the mighty Roman Empire as described by Edward Gibbon.

Indriya nigraha (sense control), *vinaya* (humility) and *atma sampadana* (self-knowledge) were important virtues prescribed by Chanakya for the Rajarshi. These values should become part of the cultural and educational milieu in which one grows up. Culture is the result of long tradition of practices and effective institutional mechanisms of checks and balances, rewards and punishments. The only measure of culture, the practice of which requires a subtle mind, is the inner peace, harmony, happiness, and clarity that practitioners enjoy.[4] As a result, social cohesion, trust, mutual respect, and creative impulses that the community engenders and nurtures contribute to greater progress and well-being. In this context, it is relevant to note the observation of Francis Fukuyama, the author of *Trust* and a leading conservative thinker, that India is a low-trust society, while Western Europe and America are high-trust societies.

The philosophy of Vedanta is built on the idea that the individual human being is a composite of body, mind and spirit, or consciousness. Mind and body are objects and consciousness is the subject. In this respect, Vedanta goes a step further than the simple Cartesian dualism of mind and body. Rene Descartes (1594–1650) in his monumental work *Discourses on Method and Meditations* concluded that 'mind is a thing that thinks and has no extension and the rock is a thing which has extension but does not think'. 'I think, therefore I am' 'my existence is the only indubitable fact', declared Descartes. 'I am imperfect and I can conceive of perfection and therefore a perfect God must exist' was the second proposition of this icon of clarity. From there it was not a big leap for the rationalist to make his third proposition that 'the world that I experience exists, for a perfect God has no reason to deceive me'. And about the world, 'the knowledge of sound, taste, smell, touch, and colour are dubitable, uncertain and doubtful', but numbers and figures/lines signified by arithmetic and geometry are indubitable and certain. Thus, with Descartes, the scientific project dealing with numbers and figures in search of measurable and empirical knowledge began.

Vedanta categorises thought as matter, a modification of food and object of consciousness. For Descartes, it is 'I am thought' but for Vedantin, it is 'I have a thought'. Vedantin has a higher perspective that empowers us to critically look at thought and be aware of our intentions, motives, prejudices, and the whole gamut of mind. Vedanta teaches that all activities of thought are prejudiced and premised on 'ignorance' or partial vision and suffers from the problem of cognitive limits. The seeing of those mental modifications from the perspective of a witness is true meditation. Even the so-called indubitable data given by arithmetic and geometry suffer from qualitative subjectivity as proved by Einstein's relativity theory, the uncertainty principle of quantum physics and the incompleteness theorem of Godel. Thomas Kuhn's theory of 'paradigm shifts' and Karl Popper's theory of 'falsifiability' are other blows on Descartes' indubitability of arithmetic numbers and geometric figures. Vedanta argues that though our true, indubitable 'I am' nature is not determined by flow of thoughts or mind, at the same time, thoughts reveals our nature in kaleidoscopically multitudinal ways. *Lakshmana vritti* (thought) points to the self as consciousness. Therefore, the Vedantic declaration, 'I am consciousness that has thoughts' is a higher and stable perspective than 'I am a thinking thing'. Rajarshi realises himself as Brahman, the infinite blissful consciousness, as revealed in the scriptures and experienced by contemplatives. Jesus Christ had declared: 'I and my father in heaven are one'. And, the Islamic Sufi saint had also said: 'Anal Haq': 'I am God'.

The Vedantic system of philosophy is based on the indubitable knowledge that I am consciousness which is the source of all mental and material manifestations. Brahman expressing its fullness in myriad manifestations or appearances is the creation or cosmos made of *karta* (agents of action), *karya* and *karana* (law of cause and effect), *kala* (duration), *indriyas* and *devatas* (instruments and fields of enjoyment), *visayas* and *karmaphala* (objects and conditions of enjoyment) etc., which Vedanta identifies as the *drisya prapancham* (the tripartite, objective world) or *samsara*, which again is defined as impermanent and which depends on the substratum of permanent consciousness for its existence. The Rajarshi draws strength and stability, motivation and energy and clarity and purpose from this philosophical foundation.

At this point, it would be reinforcing to quote David Gordon White.[5] Encapsulating the dialectical philosophy of German philosopher, Georg W. Hegel, White writes:

> For Hegel, history was a stage upon which an abstract cosmic mind called the 'World Spirit' evolved—from a state of unconsciousness to one self-conscious freedom grounded in ethical responsibility – by morphing into a succession of 'folk' or 'national' spirit-s (*volksgeist*-s) spurred by the acts of 'world historical individuals' such as Napoleon.

The Vedantin would reformulate this insight more inclusively. The Brahman (consciousness) appears as the cosmic mind and becomes self-conscious, causing a dialectical play of subject and object and the illusion of time and causality, and the same Brahman, identifying with subjects morphs into choice making individuals and their collectives, as societies and agents of historical processes, who feel a moral responsibility for their choices creating an inner world of memories, attachments and variable ego identities. For the Vedantin, unlike Hegel and the evolutionists, the movement is not from unconsciousness to self-consciousness, but from consciousness to self-consciousness and then to individual and collective consciousness. To be conscious or unconscious is not a matter of gaining or losing consciousness, but only states of appearance and disappearance of objects and thoughts in consciousness. The basis of ethical behaviour, according to Vedanta, is the individual's sense of the ground consciousness and the interdependent nature of collective consciousness, and the resultant sense of mutuality and solidarity with all life forms and the living habitat. Historical personalities like Napoleon or Gandhi represent the collective consciousness of the time (*yuga chetana* and its dharma).

Rajarshi understands his or her relationship with the ground consciousness as well the collective consciousness and chooses actions and regulates expectations and responses accordingly. Their desires spring from the fullness of being and actions become spontaneously right and contribute to the well-being of all (*lokasamgraha*). Rajarshi is the living standard of ethical values, a veritable dharma in flesh and blood (*ramo vigrahavan dharmah*). In the modern world where ethics has taken a backseat in public conduct, the Rajarshi will be a welcome presence of moral authority.

Rajarshi model and the misunderstood theory of Maya

Other much misunderstood idea of Vedanta is the theory of *maya* and the category of *mithya*. The oft-quoted sentence for this misconception is Sankaracharya's proposition, '*brahma satyam, jagat mithya/jivo brahmaiva naparah*', that is, Brahman alone is true, the world is false (neither true or untrue) and the real nature of individual *jiva* is Brahman.[6] The words maya and mithya are used synonymously. Both means indescribability. Vedanta argues that the world cannot be boxed into categories of either/or; yes or no; is or is not; with form or without form/emptiness—the experienced world defies logical categorisation. That is the meaning of saying that the world is maya or mithya. Maya does not mean that the world is nonexistent, nor does it assert that the world (as it is presented by the senses and interpreted by the mind) is absolutely true. This Vedantin worldview quite agrees with the modern scientific view of material universe.

Rajarshi, as a consequence of this view, is a 'yes and no' or '*yin* and *yang*' person. He or she sees both sides of the coin and looks for 360-degree perspectives. There are no bad apples in such a worldview, as a Sanskrit adage says: 'the problem is leadership deficit, not talent or resource deficit. It is a matter of identifying the right person for the right task; applying the right resource to work out the right solutions; and pulling out the right idea at the right time'. All the constituent elements of the world are right fits, and in the expert hands of a Rajarshi worksman the world clock ticks.

Maya also means change, nested structures and interconnected collection of objects presupposing a subject as its raison d'etre. The Rajarshi sees the world as maya, an everchanging interdependent phantasmagoria of events and thoughts. Rajarshi flows with change and is often in the forefront of change. Rajarshi is a change leader. The changing world and the unique, ever-new problems that it throws up inspire the Rajarshi to delve deep into the oceanic consciousness and fetch out-of-the-box solutions. People of average intellect respond to life's challenges from the stale storehouse of memory, conditioned by fear, anxiety and tension. They don't know any better than following others, than repeating past mistakes or parroting outdated winning solutions, or just mimicking memory, and continuing to be part of the problem. Although the Rajarshi is a risk taker, he/she interprets change as an opportunity than a calamity. New problems are seen as invitations to step out of the comfort zone of memory and call forth the infinite resources of consciousness in designing innovative solutions. Rajarshi is from the dynamic sun and others are from the barren moon! The daily prayer of the Rajarshi is: 'as you light up Heaven and Earth, O, Radiant Sun, so you light up my mind'.[7]

Successful intelligence and human motivation

Robert Sternberg defines successful intelligence as 'one's ability to attain one's goals in life, given one's sociocultural context, by adapting to, shaping, and selecting environments, through a balance of analytical, creative and practical skills' (Sternberg, 1997). In this definition of intelligence, creativity is the critical factor compared to analytical and practical skills and according to Vedanta, the source of creativity is not the unconscious process of cutting, mixing and pasting memory bits on the canvass of imagination, but contemplative consciousness and its infinite wholesome resources. Mind is not intelligence, it only invokes intelligence. At the end of the day, after all the analysis is done and all practical considerations are taken into account, what glues all the bits into a creative solution is awareness which is a result of detached contemplation.

For the Rajarshi, success is not just isolated personal success, but it is total success which is personal success aligned to collective, long-term and sustainable success. Rajarshi doesn't dissolve his/her individuality into the melting soup of the collective. The Rajarshi concept of *samashti* (collective) is that of a network. Vedanta describes it as *Indrajaal* (Indra's net), like the human brain made of trillions upon trillions of synaptic connections, creating exponential number of sites for quantum collapse and release of fresh energies. It is this networked individual who becomes the channel of creativity and Rajarshi places himself/herself in that spot.

Every act of the Rajarshi ensures personal growth along with the development of all stakeholders, while ensuring long-term collective well-being. The success of the Rajarshi is celebrated by all stakeholders, nay, by the whole universe. The Rajarshi is enemyless (the *ajatasatru*) whose success leaves none anguished behind, whose victory is not a march on the prostrated bodies of vanquished victims, whose accomplishments cause no bitterness or revenge and the zero-sum cycle of bloodletting.

The Vedanta world can be summarised as constituted of *vyashti* (unique individuals) networked as a grand samashti (universal intelligence) both grounded in and inspired by *parameshti* (pure consciousness). As an agent of action, Rajarshi is a humble devotee, as a thinker Rajarshi is a partner in expressions of universal intelligence and as consciousness he/she is the supreme creator. Rajarshi is capable of focused action (function of IQ), while part of his/her mind surveys the background, bringing 360-degree perspectives (EQ function) all the time, channelizing the infinite resources of consciousness (CQ function). Rajarshi keeps this big picture in mind while making miniscule, blow-by-blow decisions and initiating actions. The brain of a Rajarshi functions in optimal capacity and efficiency. Rajarshi does ordinary things in extraordinary ways, while others do so-called extraordinary things in ordinary fashion.

Vedanta analyses human motivation in terms of natural inclinations and urges. Humans, like any other sentient entity, seek agreeable objects and comfort and avoid disagreeable objects and discomfort. This mutually opposed activities of avoidance and courting is built into the human genes as survival instinct. But beyond the needs for survival, humans have developed needs for power, fame and pleasure to satisfy his/her ego. In present times, all these needs are reducible to the overarching need for money and consequent insatiable greed. Greed sends the greedy in a tailspin into abyss. As Gandhi had said, 'God has provided for man's need, but not for his greed'. Greed works as long as there are innocent and ignorant people to be enslaved, converted or exploited, and natural resources to be expropriated. On one hand, people the world over are getting more and more self-conscious and aware of their unique identities and rights; on the other hand, nonrenewable natural resources are getting fast depleted, while their demands are increasing. The predator and prey game is getting over and nature is retaliating in terms of climate change. Decision makers are called upon to be environment-friendly, people-friendly, and be comfortable with different cultural practices. This is the age of pluralism and a synthesising ability in harnessing diverse disciplines, worldviews and practices towards a shared, consensus vision and action plan will be a crucial capability for modern leaders. The Rajarshi would be a fit candidate for such leadership roles. The empathetic embrace of the Rajarshi encompasses not only the entire human race, but also animals, plants and insentient objects that constitute the living ecosystem. For the Rajarshi, the whole universe is a play of consciousness.

Rajarshi and the new world

According to Vedantic psychology, all human desires are motivated by one overarching desire: happiness or to be a happy person. Happiness is the ultimate human value. The powerful king and the powerless beggar, the rich and the poor, literate and illiterate: all share the same consuming passion for happiness. A careful and dispassionate analysis of life experiences lead the rational human to the conclusion that happiness is not the property of objects but is the experience of *atma nishta* (the contemplative subject). The ancient Greeks named it eudaimonic happiness apropos of *vishaya nishta* (hedonistic pleasure). A happy person is seen to be the natural source of ethical standard and moral conduct. It is impossible for a happy person to be violent or greedy. Most peccadilloes and other offences of human beings are committed by unhappy individuals, those who suffer from low self-esteem and hurt feelings. The Bhagavad Gita identifies *dharma virudha kama* (uncontrolled desire) as the source of wrong doings. Vedanta concludes that uncontrolled desire is the result of *atma ajnana* (self-forgetfulness or self-ignorance). Rajarshi is a fully awakened person, aroused with the realisation of being Brahman. Hence, Rajarshi is naturally and effortlessly happy. Rajarshi thinks and acts out of unlimited happiness, while others are breaking stones and pressing sands for happiness. Atlhough Raja captures what he or she wants, the Rajarshi leads a life of sharing and giving; the more one offers the more one receives.

However, the world has undergone several changes from the ancient times and has evolved into a new form. The salient features of the new world are:

- Unimaginable volume, velocity and variety of information and its universal accessibility
- Inconceivable volume, velocity and variety of individual aspirations and needs
- Accelerating volume, velocity and variety of change
- Foregrounding of women's rights and empowerment in gender discourse
- Individual as the ultimate value, over and above any other form of grouping like family, community, nation or religion
- Unity of matter and spirit in the human embodiment
- Legitimacy of desire and its uninhibited pursuit as means of self-realisation and happiness
- Living deeply in the moment and enjoying every moment of it rather than living for something else and that too for a chimeric tomorrow
- Invasion of machine in human life and the emergence of man–machine interfaces
- Human replacing God as the creator, sustainer-destroyer of life
- Cognitive limit and consciousness as the most important subject of study
- Gross Human Well-Being replacing Gross Domestic Product (GDP) as the true measure of human progress
- Entire humanity uniting as one people against perceived threat to human survival
- Impossibility of a Third World War
- Emergence of nature as a stakeholder in the survival discourse
- Breakdown of all forms of identities based on family, tribe, caste, ethnicity, race, language, religion, man, woman, gay, straight, rich, poor, powerful, powerless, and the rest of it; so too the blurring of logical categories like time and space, past and present, cause and effect, part and whole, substratum and substrate, substance and quality and ethical

categories like good and bad, ought and ought not; and aesthetic categories like ugly and beautiful, paving the way for the emergence of a fluid, indefinable global person as the agent of action—of knowing, willing, acting, interpreting, and being

Because of these cataclysmic changes that are happening in the environment, organisms and organisations, there have been drastic changes in the ways in which humans interact, process information and make decisions—all of this has become widely dispersed and diffused. The leader no more takes decisions, but only ensures conditions for individuals to access information freely and make decisions fearlessly. The leader makes sure that there is incessant flow of information vertically and horizontally. If individuals are the ultimate value, they should be the ultimate value creators too. Leader is only a master conductor of the orchestra, the denouement of which is open-ended. If music unfolds in a chaotically designed pattern, individual and group initiatives, innovative expressions and the director's spontaneity can ensure the flow of the performance into a grand harmony. Only a Rajarshi is deemed fit for such an arrangement.

Rajarshi and modern leadership

Rajarshi does not function from the cesspool of memories but from the vast ocean of consciousness, which is ever fresh and new. Since the functional ego of Rajarshi is not conditioned, but is informed, by past memories, he/she has the freedom to draw from the experience of memory without getting drawn into its prejudices and rigidities. Armed with the metaperspective of the Vedanta vision, the Rajarshi enjoys the inner freedom to design himself/herself moment to moment as the situations change and call for innovative solutions to complex problems. Being a proactive change agent, instead of just reacting to change, Rajarshi anticipates and often initiates change.

As Gandhi observed 'change has to begin with oneself: the heart of change is the change of heart'. Most of the present transformational leaders try to change the outer organisation—its structure, personnel, culture, behaviour, and so on—but they miss the opportunity to change themselves, so the transformation gets stuck with the leaders' needs and inner drives, with their fears and anxieties, and soon the inevitable entropy sets in. Outer transformation without the inner transformation of the leader adds an authoritarian outlook and saps the holding energy of the organisation. A Rajarshi is constantly on the move. He/she is a peripatetic leader. The past, present and future exist simultaneously within the Rajarshi. Hence, movement for a Rajarshi is moment to moment creative self-expression, because he/she transcends himself/herself, beyond the egoistic sense of doer–enjoyer continuum, in every thought and every action. Hence he/she is also called a transcendental or timeless leader.

21

The modern leader functions in an environment which is pluralistic, multicultural, multilinguistic, and having multiple perspectives. Specialists bring their specialized skill sets, visions, agendas, personalities, aspirations, and prejudices to the decision-making process. A leader must have an awareness that accommodates all these varieties and a mindset that sees value in all variations, a personal comfort level with differences, alternatives, dissent, rebellion, and disobedience. He/she sets personal standards without expecting to be emulated, without wanting to impose, but expecting to be challenged, to be excelled and exceeded. True leaders enjoy competition as a means of as well as an opportunity for self-discovery and self-expression. Rajarshi is a highly competitive leader. In fact, his/her actions are coopetition in practice. Coopetition is a positive sum game intended to create win–win solutions.

Decision-making in the present information-overloaded society is not just data crunching and adding and subtracting like a computer. Computer does not factor in emotions. All variables involved in the decision-making context are difficult to be digitised. There was a time when at least economists and some psychologists believed that decisions were products of rational thinking; now it is being realised that decisions are largely products of emotional processing. An economically sound decision can turn out to be politically unsound. This does not mean that data do not play any significant role in leadership decision-making. The problem with data is their humongous volume and making a decision based on data is like looking for a needle in a haystack. Data also become easily outdated and their veracity is at times questionable. The impossibility of measuring emotions, subtle drives, unexpressed and inexpressible motives—all make data generation and data-based information often undependable. A venture capitalist known to the writer, once confessed that he would consult all experts and then decide according to his gut feelings. Another problem with data is that experts speak different tongues and the data they collect and interpret are often unintelligible to each other. Decision-making requires that these experts understand each other and agree on fundamentals so that the decision that emerges has a wholesome flavour. Computer spaces and languages are being designed for these experts to meet and converse intelligibly. All these require stewardship of a leader who cannot, and even is not, expected to be a master of all trades. What the leader requires is awareness and not just information; compassion and not just courage; empathy and not just expertise; humility and not just confidence. Only a Rajarshi can match all these requirements.

The invasion of machines into the inner world of humans—through medicine and treatment modalities on one side and production processes, information collection, data generation, and thinking processes on the other—are epoch-making developments and call for serious philosophical reflection. Are humans losing their self-identity and becoming just a composite of chemicals and brain processes amenable for manipulation by medicines, machines and their masters, or is there an individual core inviolable and sacred and accessible only to the individual concerned? It will be revealing in this context to read the statement of Sally Greenberg, executive director of the National Consumer League, USA, in support of the female Viagra 'flibanserin', a drug touted as an effective cure for women diagnosed with low sexual desire, and newly approved by the U.S. Food and Drug Administration. Sally says:

> It [low sexual desire] is very destructive to their relationships, their families, and their self-image. We know this is a problem with their brain chemistry, just like depression and just like depression their brain chemistry can be adjusted. We can treat it and we should treat it. I think it is a historical moment, a huge moment for women's sexual health, in the way that the pill was for women's sexual health and ability to control their own destiny.

This is a machine mindset that persons are just a composite of chemicals. That there is no core self which can ensure the well-being of an individual by positive imagining and healthy thoughts and lifestyle changes. The march of the machine is unstoppable, but the retreating self instead of getting overrun needs to enlarge and encompass the powerful machine and give it purpose and meaning; this can only be accomplished by an awakened Vedantin Rajarshi. The Rajarshi clearly sees that machines and their interactive spaces invoke consciousness and intelligence and do not create them and that machines themselves are modification of intelligence, hence, not an invader but only an enhancer and facilitator. Such a vision gives the Rajarshi the inner leisure and freedom to deal with machines proactively and innovatively. The man–machine entanglement will continue forging a new individual who has the power and omniscience of machines and wisdom and interiority of self: the modern avatar of Rajarshi.

Fifty percent of human potential had been locked up in menial homebound preoccupations, dictated by the misogynist perspectives and expectations of a patriarchal society. But because of the revolutionary changes that has happened during the past hundred years in science, technology, production processes, and social mores, women are emerging out of their closets, coming forcefully to the forefront, demanding equality with men, in decision-making, production processes and in sharing the rewards. Women want to be the sole owner of their bodies and the sole determinant of their future. This rebellion of women is an existential threat for men and the traditional model of the Rajarshi is not immune from the bruises caused by the feminine revolt. Patriarchy, patriotism, hierarchy, elitism, discipline, character, and the 'honour your gods, love your women, fight for your country' kind of chivalry were all built into the Rajarshi model of yore. Treating the feminine on equal footing and integrating the male and female energies into wider dynamics though is not a new challenge to the Rajarshi tradition. In the concept of the Shiva–Shakti union and the ideal of *ardhanarishvara*, the Vedantin has already envisaged male–female union and has also realised it in mystical states. Shiva is powerful only in association with shakti.[8] The *lasya* of Parvati and the *tandava* of Shiva in a competitive mode create spirals of energy, beauty and happiness. The future Rajarshi leader should be able not only to creatively integrate the rousing female energy, but also to find such confluence of polar energies in his own psyche. Similarly, females have to integrate the male energy in unique ways. The Rajarshi will be a male/female leader, rather than just a one-sided, emotionally disabled, male alpha gorilla or rationally deficient demure female kitten. Conversely, the males becoming timid and apologetic and the females becoming ogre-like and vengeful also do not bridge the gender divide. Only the Rajarshi, who knows himself/ herself to be neither male nor female (or as both male and female), can take up the challenge of the gender revolution sweeping the world today.

Rajarshi leadership alone can save the world

The democratic principle of majoritarianism, that is, imposing the decisions of the majority on the minority is unacceptable to the modern world. Majoritarianism is morally wrong and dangerous in practice, logically self-contradictory and politically unsustainable. It is morally wrong because majoritarianism ignores voices of minorities; dangerous in practice because it leaves minorities disgruntled and discontented; logically self-contradictory because majority opinion in the name of democracy ends up as dictatorship of many over few, politically unsustainable because of the rebellion or noncooperation of the minority. At the same time, a politically organised and armed minority on sectarian ground is a serious threat to democracy, its institutions and practices. Rajarshi listens unconditionally to the voices of all stakeholders and also of those who are outside the system (*avarnas*). Rajarshi has an acute ear for the muted voices of the voiceless and the unrepresented (before the whisper becomes a scream). Rama made friends with Guha, the tribal leader; Jatayu, the bird; Hanuman, the monkey; Jambavan, the bear; Sabari, the outcast; and Vibhishana, the rakshasa outsider. Rajarshi is a conciliator, mediator, negotiator, persuader, and consensus builder. Rajarshi wins without fighting which is the highest form of strategy. Rajarshi wins without defeating which is sustainable victory. In a nuclear-armed world, capable of destroying the planet with the press of a button, no other victory is sensible nor sustainable. Rajarshi leadership alone can save the world from a third world war and its aftermath—the inevitable end of humankind.

To deal with the explosive energies of the new individual (and at present there are seven billion of them and will get stabilized only at 12 to 15 billion by 2100 AD) powered by unrestrained imagination combined with unimaginable computing power of machines is a task that calls for the depth and width and wholeness of Brahman consciousness. Let the individual pursue their self-interest to the best of their wisdom and capacity and as Adam Smith, the father of modern economics, said the 'invisible hand' of the market will regulate those activities to the best advantage. Rajarshi represents that invisible hand; he/she is nowhere in particular and yet is everywhere, like Lord Vishnu, lying on the serpent bed, floating in the ocean of milk (symbol of consciousness) Vishnu is present everywhere. Such nimble-footedness of backgrounding and foregrounding oneself as per need of the hour is the secret of Rajarshi vitality. The spacelike invisibility of Rajarshi assures that all get their voices heard and aspirations fulfilled: Rajarshi becomes the thread that holds all individual flowers into the organisation of a garland. The spacelike consciousness of the Rajarshi has individual places for all.

The power and the palpable truth of the moment, which holds the dead past and unborn future in its tight pulsating grip, collapses into the focused intensity of human action making the embodied individual the only reality and the satisfaction of the moment the only freedom. God, heaven, sacrifice (for the other), and the rest of it have been tossed into the blazing fire of the moment. The poignancy and the urgency of the moment is what drive humanity now. Vedanta alone, of all worldviews, is equipped to deal with this situation. For the Vedantin, the happiness that one seeks (a seeking which causes efforts and creates time, in terms of past, future, memory, anxiety, and angst) is actually 'here and now' and the realisation of which requires no effort because it is not a product to be manufactured. Happiness being an ever-existing reality (*vastu-tantra-tvad*) and which exists nonseparate from the seeking individual (*tat tvam asi*) has to be known as such. In this case, knowledge means awakening, which takes no effort or time. Effort based on expectation is time. Living in the moment means living happily and not living for happiness. Rajarshi is an embodiment of happiness and he/she alone has the philosophical and psychological wherewithal to deal with the demand by billions of individuals for instant satisfaction. A happy leader lives in timelessness and radiates happiness to all. The Rajarshi sees life as a play and the world as a playground and not a battleground or burial ground.

One of the paradoxes of human existence is that though on one hand, the human is physically and cognitively (includes affection and conation) limited and acutely conscious of such limitations, on the other hand, the sense of limitation happens in the context of a vague feeling of perfection and limitlessness. As Blaise Pascal, the French mathematician–philosopher articulated: 'from the physical body standpoint the world reduces me to a pinpoint, but from the consciousness standpoint I reduce the world to a pinpoint'. This dual nature makes the human condition unique and a creative space of tension. Universally, human beings want to be perfect, be free from all limitations, spread their wings, and fly out of the cocoon. This hunger for perfection can be quenched only by awakening and not by any amount of efforts. Efforts are necessary to maintain the body but are of no value in awakening to consciousness and to *sahajananda* (natural bliss). Modern science has proved that humans have cognitive limits, human knowledge and its reach is limited by the speed of light, physically humans are determined by the laws of physics and biological evolution and life has to be organised within that limit. Hence, true freedom is the result of an awakening, a freedom that accommodates limitations and uses limits and boundaries for self-expression. Only an awakened Rajarshi can accomplish this magic of making elephants dance on needle tip, or see the ocean in a drop of water, or see the whole universe in a grain of sand.

However, in spite of sporadic violence and skirmishes here and there in the name of religion, ethnicity, national boundaries, and inequality, a global consciousness-based consensus is emerging that call for united action to ward off the threat to human survival—threats like climate change, inequality, poverty, nuclear war, over exploitation of scarce natural resources, and the pervasive sense of meaninglessness. The pope and the mulla, the rabbi and the pandit, presidents and prime ministers, kings and dictators, scientists and activists, businesspersons and politicians are all in agreement that humankind faces an existential threat due to competitive human follies and greed, and that unless urgent remedial actions are taken, human survival will be in dire peril.

Rajarshi and the vedantic vision

To galvanise this global awareness into a culture of proactive policies and institutional action requires the wider vision, personal conviction and persuasive skill of a Rajarshi. Vedanta alone can provide that vision, skill, vocabulary, and stamina to launch a sustained campaign against the aforesaid perils, till it gains a critical mass of appeal to become part of mainstream discourse. Leaders who can rise above narrow sectarian considerations, be it religious, ethnic, ideological, or nationalistic, alone can be in the forefront of this campaign. The world needs Rajarshi leaders who can foresee this calamity and lead humanity away from the brink of total annihilation.

The traditional image of Rajarshi leader is that of a single-person authority assisted by a small group of advisors and supporters. Even today, whether he/she be a family head, a community leader, corporate CEO, or a country's president, they all are still single individuals at the top of the heap. Fortunately, the days of the infallible Pope, the all-knowing ideologue, the all-powerful general, or absolute monarch or dictator are over. These days individuals have become self-assertive, their aspirations soaring to the skies; organisations have become intractably complex and issues beyond logical analysis; and the cure offered by science and technology often are worse than the disease. The debate over GDP versus Gross Domestic Wellbeing (GDW), or development versus environment, or science versus wisdom, or technology versus the self, and individual versus the state are indicative of a catch-22 situation that responsible leaders face today. Is morality the exclusive preserve of the individual; does he/she have unfettered freedom to pursue personal desires and goals; does the family, community or state have any right (or even responsibility) to impose discipline on the individual; and who will decide and by which process and standards? Can research, especially in humanities, be free from personal and social biases, prejudices and business interests and political influences? These are some of the questions that still beg answers.

Authority used to be inherited, along the line of biological succession. Those who learnt the trick of the trade disciplined themselves to positions of knowledge, power and influence, acquiring enormous authority and control over the decision-making process. Whichever way one chooses to explain the emergence and exercise of authority, presently it is seen as an unacceptable, demeaning and self-serving, though unavoidable, imposition on individual freedom of self-determination, and hypocritically and selfishly exercised in the name of collective security and survival.

Thus, in the 21st century we have individuals who refuses to be led or to lead; wants to walk the untrodden path; lives in a universe of friends with shared interests; whose bonding and bonds are subtle and subliminal, free from authority, conversion and apostasy; who lives, communicates, shops, expresses opinions, operates, and organises protests in the virtual internet space. Most of the younger generation leaders whether in politics, business, or religion operate in the virtual space. Social media has liberated the individual follower from the leader and the leader from the follower. Their connections have become invisible and free flowing. Every empowered individual has become a centre of authority and source of unique values. Postmodernism, with its visceral distrust of grand narratives, has ushered in the pluralism of autobiographical narratives and the practice of multiculturalism. Though the exclusivist pope has condemned this movement as the tyranny of relativism and atheism, the celebration of pluralism and diversity has released vibrant spurts of creative energy, individual imagination and customised solutions.

All these developments make the world chaotic, ambiguous and messy. America thought that they will once for all solve the problems in Vietnam, Korea, Middle East, Afghanistan, and Iraq, but landed in messier situations. Asked about the fundamental difference between the Chinese and Americans in their approach to world problems, the redoubtable scholar–diplomat–statesman Henry Kissinger, in an interview to *Time* magazine said that the Americans believed that there was a final solution to every problem, whereas the Chinese believed that there were no final solution to a problem and that solutions are only provisional. This reminds us of the Bhagavad Gita's teaching that 'there is no action and solution thereof that is free from defect, just as there is no fire without smoke' (Ch: 18: 48).

Vedanta teaches that the world is always a work in progress and will never attain perfection; that growth is ultimately towards decline and disintegration; just as the day is followed by night, evolution has to necessarily be followed by devolution—the Big Bang comes in the end to a big crunch. Progress is not linear, but cyclical. 'The born shall die'!

The Rajarshi armed with the wisdom of Vedanta is well equipped to deal with this chaotic situation. For the Rajarshi freedom is not from action, but in action; liberation is not from the body, but in the body; salvation is not outside the world but challenging and being challenged by the world; problem solving is not the end of the game, but the beginning of another game; and so on. All this is possible because the Rajarshi identifies with Brahman, the consciousness that shines on phenomena and, by virtue of that transcends all phenomenal events.

Rajarshi Janaka, the wise king of Videha, rumoured to have famously said, '*mithilayam pradiptayam na me dahyati kaschana*'—if Mithila, (his capital city) burns, nothing of mine is burnt. This appears to be an irresponsible statement of a ruling king. But what Janaka actually meant was that he was prepared to measure up to any challenge, that no untoward event could paralyse him. The same was said about Emperor Nero (37–68 AD) of Rome, that he fiddled while Rome was burning. Later, however, it was proved that all of that was mainly malicious Christian propaganda. Nero persecuted Christians for denouncing Roman gods and they in turn took revenge by blackening his name in history. Historians now say that in the first place, there was no instrument fiddle in use during Nero's time. Second, Nero was not in station while Rome burnt. Third, Nero ordered immediate relief to suffering citizens. Fourth, Nero rebuilt the city to its original glory in no time. But at the end, Nero committed suicide, which shows there was some flaw in his personality. But Janaka went on to rule. Perhaps the problem was that Nero had no advantage of Vedantic learning.

The modern Rajarshi

In this chaotically complex world where human desires and efforts, supported by ever-sophisticated machines and appliances, are running round and round chasing each other in circles, leadership and decision-making have become the theatre of the absurd. Modern political, business, cultural, and religious leaders look comical. Their empty, nervous smiles betray their insecurities and anxieties. They neither have the authority of pedigree and tradition nor the strength of integrity and character; nor the encompassing depth of vision and compassion to lead the world with moral conviction and personal dedication. The world has to resurrect the Rajarshi ideal to deal with this messy situation.

Change has to be dealt with vision, complexity with clarity, uncertainty with conviction, chaos with purpose, anarchy with determination, loneliness with meaning, wretchedness with nobility, greed with charitableness, rebellion with understanding, dissent with accommodation, mindless machines

with mindful self, mass madness with individual sanity, decadence of prof-
ligate consumption with the efflorescence of voluntary poverty: every problem comes with its solution.

Our image of the Rajarshi also has to change pari passu with the problems
of the world. The modern Rajarshi could not be an individual or a collegium
or class of individuals. The modern Rajarshi has to be a social network, or
system or an institution – a living, smart and wise organisation that ensures
uninhibited flow of information. The need of the hour is an institutionalised
Rajarshi, a network of self-aware, empowered and empathetic individuals
and levels of deliberations, with effective moral and legal checks and balances, a sort of a global institutional brain that can think and feel, will and
wish, that beats the heart beats of all stakeholders. The modern Rajarshi will
be analogous to the cosmic person of the *purusha sukta* (Rig Veda 10–90) or
the *visvarupa dhara* of the Bhagavad Gita (Ch: 11).

A Rajarshi in the mould of an ayatollah (combines religious and state
authority in one self-appointed, unelected, manipulator á la Iran) or a general secretary (combines ideological and state authority in one person who
emerges on top after a series of clandestine wheeling and dealing in the
ruling party that has forced itself on the people á la China) is unacceptable
to the modern sensitivity nor will it be up to the challenges of the modern
world. A command economy like China might flourish in the short term,
serving the consumption needs of the rich minority of the affluent world,
but the contradictions involved in such an exploitative relationship would
culminate in its inevitable collapse under its own weight. China cannot grow
without America and America cannot and will not let China grow beyond a
toleration point. When the branch grows thicker than the trunk, tension is
inevitable. China will either implode or come to direct confrontation with
America and self destruct, pulling down the world economy along with it.
Either way, China has no alternative but to fall off the cliff, unless, of course,
China comes to embrace the Rajarshi model of enlightened leadership. Iran,
being a minor backwater power, may or may not carry on with their outmoded Rajarshi style of leadership. The Rajarshi model that the RSS recommends for India will have the same defect that of Iran and China. Therefore,
India will have to think twice before it defines its Rajarshi model.

The main challenge for the updated Rajarshi model would be incorporating ethics and morality, integrity and character, empathy and compassion,
and all that has to deal with emotions. An individual with effort can be
disciplined to combine efficiency and empath—but how to build a network
of institutions that function with empathy and compassion, with integrity
and character?

India has to build on the democratic and parliamentary institutions that
it has partly borrowed consciously from the west and partly inherited from
its colonial masters. The market economy, civic freedoms, rule of law, and
application of reason to decision making and problem solving go hand in

hand with the political institutions. But they have to be grafted on the Indic roots and those institutions and practices have to be interpreted in and by Indic/Vedic/Vedantic terms. The same applies in the remodelling of the Rajarshi. Will he/she/it be a 'coated booted', 'English-speaking' Rajarshi? Or a dhotiwala, Hindi-speaking Rajarshi? Or a Persian-Urdu speaking Rajarshi? Or may be a Hindi-Urdu-English speaking-dhoti-coat-boot-topi–wearing Rajarshi! One significant phrase in Advaita Vedanta is '*taira-yam na virudhyate*', we are opposed to none (Mandukya Upanishad Karika: 2–17). Vedanta being an inclusivist world view is not opposed to any other exclusivist world views. Hence, Vedanta is *samanvaya darsana* (an integrating vision). The story about Ramakrishna is relevant in elucidating this point. An atheist engaging in a debate with Ramakrishna convincingly proved that there never ever was such an entity called God. Ramakrishna heard him with rapt attention and great admiration and appreciated his stand with deep reverence. On being asked by his baffled devotees, Ramakrishna averred that the atheist was greater than the theist because theist had renounced only the world whereas the atheist had renounced even God, which was much more difficult and deserved to be called supreme renunciation. For a Vedantin, even absolute negation is assertion.

Such comfortableness with negation is an asset for Rajarshi leader. He/she will encounter stringent opposition to propositions. Just as democracy is an uneasy, dynamic, balance between proponents and opponents, Rajarshi is a pulsating balance between negation and assertion. This makes the inner balance and peace of Rajarshi undisturbed in all conditions. An inclusivist world view cannot be challenged by an exclusivist worldview just as space cannot be sliced by a sword or punctured by a needle. This vision gives Rajarshi enormous strategic depth and incredible range of tactical choices.

The characteristics of the future Rajarshi is unpredictable; so, too, is the definition of the unfolding world. Arjuna asks the same question to Krishna: 'How does one define a Rajarshi'? 'Simple', said Krishna. 'Rajarshi is happy in the self by the self.' 'Then Rajarshi will be inactive', quipped Arjuna. 'No'! Krishna reassured. 'Rajarshi will be happily active, not active for happiness'. That would be the sum and substance of Vedanta and the Vedantic model of Rajarshi leadership. Be happily active!

Notes

1 *Karmani akarma yah pasyet/akarmani karma yah/ sah buddhiman manushyeshu/ sah yukta krisna karmakrit* (B. Gita Ch: 4–18). Tranlsation of the Gita verses are of the author.
2 *Sa kaleneha yogo nashtah parantapa* (B. Gita Ch: 4–2).
3 *Anushtradrinam kamodbhavad, hiyamana viveka vijnana hetukatvena.*
4 *Sukshmatvatad dharmasya* – Mahabharata.
5 Cited from his book titled *Yoga Sutra of Patanjali—A Biography,* published by Princeton University.

6 Brahma Jnanavali Mala, verse: 20.
7 A free rendition of gayatri mantra given by Sanyal (2012).
8 *Shiva Shaktya Yukto Yadi Bhavati Shaktah* – Soundaryalahari.

References

Mueller, M. 1899 (first published). *The Six Systems of Indian Philosophy.* Chowkhamba Sanskrit Series. London: Longmans, Green, https://openlibrary.org/publishers/Chowkhamba_Sanskrit_Series_Office (accessed on 2 October 2018).

Nehru, J. 1947 (speech first delivered). 'Tryst with Destiny' Address to the Constituent Assembly of India in New Delhi. https://www.americanrhetoric.com/speeches/jawaharlalnehrutrystwithdestiny.htm (accessed on 27 August 2019).

Sanyal, S. 2012. *The Land of Seven Rivers: A Brief History of India's Geography.* UK: Penguin Books.

Sternberg, R. 1997. *Successful Intelligence.* New York: Plume.

3

MANAGEMENT AND RAJARSHI LEADERSHIP

R. Narayanan

Yatra yogesvara Krishno yatra Partho dhanur dharaha
Tatra Sree(r) Vijayo bhuti(r) dhruvaa neethi(r) matir mama
Bhagavad Gita 18:78

The combined teamwork of contemplative Krishna, the Rishi
and proactive Arjuna, the Raja ensures prosperity, success,
wellbeing and universal justice.

Introduction

It is a widely held belief that the future lies in the past. We need to be respect-
ful of the past while charting the future, just as we need to use the rear-view
mirror as much as the front windshield while driving. Those who forget the
past have no future and those who do not care about future become fossils.
It is from this perspective that we discuss the role of classical wisdom in
helping us draw the contours of effective management and leadership.

The words 'raja' and 'rishi' appearing in this chapter do not necessarily
connote persons. They refer to a set of attributes characterising the person.
We will attempt to identify the set of attributes that depict rajarshi in the
domain of management. Rajarshi, as a metaphor, stands for a combination of complementary attributes—feminine and masculine, satva and rajas,
intelligence and emotion, action and thought, knowledge and skills, innovation and production, strategy and execution, analysis and synthesis, prose
and poetry, and so on. The term rajarshi is gender neutral; hence the pro-
nouns 'he', 'his', etc., may be interpreted as a shorthand notation for he/she,
his/her, etc.

Raja and Rishi: complementary attributes

In our ancient tradition as well as in recent history, we have had great rajas
and rishis in separate silos. The raja seeks new routes to a given destination
while the rishi seeks new destinations. The raja crunches data using the left

brain, the rishi reflects on intuition using the right brain; raja focuses on doing a thing right driven by efficiency considerations, rishi concentrates on doing the right thing, thereby achieving effectiveness. In modern jargon, we can say that raja is obsessed with output while rishi sets his eyes on the outcome. For example, the raja may take pride in declaring that they have built 20 new hospitals, achieving a ratio of one hospital bed for every 1000 citizens. Rishi may silently work towards creating conditions that would make hospitals redundant. An ordinary manager worries only about growth while a rajarshi manager is mainly concerned about development.

Growth and development

Russell Ackoff, one of the most profound thought leaders, makes the distinction between growth and development in a clear manner (Ackoff and Rovin, 2003). A rubbish heap grows, it does not develop. Many geniuses develop without necessarily growing. Senseless growth results in crony capitalism while development leads to compassionate capitalism. Third-world nations can justify growth only if it contributes to development. Development reflects in the quality of life and not in the standard of living index. Quality of life can only be perceived and cannot be quantified, while standard of living can be quantified, hence, prone to fudging. A state of good health and well-being, for example, indicates a better quality of life. The increased ratio of 'hospital beds per thousand population' may at best indicate growth. The chief economic advisor of an African nation once remarked to the author that their country's target was fewer hospitals and a better state of health. Bhutan claims to measure gross domestic happiness in addition to GDP. The pursuit of development is always accompanied by *satyam* (truth), *shivam* (goodness) and *sundaram* (beauty). Managers need to get a grip on the humane and aesthetic aspects of development.

Even as early as 400 years before Christ, the Greek philosopher Plato had said that there will be no end to the troubles of states or of humanity itself till philosophers become kings or till those whom we call kings truly become philosophers, and political power and philosophy come into the same hands. He coined the phrase 'philosopher king' which echoes the ancient Indian references to 'rajarshi'. In the rajarshi style of Indian management, we shall seek to synthesise and seamlessly integrate these bipolar qualities. The end result would be a smooth flow of management vocabulary and spiritual traditions.

Classical Indian wisdom

The Vedas, Upanishads, Puranas, and Neeti sutras have given us loads of wisdom; these are in the nature of items on an a la carte menu. Depending on our needs, goals, capabilities, constraints, and the environment amidst which we are placed, we have to choose the appropriate items and synthesise into a full meal. Enjoying the honour of being the most developed species in creation's evolution, we have the freedom and responsibility to make the choice. There is no imposition of another's will here; it is all about each individual manifesting his innate consciousness. In fact, heaven is a metaphor for such a freedom of choice, although religions wrongly project it as a geographical destination somewhere up north.

The core concept of the rajarshi model of ancient Indian wisdom is cognisance of unlimited individual potential energy and its conversion to kinetic energy through work and sadhana. Several instances could be cited of those who achieved such a state; for example, Alexander Fleming, Lata Mangeshkar, Bill Gates, and Martina Navratilova. When everyone is working towards giving concrete shape to his potential, conflicts of interest are bound to rise. Maximising the potential of a large group should not be allowed to become a zero-sum game. In order to minimise the pain of one losing out, tradition has created the concepts of *svadharma*, *lokadharma* and *apat dharma*. Svadharma is personal and specific to each individual while lokadharma is universal and absolute. Apat dharma makes provisions for behaviour during emergency situations. Ordinary managers practice svadharma and lokadharma separately whereas a rajarshi *embeds* svadharma in lokadharma. An ordinary manager may be ossified in complying with processes. He or she may be doing a causal analysis simulation when the house is burning. A rajarshi manager knows when to flout processes namely when to bring apat dharma into play.

Highly enlightened rajarshis are the most relaxed people—Vishnu, the CEO with the responsibility for the well-being of the entire cosmos, relaxes comfortably on the smooth surface of a snake but never fails to intervene when the situation enters a crisis phase. He may be mistaken for being asleep, but he is constantly watching a dashboard displaying the key performance indicators of every major project. He lets junior managers handle day-to-day issues; he does not micromanage but intervenes when the brand image is about to take a beating. How does this translate into empowerment, delegation and accountability in the modern management scheme?

No hard slots

A pure rishi may not prove to be a good manager; his areas of strength are in assignments such as innovation and strategising. He or she may be too indifferent to the nuts and bolts of execution. He or she will drown himself in analysis paralysis. He or she may not have the heart to make harsh decisions even if the situation warrants. Without possessing down-to-earth skills, he or she may not be able to produce tangible results. A great automobile designer will be clueless when the tyres of his car go flat; a capable electrical engineer may not know how to change the fuse. That is why we need an automobile designer and a mechanic; we need electrical engineers and electricians. The rishi is like the bow that provides the necessary tension and support for the arrow (raja) to travel and destroy the target. The rishi is the software architect who designs complex software ('apps') but needs a raja in the form of a hardware platform (say, a smartphone) to 'execute' the code and bring the benefits of his contemplations and creative ideas to the end-users. While the rishi uses the telescope to get a 30,000 feet above-the-ground macro vision, the raja uses a microscope to delve deep into finer details.

There are no pure rajas or rishis. It is always the dominant component that determines one's slot. The proportion could vary because of training and passage of time. Bill Gates was perhaps 90 percent raja and 10 percent rishi in his initial days at Microsoft, but today he is 20 percent raja and 80 percent rishi. As raja he created enormous wealth and as rishi he is distributing the wealth in the most appropriate manner for procuring maximum good for the most people. Several characters from epics and history have demonstrated that complementary traits could be acquired through training. King Janaka, tired of day-to-day chores, is believed to have taken sabbatical for a month, apprenticed under Sage Yagnavalkya in the forest, and come back fully charged to resume his duties. Senior executives make a beeline to Davos to attend the World Economic Forum to learn through networking.

The mutuality of relationship between a pure raja and a pure rishi is interesting. The compassionate rishi intervenes whenever the raja gets into the habit of possessing and perishing. The rishi brings the raja into the habit of sharing and flourishing. In the Mahabharata, Draupadi argued for revenge when she was ill-treated in Duryodhana's court. She kept egging on her husbands to wage war. At the end of the war, she chose to forgive Asvattama, who had killed her children in a midnight massacre. What a change of mindset over just a few years! Manuneethi Chola was very fond of his son, but he did not hesitate to drive a chariot over him because of a complaint received from a cow that his son's chariot had killed her calf. Today, we see competing companies that had fought street battles for market share cooperate with each other by sharing expensive facilities and probably tackling a more powerful common enemy.

Ambassadors on the move

Rajarshis are temperamentally hardwired to accept the Law of Constant Change. They believe that only a state of unstable equilibrium triggers dynamic activity. A rajarshi CEO thus would create a product, expand its features and functionalities and, at the right time, withdraw the product; concurrently, R&D on the next-generation product would be happening in the background. Apple frequently releases new models of iPhones, just as Microsoft releases newer versions of Windows with predictable periodicity. The absence of rajarshi mindset results in companies becoming stagnant and ultimately irrelevant. Even a company such as IBM swore by mainframe computers but woke up to the potential of personal computers at the right time. It had the resilience to dominate the PC market before hiving it off to Lenovo.

Rajarshis can be identified through their humility, brevity of speech, frugal living, and high integrity. They don't hang on to institutions they create. After taking the organization to a level of maturity, they withdraw. Several kings, such as Raghu and Yudhishtra, conquered everything and, at the apex of their glory, decided to renounce them all. Angel investors today provide funding for start-ups, mentor the budding entrepreneurs during the early stages and, when the company starts standing on its own legs, withdraw so as to help another outfit to find its feet.

Rishis, while interacting with several rajas, act as carriers of best practices from one kingdom to the other, thereby creating a healthy competition among the rajas. As roving ambassadors, they do not believe that best practices should remain the copyright of specific kings. The idea is not to be misinterpreted as espionage. Rajarshis are open-source evangelists. The noble aim is to harness individual excellence into global excellence. The global well-being has been repeatedly emphasised in our ancient wisdom through such phrases as

Loka samasta sukhino bhavantu
Bahujana hitaya bahujana sukhaya
Yogakshemam vahamyaham
Atmanastu mokshartham jagat hitaya cha

Medium is the message

A rajarshi is not just a medium but a message. He or she does not *convey* virtues, he or she *embodies* them. It would be futile to expect do-it-yourself formulae from him. His messages are implicit. As a teacher he or she sets out the *arohana* and *avarohana* (ascending and descending sequence of notes) of, say, the Todi raga. It is left to the *manodharma* (improvisation or spontaneous creative interpretation) of the student to indulge in permutations and combinations of the notes to produce an aesthetically pleasing music. Each student may do it differently. Again, the same student may do it differently on two different days. Adhering to the basic non-negotiable definition of the arohana and avarohana, a thousand varieties of Todi raga emerge. A teacher who achieves the blossoming of a thousand lotuses from a single seed is a rajarshi teacher.

Personal mastery

A conscious manager realises the importance of personal mastery of his team members. He or she lays emphasis on personal goals. He or she believes that a person who cannot decide his goal cannot win. Since knowledge is the key asset today, developing talent is the main challenge for the corporate sector. Therefore, organisational criteria should ensure that human resources work smoothly and their talents are constantly enhanced. In fact, there is ample evidence to show that personal mastery is a prerequisite for effective teamwork. One of the underlying principles behind this effect is respect for meritocracy, the primary reason for knowledge workers migrating to the West. Peter Senge (2006), a contemporary Systems Thinker, places personal mastery ahead of higher-order values such as shared vision and teamwork.

'Live as if you were to die tomorrow. Learn as if you were to live forever', Mahatma Gandhi, a great rajarshi in every sense of the term, commented. A rajarshi manager's primary responsibility is to gauge the potential of his protégés and enable their professional advancement through customised learning opportunities. Such a manager uses all possible modes of knowledge acquisition in improving the competencies of his team members namely, *pratyaksha pramanam* (experiential learning through sense organs), *anumanam* (inference of new knowledge derived from existing knowledge), *upama* (learning through similes and metaphors), and *sabdabodham* (sayings of trustworthy people). He or she is enrolled in training programs and allowed to experiment. His learning is enhanced through apprenticeship with seniors and the study of previous case instances.

Moreover, the manager himself has to constantly update himself. A conventional manager uses the first two steps prescribed in the traditional wisdom, namely *sravanam* (listening) and *mananam* (critical reflection). A rajarshi manager goes one step further in *nididhyasanam* (practising meditation); it is through meditation that one attains the capability to draw inferences. The rajarshi model of human talent management ensures that inherent potential is transformed into self-confidence. The newly acquired confidence, in turn, increases the potential stock. Thus 'potential' and 'self confidence' begin to operate in a virtuous cycle each reinforcing the other.

During the Industrial revolution, individuals were referred to as 'hands'. In the context of a growing population, governments worried about feeding 'mouths'. Corporations hunted far and wide for 'heads'. However, in a rajarshi model, the individual is not a hand, mouth or head but the mind, spirit, emotions, and aspirations. It is highly gratifying to note that in recent times, we find a sort of awakening among the enlightened youth. The sounds of *Shivoham* and *Tatvamasi* seem to be ringing loud. We see more youngsters taking the entrepreneurial route or following vocations dictated by their heart. The environment and technology are also favourable to encourage the trend. Youngsters today are e-tailers, mobile app developers, animators, yoga teachers, concert artistes, script writers for films, and owners of restaurants serving authentic ethnic cuisine. They enjoy the freedom of working from home; they are doing financially well too. Similarly, on the side of management, the focus is shifting towards soft factors such as meritocracy, harmony, adjustment, coopetition, gender neutralisation, and cultural diversity alongside hard factors such as productivity, efficiency, market share, and quality. There is ample evidence that the rajarshi has started to play his role.

Yajna model of work

The yagna model of work culture is an inseparable aspect of the rajarshi model. In the yajna model of management, the chief executive of an organisation assigns responsibilities to individuals matching with their *gunas* (natural traits). He or she also empowers them to function in an unfettered environment. Given the required creative space, individual competence manifests in all its fullness. The individual energies of the employees are synergised into the composite energy of the organisation. Products and services produced by passionate employees result in delighted customers. The opportunity to manifest individual consciousness inspires employees and they remain loyal to the organisation. The focused channelling of individual competencies raises the financial status and brand image of the organisation.

Global corporations such as IBM and Microsoft bring together diverse talent from different backgrounds, countries and cultures to create products that even lay people can use. Thus, they contribute to narrowing the chasm between the digital haves and have-nots. As a byproduct, wealth gets created. Wealth includes material assets and intellectual property rights in terms of patents. The wealth so generated is shared among all stakeholders— shareholders, employees, suppliers, and society at large through Corporate Social Responsibility (CSR) initiatives. The residual wealth is enjoyed by the owners of the enterprise. The model closely follows the yajna style where the *yajaman* (owner) enjoys only the *yajnasishtam*, namely, the residue after giving away the benefits to all other stakeholders.

The Indian Space Research Organization (ISRO) brings together multidisciplinary talent, such as academia and industry, from all over the country. ISRO has fostered the culture of performance-based management to fulfil missions of national importance. These include telecommunication, remote sensing, weather forecasting, tele-education, telehealth, and so on. Such missions are accomplished in true yajna style. The fruits of the yajna not only earn a sense of pride for the employees but also earn the respect of the world towards India. The world respects technological strength even more than military and financial strength.

It should be noted that in the rajarshi model, desire forms the stimulus for action and creation. The competition too provides a stimulant for more vigorous work. Spiritual experience acts as a catalyst and further aids in attaining fullness. A rajarshi cannot afford to be risk averse. He or she believes that we develop and prosper as long as we have fire in the belly and not butterflies in the stomach, else we decay and can only envy our neighbors who continue to develop. It is only the weak who pass the buck on misfortune or karma.

Cause–effect duality

'*Dharmat arthascha kamascha tatah dharma kim na sevyate*'? ('Dharma brings wealth and happiness; therefore why not live life according to Dharma'?), asks Sage Vyasa at the end of the Mahabharata. On the other hand, Chanakya in *Arthasastra* boldly asserts that '*Dharmasya moolam arthah*' ('Wealth is the root of Dharma'). Thus we are led to believe that Dharma and Artha share a bidirectional and mutually influencing relationship. A rajarshi manager is one who is comfortable with the bidirectional nature of cause–effect relationships. This sense of comfort enables him to avoid knee-jerk reactions and make sustainable decisions. The inseparability of cause and effect has been stated in the ancient texts as *karyakaranayoh(r) abheda*.

Managers trained through the Western reductionist philosophy would find it difficult to digest the concept of mutual reinforcement of cause and effect. Chanakya further adds *sukhasya moolam dharma* (dharma causes happiness). It follows that if the goal of an organisation is to create happy customers and employees, it has to crate enormous wealth and adhere to dharma. Managers in every organisation should set *abhyudaya* (worldly achievement) as their goal.

Even the Buddha advocated that material well-being is necessary for spiritual advancement. He has been wrongly understood as having favored renunciation. He, however, advocated moderation in consumption, and so did Gandhi when he said that we have enough to satisfy everyone's need but not anyone's greed. The extent of need is to be determined by each individual depending on the stage of life (student, householder or retired person), level of spiritual advancement, and timeframe of existence. For example, the needs of a satvic retired person in the 19th century would be different from those of a rajasic student of the 20th century or a tamasic householder of the 21st century.

Wealth is the root of happiness. Wealth creation involves action. Action has to be preceded by volition; namely, the mental preparedness to plunge into action. The mind gets prepared for action through desire. Desire is the result of knowledge. Unless one is aware of the benefits of an action, how can one cultivate a desire for it? Hence, we have the virtuous cycle wherein freshly found happiness kindles further quest for new knowledge (Figure 3.1):

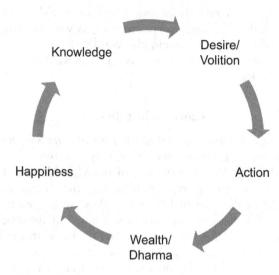

Figure 3.1 The Virtuous Cycle

Aurobindo in Savitri says that behaviour of all living beings is influenced by Thought, Intelligence and Reason. *Pravruthi* (acquisition), *nivruthi* (disposal) and *audhaseenya* (maintaining status quo) are instruments we use while working towards our objective. Intelligent business leaders trained in the rajarshi model know precisely when to acquire another business and at what price, when to exit from a current business and when to lie low.

The complex world

We can easily recognise how complexity has enveloped our everyday lives—there is a large variety of cars to choose from, there are plenty of choices when it comes to selecting an educational stream, the menu card in restaurants offers hundreds of dishes. The way we do banking (through the Internet), the means through which we communicate (through e-mail, SMS, WhatsApp, and video conferencing) and the manner in which we receive medical care (super specialists, variety of diagnostic instruments) have all changed in the last two decades. Often we are baffled by the variety of services available to us and the type of access mechanisms present for availing the services. Abundant variety contributes to complexity, leading to rational decision-making difficulties. If each member of a family wants a different food item, it makes life complex for the housewife. If students of a class possess different types of intelligence and, consequently, need different learning modes, it makes the job of the teacher complex.

We cannot wish away complexity because we have no control over it in most situations unless we choose to live in a Himalayan cave. It is useful, even necessary, to have the ability to recognise complexity before we can cope with it instead of running away from it. This will help us tame complexity and make it dance to our tune instead of succumbing to it.

In the realm of physical sciences, the science of the 'big' (cosmology) and the science of the 'small' (quantum physics) have given way to the science of the complex (superconductivity, for example). Chaos is another emerging discipline which studies systems comprising a large number of parameters and in which a small perturbation in one of the parameters results in a disproportionately large change in the system's behaviour. Long-term weather prediction is an example of a complex system where the effect of chaos is clearly visible. A small change in the atmospheric conditions in the Mexican coast (El Nino) results in a large change in the monsoon pattern over India.

Increased focus on rights and privileges at the expense of duties and responsibilities also enhances the complexity of a society. The increased levels of consumer awareness and consumer protection laws make things difficult for service providers. The telling effect of this can be seen in the conservative style of medical treatment in the West because the threat of litigation hangs like Damocles' sword over doctors.

A manager can be assessed only when he or she is exposed to handle complexity. Some managers may adopt a conservative posture and rely on past precedence. Others may exhibit daredevil tendencies and take risks. The senior leadership team of a company should contain a mix of people sporting different mindsets. It is the responsibility of a rajarshi manager to assemble such a heterogeneous team. Rajarshi managers develop the ability to see the big picture, understand the needs and constraints of all the stakeholders and design a solution that will not have undesirable side effects. Krishna's handling of the feud between the Pandavas and Kauravas illustrates the behaviour of a rajarshi manager.

Problem solving and systems thinking

Rajarshi manager is a systems thinker. Very often, the problem, in spite of being an inanimate entity, wants to convey a lot of information to us but we turn a blind eye and do not listen to it because our eyes and minds are blocked by filters such as our education, specialisation, political ideology, religious beliefs, and media influence. As a result, we end up finding brilliant solutions to some problems, namely, the problem as perceived by us and not the problem for which we are expected to find a solution. A rajarshi manager develops the skill to engage in conversation with the virgin problem. This gives him insight into the problem and not mere understanding of the problem. He or she believes that by doing a right thing wrong we have an opportunity to learn; but by doing a wrong thing right we make it 'wronger'. The epics Ramayana and Mahabharata are full of anecdotes in which wise people have invested time in identifying the right problem without rushing to solutions.

41

Managers cannot shirk the responsibility of making decisions; they cannot procrastinate, claiming that the issue is too complex. However, they should realise that their decisions may not be perfect all the time. The decisions are made with the information available at a given point in time, in the given context, and at the available level of understanding the interrelationships among various factors. In one of his sutras, Chanakya says that the conscientious ruler must resolve complex issues by careful and thorough analysis of all perspectives and the consequences of each including side effects before making his decision. He advocates harnessing the help of ministers, and individuals who are famous, wise, prosperous, enthusiastic, impressive, hard-working, well intentioned, and well behaved. In the current context, we see that the board of management of a company includes independent directors who possess diverse competencies. The sustained growth of the company emerges as the synthesis of these competencies. Moreover, we have consultants who are not attached with any single organisation and offer their services to anyone who cares to consult them.

A rajarshi manager never exhibits knee-jerk reaction to problems. He or she does not react to one-off events; he or she is not interested in answering what happened. He or she does not even respond to a pattern of events; he or she is not interested in any discourse on what has been happening. His thought process goes one step higher into the realm of generative thinking; he or she wants to know why something had been happening. This leads him to inquire about the structure behind the problem. Present-day systems thinkers believe that it is the structure that drives a system's behaviour. For example, if we consider governance systems, the democratic structure behaves differently from an autocratic structure. An enterprise that has a hierarchical structure is risk averse while one with a radial or flat structure is more innovative. The behaviour of members in a joint family is different from that in a nuclear family. The absence of generative thinking is responsible for solutions that

- Prove to be quick fixes that fail (also called Band-Aid solutions)
- Escalate the original problem
- Do not solve the given problem
- Degenerate into erosion of goals
- Result in the 'tragedy of commons'
- Bring success to the already successful and so on

We can see everyday examples when water pipes burst, roads develop potholes, inflation soars, bright students monopolise a teacher's care and attention, a bypass road soon becomes as congested as the main road whose congestion it was supposed to ease, or when tensions build up at the borders of neighbouring countries.

Fritjof Capra (1996) argues that the whole universe is an interconnected web; the web includes not just humans but also flora and fauna. In today's digital world, ordinary objects such as chairs are empowered to generate information and access and utilise information generated by other sources. We are referring to the technology behind the Internet of Things (IoT). Goods and services are marketed in a targeted manner based on intelligence gathered from shopping and web browsing patterns. The delinking of even one strand in the chain may result in the collapse of the web. The vision of oneness is a core concept of the rajarshi model of management as it is of Advaita. The vision helps cope with change in an orderly manner and build networks among seemingly disjointed entities. In such a unified world, the norms of ethical and social behaviour need to be rewritten. This is a task awaiting the rajarshi of this century.

Conflict resolution

Conflict between two entities arises when there are opposing views on issues of significance or when two people covet the same object. The nature of issues could be material, intellectual or spiritual. Managers in every domain of activity spend a considerable proportion of their time in resolving conflicts. Conflict resolution is the art and science of resolving differences and implementing resolutions to the satisfaction of all parties involved while staying within the boundary of dharma. A true conflict resolution manager is a participant in the process of resolving the differences and implementing the solution. He or she is committed to the cause of arriving at a solution and is willing to pay the price of the outcome. He or she is unlike a consultant who flaunts a set of recommendations and has no stake in the outcome. An ideal conflict resolutions manager separates himself from the immediate issues at hand and looks at the overall picture, including historical and cultural nuances behind the conflict. He or she studies the issues from a detached and balanced perspective.

A person genuinely interested in ending a conflict allows normal diplomacy to run its course first. This gives him or her time to study the motives and the stated position of each participant. It also helps to let the emotions subside. He or she then listens to each participant in the conflict carefully, avoiding his own biases. He or she carefully analyses the strengths and weaknesses of arguments offered by each participant. He or she reverse-engineers the weaknesses behind each rationale and interacts with each participant in a manner customised to the intellectual and emotional make-up of the individual. With some individuals he may find it productive to have direct interaction while with some others his interaction would be through intermediaries. He or she systematically develops multiple potentially acceptable solutions that are also amenable for practical implementation. He or she studies the consequences of implementing each of these alternatives. He or she also is ready with a set of offers to be used during negotiation. These offers, in addition to being logically sound, have to appeal to the cultural and emotional make-up of the participants. When the offers are rejected, he tries to threaten and create differences within a party. As an extreme measure he may even inflict punishment. The idea is to arrive at a final state—a solution through whatever means—buying peace, negotiating a trade-off, threat of dire consequences, or use of aggression. Thereafter, he devises a plan to implement and monitor the process with a definite timetable. Last, but not least, he or she is committed to the process in the sense that he is willing to pay the price personally during the course of conflict resolution. Ancient wisdom had paraphrased the above process as the sequence *sama – dana – bheda – danda*, meaning collaboration, accommodation, avoidance, and competition, respectively.

The conflicts between religious groups, political ideologies, development, and environment are all manifestations of inadequate capacity and mindset in resolving them in a rajarshi way. Krishna in the Mahabharata played the role of an ideal conflict resolution manager as seen from his behaviour preceding the war, during the war and after the war. He or she adopted different strategies while dealing with Duryodhana, Vidura, Draupadi, Kunti, and so on. He or she could act as an ideal rajarshi because he was a *gunatita*, someone who cannot be typecast as soft or hard or dark. Depending on the demand of the situation, he or she could be constructive and creative (*satva*), or he could be egoistic and passionate (*rajas*). On rare occasions, he or she may not hesitate to behave in a negative and lethargic way (*tamas*).

Abstraction

Everyone understands that good decisions cannot be made when key information is missing. An intelligent manager is one who understands that the presence of unwanted, redundant and irrelevant information is as injurious to the process of decision-making as the absence of required information. Such a rajarshi manager focusses on a few key performance indicators to get an overall feel of how the company is doing; he or she does not overload him- or herself with information. A typical relaxed CEO would only want to know the cash-flow position, the profitability projection for the next two quarters and the satisfaction levels of the employees and customers. He does, however, have access to all the data, should he choose to drill down for the details of any particular area of concern. The mindset required to separate the signal from noise, separate the grain from the chaff and separate the essence of an issue without being sidetracked into irrelevant details is called abstraction.

The process of abstraction implies not finding a solution to the problem at hand. It seeks to elevate the problem to a higher plane and then find a solution. By doing so, a reflective manager solves not just the given problem but a whole class of problems that are structurally similar (isomorphic) to the given problem, although they may use different vocabulary to describe them. Abstraction enhances the productivity of an operation by preventing the syndrome of reinventing the wheel and encouraging reuse of earlier designs and solutions.

The entire Bhagavad Gita can be viewed as an excellent case study in the art and science of abstraction. Its passages contain situations wherein abstract concepts are translated into concrete scenarios (analysis) and concrete attributes are aggregated into abstract concepts (synthesis). Several concrete roadmaps such as Bhakti Yoga (path of devotion), Karma Yoga (path of action) and Jnana Yoga (path of knowledge) are described in prescriptive explicit forms for realising the abstract concept of dharma. At another place, the Gita describes several desirable attributes, provides benchmark examples for them before synthesising them into the abstract concept of sthitaprajna. Similar pedagogy is used while expounding the form of *Viswarupa*.

The principle of abstraction is implicit in the Law of Life. All objects have essential properties and nonessential properties. An object cannot live without the essential properties but can live in the absence of nonessential attributes. For example, heat is the essential property of fire and sweetness is the essential property of sugar. The length and width of the tongues of the flame or the shape and particle size of the sugar lump are nonessential properties. The colour of skin, educational qualifications, height, weight, IQ, and EQ are nonessential properties of a human being while the essential property is divine consciousness which may get reflected in the above attributes.

Conscious corporation

We call some people like Kanchi Paramacharya and Ramana Maharishi, 'enlightened' because their consciousness quotient is higher than that of others. They know the purpose of their creation and they know what is to be done to fulfil that purpose. The same principle applies to enterprises too. If we look at enterprises that have sustained themselves for hundreds of years, one common thread is their level of consciousness. They know what they are doing and why they are doing. In other words, they have a mission and a vision. They continuously keep asking 'why does our business exist' and 'what is it we strive to achieve'. It does not matter if the objectives are self-centered or directed towards social responsibility as long as they conform to a set of values that they have set for themselves.

Physicist and philosopher Sir Roger Penrose (2002) argues that human consciousness is non-algorithmic and thus is not capable of being modelled by a conventional digital computer. At the level of society, consciousness level is determined by a number of 'soft' factors, such as political ideologies, media influence, adult education, opportunities for cheaper travel, and so on. Civil society movements—such as the one Jaya Prakash Narayan led in the 1970s or the initiatives of Anna Hazare against corruption, the Nirbhaya movement in the wake of a gruesome rape incident in Delhi or the enactment of the Right to Information Act—have helped the upward movement of the consciousness index. The rise and fall of empires and civilisations can be attributed to the rise and fall in the collective consciousness index. One of the most eminent attributes of a rajarshi is that he or she fosters the spirit of consciousness among individuals, kingdoms and nations so as to keep the development trajectory on course.

Consciousness is never designed. One cannot issue an office memo saying that with effect from 1 July 2017 this company shall behave like a conscious corporation. Enterprises that constitute task teams to drive consciousness across the organisation fail miserably. Consciousness is an emergent property of the interplay of several factors. We can recognise a conscious corporation when we see one. But it is difficult to lay down specifications. Consciousness shares this property with other notions such as beauty, obscenity and quality. However, we will attempt to list some tell-tale signs of a conscious corporation.

To achieve business goals such as profitability and market share, one can design suitable organisational structures and work out empowerment and accountability criteria. There is no specific organisational structure associated with a conscious corporation. There are no recipes for empowerment and accountability to achieve consciousness. A conscious corporation goes through a feedback cycle, comprising perception → knowledge management → creating world view → learning, which can give lead to a new perception and so on. Typically, a manager moulded in the rajarshi tradition would increase the consciousness level of a corporation through the following means:

- He or she evolves short-term and long-term strategies for the corporation taking into due consideration the competencies available within the organisation, the quantum of finance available for investment and the market conditions. Almost 2000 years ago, the great Tamil poet Tiruvalluvar in his magnum opus *Tirukkural* had said that during project execution one should take into consideration a) competencies needed to perform the job, b) one's own personal competencies, c) competencies of the support groups and suppliers, and d) competencies of the competition.
- He or she enunciates a statement of mission that is socially relevant and sensitive to ecological and ethical issues. He shares the strategy with his peers, superiors and subordinates so as to create a common and consistent alignment across the organisation. Otherwise, there will only exist silos of excellence working at cross purposes.
- A primary requirement of the rajarshi model in management is to state clear goals in most unambiguous terms. Goals should not be chosen just because they are convenient to measure. A rajarshi manager works out measurable targets for those down the line meshing seamlessly toward targets of those higher in the ladder. This provides scope for interdepartmental collaboration and collective problem solving. It avoids the common practice of passing the buck and finding scapegoats.

- He or she makes all business decisions (marketing, sales, production, HR) using reliable and up-to-date data. He or she builds models for assessing alternative business strategies. For strategic, tactical and operational initiatives, he uses quantitative data as well as qualitative perceptions.
- He or she chalks out a career development plan for all employees reporting to him or her. He or she helps them diagnose their current level of competence and compare the same against levels of competence required to shoulder higher responsibilities. He or she helps them bridge the gap through training, job rotation and any other means.
- He or she sets up a credible mechanism to address grievances of customers, employees and suppliers.
- He or she does not become a victim of mindless compliance with processes. He or she knows when to flout processes and when to rewrite processes. He or she does not allow him- or herself to be deluged in oceans of data. He or she values anecdotal evidence and emotive considerations.
- He or she uses field data and company targets to assess if any midcourse correction is called for. He or she does not hesitate to terminate projects that have reached irreversible levels of slippage.
- He or she appreciates how the industry is moving, guesses how competition is strategising and comes with R&D plans for new value-added products and services that will enhance the market share of the company. He or she constantly benchmarks his or her own performance against his peers from other organisations.
- He or she evolves an optimised organisational structure so as to offer independence to employees giving them creative space and at the same having checks and balances to see that the targets are met. Every employee knows to whom they are reporting and who are the people for whose performance they are responsible.
- He or she has mechanisms both overt and covert to smell any illegal acts such as evasion of governmental levies, corruption and nip them in the bud. He makes it known to all the zero-tolerance policy against dishonest acts.
- His or she actions are not conditioned by his mental models. He or she looks at the world as it is and does not see it as he or she wants it to be. He or she does not let tradition, past practices and media to influence his or her decisions.

A company with a consciousness deficit will look at targets but fail to see soft factors such as fatigue, and inappropriate staff welfare measures. For example, a scholarly employee would need membership in a professional society while an extrovert in corporate marketing division would prefer a social club membership. A manager in a conscious corporation has the ability to weave the company's fact file into a script, a story, a metaphor, and so on.

In any organisation, business models are valuable only if they continue to co-evolve with shifting trends in consumer preferences and technology. If they are etched in stone, it is a sure recipe for an organisation's extinction. The model should evolve as a result of wide consultations with diverse interest groups. Models can usefully be simulated for predicting outcomes. Good models comprise Reflection → Action → Reflection cycle. In the metaphor of the goose that lays the golden eggs, greedy business is over obsessed with getting their hands on the eggs. A conscious corporation believes that eggs will follow if attention is focused on the care and feeding of the goose. This is the real import of the oft-quoted verse from the Bhagavad Gita: *Karmanyeva adhikaraste maa phaleshu kadhachana*, meaning that we can exercise control only on our actions but we cannot influence the results thereof.

A conscious corporation assigns great importance to succession planning. If overnight the management team is changed and if the consciousness levels of the members of the new team are less than that of the enterprise at the time of change, there is a certain imbalance and disturbance. This results in frustration, staff turnover and a decline in the fortunes and brand image of the enterprise. We have seen such a phenomenon in semigovernment institutions such as universities and public sector undertakings. Whenever a new vice chancellor is appointed whose academic credibility is in question, the standing of the university falls, leading to faculty members with a higher level of consciousness leaving for other avenues. This further reduces the consciousness level of the university, cascading into a vicious cycle. Even reputed private enterprises had to face the consequences whenever there was an imbalance in the consciousness quotient of the outgoing and incoming teams. The Tata group and Infosys are two of the most respected business houses of India known for their impeccable standards of corporate governance. In spite of exercising due diligence in the succession planning process, conflict arose between Ratan Tata and Cyrus Mistry at the Tata Sons and between Vishal Sikka and Narayanamurthy at Infosys. One could clearly see the imbalance in the consciousness quotient of leaders from two different generations.

Spiritual quotient as figure of merit

The economic crisis brought about by greed has resulted in an emotional vacuum in the marketplace. Consumers and sellers do not trust each other, employers and employees are no longer mutually dependent. Rajarshi managers realise that profits are not the only purpose of business. They nurture a people centred culture; they not only seek feedback from consumers but also invite them as cocreators of products and services. In a transnational environment, formal encoding of ethics in statute books alone does not suffice.

Ethics needs spirituality as a driver to find its inner purpose and meaning. It needs the commitment of business managers driven by spiritual, environmental and societal considerations.

Prof. Laszlo Zsolnai is the chairman of the Business Ethics Faculty Group of CEMS, the global alliance in management education. According to Prof. Zsolnai, a more inclusive, holistic and peaceful approach to management is needed if business and political leaders are to uplift the environmentally degrading and socially disintegrating world of our age. 'We have several theoretical models of ethics. But from practice we know that the main problem to behave ethically is not knowledge but motivation' (Zsolnai, 2004). He further says that 'Empirical evidence suggests that spiritual experiences help the person transcend his narrow self-conception and enable him to exercise genuine empathy with others and to take an all-compassing perspective'.

According to Prof. Zsolnai despite the rich diversity of spiritual experiences, the main ethical message is always the same namely love and compassion, deep reverence for life and empathy with all. We need to realise that the rest of the world is as much an integral part of creation as we ourselves are and that by hurting others we would be hurting ourselves. The way we manage will be influenced by the way we lead our lives. Spirituality cannot be appended as an additional fixture to management: if spirituality is in our nature, it will manifest itself in our management style.

Scientific studies conducted in the West have confirmed the hypothesis that spiritual practices help the ethical part of the self. In early days, ethics was equated with compliance with the law of the land. Thus, if one declared all his or her goods at the customs and paid taxes correctly, he or she could call him- or herself ethical. In recent times, however, the character traits of managers are closely watched in the presence of group actions. For example, one can see that co-workers show solidarity when one of them is sacked. Similar considerations explain the large response to the prime minister's exhortation for well-to-do people to voluntarily give up the cooking gas subsidy. Short of using the phrase rajarshi, Prof. Zsolnai has captured the spirit of rajarshi in his writings and speeches. He quotes Socrates, Aristotle, Albert Schweitzer, Mother Teresa, Immanuel Kant, Gandhi, St. Francis of Assisi, and the Dalai Lama, among others, as examples of rajarshis.

The philosopher king is the cornerstone of Plato's aristocratic philosophy of governance. Managers who exhibit a fair, compassionate and consistent behaviour have their background solidly established in spirituality. Their empathetic mindset rubs on fellow managers and team members contributing to a great organisation and society. Spiritual quotient measures our ability to understand situations and systems in their entirety and come up with creative and appropriate solutions. It is not of much value when applied at the level of transactions. Spirituality has brought comfort for some individuals pursuing a quest for meaning and relevance of their existence. But at the world level, institutions such as the UN have not succeeded in preventing the destruction of the environment, or the perpetuation of inequality. If spirituality has to deliver maximum good for maximum people, we need to document a rajarshi model with codes, anecdotes and case studies.

Contemporary case studies

We shall not narrate stories of historical personages such as Akbar and Asoka nor shall we talk about mythological characters such as Janaka and Vasishta. We shall discuss a few examples of contemporary initiatives that exhibit *rajarshitvam* at its best. These anecdotes have happened right in our lifetime and in front of our eyes.

I too had a dream

His patriotic outlook, enviable self-confidence and "we can" attitude made Verghese Kurien achieve his self-imposed goal to make India the largest producer of milk in the world. From a milk-deficient country, India is today a milk-surplus country. We cannot but admire the process Kurien employed to overcome obstacles that came from far and near. Kurien considered himself an employee of the poor milk producers in the villages. He brought them under an umbrella of cooperative movement. He used to say that the farmers had employed him as their spokesman for synthesising market, technology, government, and society. The emergent benefit was a win–win situation for both the producers and the consumers of milk and milk products.

Kurien's crusade and evangelism were initially enacted around Anand in Gujarat and later spread throughout the country. This is a trait of rajarshis: they start solving local problems and subsequently enter the national/global scene. With vehemence, he opposed the efforts of vested foreign interests who wanted to dump inappropriate technology into India. For example, he had to explode the myth that milk powder can be made only from cow's milk and not from buffalo's milk. Kurien's tough stand accompanied by confidence in Indian expertise resulted in a sustained campaign which came to be called 'Operation Flood' or the 'White Revolution'.

In a letter to his grandson, Kurien says, 'Life is a privilege and to waste it would be wrong'. He wanted to utilise his native instinct to produce maximum good at minimal cost to maximum people. According to Kurien, failure is not about not succeeding—it is about not putting in one's best efforts and not contributing to the common good. Kurien behaved like a rajarshi.

In his autobiography, Kurien says,

> While integrity and loyalty are core values, there are other values, too, which are a prerequisite to achieve success in any field. For example, the leader has to set a personal example and make others understand in what ways 'change' is going to be useful. I believe

that professionals working in our organisations must have clarity of thought combined with passionate pursuit of mastery of their subject. I have always emphasised that large endeavors are only the sum of many small parts and, therefore we must keep in mind not just where we are going but how we are going to reach there successfully.

(p. 216, 2005)

A perfect paraphrase of contemplation and action needed of a rajarshi by one who walked the talk.

Infinite vision

A stint at Aravind hospital enhances the intrinsic value of the resume of any ophthalmologist. Some people answer questions, believing that no question should be left unanswered. But there are a few who feel that no answer should be left unquestioned. They challenge age-old wisdom, and seemingly unalterable constraints.

Dr. Venkataswamy was one such 'visionary' (the pun should become clear soon). Dr. V, as he was fondly called by colleagues, was an ophthalmology doctor with the Madras Government and had performed more than one lakh sight restoration surgeries. Upon retirement, he decided that the prevalence of avoidable blindness (or 'needless blindness', as he called the condition) should be eliminated. Accessibility to medical care and affordability stood as barriers for those needing surgery for cataracts. Dr. V was determined to convert the constraints into opportunities—not for making profit, but for eliminating needless blindness. Thus was born Aravind Eye Care. He showed that more quantity need not mean less quality; in fact, he established that higher quantity is a prerequisite for maintaining better quality. The Aravind Eye Care System he founded in Madurai is believed to be the world's largest provider of high-quality eye care which has treated nearly 35 million patients and performed nearly 5 million surgeries.

It is a revolutionary system as it performs cataract surgeries using a highly productive work flow model, with quality outcomes exceeding those in the West. Dr. V, it seems, was impressed with McDonald's assembly-line model. It achieves the results at a small fraction of the cost elsewhere. Poor patients enjoy free transport to and from the hospital, free surgery, free medicines, free post-care stay, food, and everything else. The paying customers subsidise the cost incurred by 'free' customers. But there is no difference in the treatment of these two categories of customers.

Pavithra and Suchitra in their book *Infinite Vision* capture the enigmatic business model of the system, the dedication of four generations of one family and the spiritual quotient underlying the phenomenon (Mehta and Shenoy, 2011). If one Venkataswamy wanted to serve humanity, how did all his siblings, their spouses, the spouses' siblings, the nieces, and nephews all

51

got hooked on to the Good Samaritan's trail? Perhaps rajarshitvam begets rajarshitvam. It is a highly infectious mindset.

Dr. V was an epitome of innovation and always went against popular beliefs and intuition. Instead of outsourcing, he believed in doing things internally. When the world's manufacturers of intraocular lenses refused to take the Indian market seriously, he had the gumption to start a manufacturing facility in-house and started exporting to the very societies that ignored his earlier proposals for partnership. When girls from urban areas did not stay long as nurses, he instituted a captive system to train girls from villages after their school education. They were given a career path where they got opportunities to perform several paramedical procedures.

The Aravind model has remained a constant case study at Harvard to demonstrate that business practices and community needs need not be antithetical. Peter Drucker and C.K. Prahalad have influenced and in turn have been affected by the Aravind model. Dr. V felt that if needless blindness has to be eliminated all over India and the world, there is space for a thousand or more Aravinds. Ignoring the business advantages of being the first mover, Dr. V freely shared all his knowledge with everyone. Several hundreds of institutions and individuals from all over the world have benefited by Aravind's give-all mindset. Aravind has a consultancy wing where they handhold start-ups to develop into quality eye care institutions.

The Aravind story is indeed a real 'eye-opener'. Dr. V's seemingly reckless initiatives backed by counter-intuition succeeded because they were tinged with compassion with the motto of doing maximum good to maximum people with minimum resources. Dr. V comes out as a benevolent dictator and benign egotist. In their book *Infinite Vision*, the authors quote Dr. V's own words, 'When we grow in spiritual consciousness, we identify with all that is in the world. . . . It is ourselves we are helping. . . . ourselves we are healing.'

Reinventing India

It is rare to find a prescription that offers guaranteed recipes for institutional or national excellence. Raghunath Mashelkar is a 'dangerous optimist' who was possessed by a spirit to restore the glory that India had enjoyed in an earlier era. Passion would be an inadequate word to describe what drove Mashelkar to do what he did. He does not support breast-beating of India's achievements in various fields such as medicine and agriculture 500 or 5,000 years ago. His chronicle *Reinventing India* is all about what he could achieve in the past 30 years, the India of the present (Mashelkar, 2011).

During the 1960s and 1970s, the Council of Scientific and Industrial Research (CSIR) laboratories in India were described as 'White elephants'. They were operating in silos, staffed by '9-to-5' scientists with no vision and mission to drive them. 'Made by an Indian' was globally acceptable but 'made in India' was not. According to a popular mythological story, when devas fell into a state of decadence, Vishnu wanted to get them back into glory. His strategy was to engage them in a goal-oriented mission (churning the ocean). He also created an ecosystem with appropriate processes and tools to accomplish the same. Similarly, Mashelkar went about performing a churning operation at the National Chemical Laboratory (NCL) to which he had been appointed director. He renamed the laboratory the International Chemical Laboratory. Cynics called it a cosmetic change, but it brought about the needed change in mindset—of thinking global, of exporting scientific research instead of being at the receiving end. This resulted in authors writing articles worthy of being published in magazines such as *Nature*. Indian scientists began filing dozens of patents. Indian scientists started bidding successfully against stiff international competition for projects to establish scientific research infrastructure in other countries. Suddenly the 9to-5 scientists were turned into zealots who became 24/7 research workers.

These extraordinary achievements could not be rewarded appropriately under the then-existing rules and regulations of the government. Mashelkar was not given to blink at constraints. He created a trust financed by corporates outside the CSIR system and used the fund to reward outstanding work in an appropriate manner.

When he became director general of CSIR, Mashelkar replicated the NCL model of rejuvenation across all the 40 laboratories comprising CSIR. Scientists across the laboratories started talking to each other, engaging in healthy competition and at the same time, fostering interdisciplinary research. There was alignment of goals and a sense of purpose. It was yet another instance of a rajarshi operating in a limited area and graduating into a wider arena. Effectiveness and outcome replaced efficiency and output. Imitation gave place to innovation; reverse engineering was replaced by forward engineering. There are several real-life examples meticulously narrated in the above-mentioned book, showing a quantum leap in the quantity and quality of scientific research in India. Mashelkar comes out as a scientist, technocrat and corporate executive rolled into a Rajarshi. In simple terms, the mission of the rejuvenated CSIR became 'first reflect and then act'.

Mashelkar was instrumental in convincing the West about India's traditional knowledge which resulted in the revocation of patent wrongly granted on the healing properties of turmeric. Mashelkar became an evangelist in spreading the awareness and the crucial economic value of intellectual property rights (IPR) among Indian scientists and innovators. Instead of fighting cases post facto, he thought of doing something to prevent wrong patents being granted in the first place. The result was the creation of a huge database encoding Indian traditional wisdom in several domains. This digital library is accessible to patent inspectors across the globe who can check the claims of patent seekers against the triple virtues of novelty, non-obviousness and utility, immediately. There are cases where the royalty from patents based on traditional Indian knowledge has flowed back to the traditional Indian people who are the repositories of such knowledge. Soon several companies who had filed patent applications based on Indian knowledge hastily withdrew their applications. While the raja in him reacted to the turmeric case, the rishi in him spurred him to take proactive preventive measures.

He transformed open-ended research into value-added innovations which could be globally marketed. Several countries, including Russia, sought the Indian model of transforming scientific research. Several others invited Indian science administrators to formulate IPR regulations for global use.

Affordability, inclusivity and sustainability are the mantras for the 'More for Less for More' (MLM) paradigm. Innovation needs to be brought down from ivory towers to terra firma. Several grassroots innovations touching the lives of the common people are described in the book that serves as a spring for inspiration. Tata Nano and the chhotukool refrigerator are instances of MLM product innovation; high degree of mobile penetration and cheap telecommunication costs are the result of MLM business process innovation.

Denial of technology led India to develop her own supercomputer called PARAM and ISRO to develop her own cryogenic engine needed for its Geosynchronous Satellite Launch Vehicle flights. Thus, India has been able to convert adversity into opportunity thanks to rajarshis such as Mashelkar.

Antifragility: celebrating uncertainty

Nassim Nicholas Taleb is respected as the most profound thinker, philosopher and author of modern times. With his incisive out-of-the-box observation of life around him, he advocates a worldview that is counterintuitive but obviously significant. Having soiled his hands as a stock trader and an academic researcher, he has authored several philosophical essays that make readers sit up and take note. His thoughts on life processes are focused around uncertainty, probability and opacity, as opposed to the common wish-view of the world based on certainty, determinism and transparency. He established that life situations revolve around highly improbable and unpredictable events (2007). He even gives a prescription for not only surviving but prospering in such a world (2012).

Glass is fragile. This means that a slight disturbance will cause it to break. What is the antonym of 'fragility'? Normally we respond by saying 'robust' or 'resilient'. If we extrapolate our thinking beyond robustness, we should say that the opposite effect is one where the object becomes better (stronger, wealthier or wiser) when subjected to disturbances. This property, for want of any other word in the dictionary, is called 'antifragility'. We accept that our bones get stronger when subjected to stresses. We see that books and films that are banned gain better traction.

The tragedy of modern life—be it in economy, governance, education, or health—can be traced to policies that promote order and status quo. We call it a bureaucratic mindset. If a train is stranded at a remote station, a young man in the neighbourhood sees an opportunity and sells a bottle of water for Rs 50. More sellers even from adjacent villages arrive and sell biscuits and fruits making a fortune. The local community has harnessed the unpredictable event of the stranded train to become prosperous.

Innovation has been the major victim of a fragile mindset. Scientific inventions and technological breakthroughs can be traced to antifragility rather than sanitised and compartmentalised formal education. Nature understands and handles antifragility much better than humans. That is the secret of our planet surviving for millions of years. Nature does not use linear simulation models with stability and order as objective functions. Nature practices continual regeneration, a process that exploits random events and unpredictable shocks. If Nature had chosen to silently tolerate the stresses or tried out to nullify the random events seeking a state of equilibrium, we will not be around today. Uncertainty is not only desirable but necessary for life.

Those afraid of fragility devise solutions that may have small, visible and short-term benefits; but such solutions will produce large invisible long-term harm, euphemistically called 'side-effect'. We can readily think of doctors, plumbers, finance ministers, and investment consultants who prescribe quick fixes that not only fail to solve the problem but end up in escalating them.

Hydra is a serpent-like creature with multiple heads; every time a head is severed, the Hydra sports two new heads. Hydra loves harm. It represents antifragility. Several religions have encouraged followers to embrace adversity so that they will have an opportunity to remember God. Taleb advocates courting uncertainty to reap tangible material benefits right here and right during one's lifetime. Taleb's thoughts embody the attributes of a rajarshi: deep contemplation and vibrant action mutually reinforcing each other.

Collective endeavour

The problems of today's complex world cannot possibly be handled by an individual. Therefore, our quest is not directed towards individual excellence, not even towards organisational excellence. We believe that several like-minded organisations have to come together with a common agenda of values so as to establish sustained development. Two recent examples of such collective endeavor readily come to mind.

The Global Alliance for Banking on Values, or GABV (www.gabv.org), is an independent network of banks founded in 2009. It has a shared mission to use wealth to deliver sustainable economic, social and environmental development. The consortium takes a leading part in bringing together members, experts and partners in defining and managing joint projects. The focus of these projects is to design a model of a sustainable financial future and help deliver this future by evangelising change. This consortium holds great promise as a think tank and an implementing agency that benchmarks itself through outcomes rather than throughput.

A second example of a beneficial consortium is SVN, or Social Venture Network (http://svn.org), a community of the world's leading influential business leaders, social entrepreneurs and impact investors working together to create transformational innovation, growth and impact. SVN's mission promises to support and empower diverse innovative leaders who leverage business to serve the greater good. The charter expects the leaders to support a triple bottom line: people, planet and profit (and in that order). Out of the high-impact collaboration would emerge a just, humane and sustainable world.

The emerging rajarshi model is manifested in the convergence of mindsets. If we pose the question 'how can I be creative and ethical and still generate wealth'? to an MIT professor, an Indian Vedantic scholar, or a successful business tycoon, we will receive answers that are semantically identical though the vocabulary may be different. All of them will probably say that when consciousness (strategy) and action (execution) are aligned and synthesised, wealth, success, and rule of law will surface as emergent properties.

Yatra yogeshwara Krishno yathra Partho dhanur dharaha
Tatra Sree(r) Vijayo bhuti(r) dhruvaa neethi(r) matir mama

The combined teamwork of contemplative Krishna, the Rishi and proactive Arjuna, and the Raja ensures prosperity, success, well-being, and universal justice.

Summary

To summarise, a rajarshi manager:

- Combines in himself complementary attributes
- Gets a total insight into the problems before finding a sustainable solution
- Copes with complexity in all its dimensions without compromising
- Abstracts a given problem into a large class of problems
- Possesses a large consciousness quotient and a large spiritual quotient
- Continuously enhances the personal mastery levels of his or her protégées
- Becomes an active participant while resolving conflicts between two parties
- Starts operating at a local level and later enters a larger arena
- Works to produce maximum good for maximum people
- Shares best practices with others and adopts best practices from others
- Believes that creating wealth and following ethics need not be antithetical

References

Ackoff, R. and S. Rovin. 2003. *Redesigning Society* (1st edition). Stanford, CA: Stanford Business Books.

Capra, F. 1996. *The Web of Life: A New Synthesis of Mind and Matter.* London: Harper Collins.

The Global Alliance for Banking on Values, www.gabv.org

Kurien, V. and G. Salvi. 2005. *I Too Had a Dream.* Delhi: Roli Books Pvt. Ltd.

Mashelkar, R. 2011. *Reinventing India.* Pune, Maharashtra: Sahyadri Prakashan.

Mehta, P.K. and S. Shenoy. 2011. *Infinite Vision: How Aravind became the World's Greatest Business Case for Compassion.* California: Berrett-Koehler Publishers.

Penrose, S.R. 2002. *The Emperor's New Mind: Concerning Computers, Minds, and the Laws of Physics.* Oxford: Oxford Paperbacks.

Senge, P.M. 2006. *The Fifth Discipline: The Art & Practice of the Learning Organization.* New York: Random House.

Social Venture Network, http://svn.org

Taleb, N.N. 2007. *The Black Swan.* New York: Random House.

Taleb, N.N. 2012. *Antifragile.* New York: Random House.

Zsolnai, L. 2004. *Spirituality and Ethics in Management.* Boston, Dordrecht, and London: Kluwer Academic Publishers.

4

LEADERSHIP PRINCIPLES FROM YOGA

Shriram Sarvotham

Introduction

The fundamental trait of a leader is his or her ability to influence people in their thoughts, words and actions. A leader specifically rallies support through the art of persuasion. The leader's persuasive power inspires people to action towards the chosen ideals, goals and objectives. According to the great Greek philosopher Aristotle, the art of persuasion has three distinct attributes namely, ethos (appeal to one's credibility), logos (appeal to the intellect) and pathos (appeal to the emotions). Yogic wisdom from authoritative yoga texts such as Patanjali's Yoga Sutras enunciate systematic methods to cultivate these triune attributes of ethos, logos and pathos (Jnaneshvara, 2019). In this chapter, we explore these tenets of leadership from classic yoga scriptures.

Ethos is the power that comes from personal ethics and the pursuit of excellence. Ethos provides credibility to the leader and creates an aura of powerful presence. A simple high school science experiment of bringing a magnet towards iron filings demonstrate the power of presence: the mere presence of the magnet organizes the iron filings in perfect order. In a similar manner, the mere presence of a leader invokes respect and inspiration. How does one cultivate this ethos? This is possible through strong foundation of ethical principles which is manifested as excellence in action. We explore these principles based on yogic wisdom and how to cultivate them in our own lives. Logos is the logical organization of goals and ideas, which provides clarity in communication. To communicate clearly, the necessary prerequisite is clarity in one's own mind. According to Maharishi Patanjali, the mind of a yogi is like a blemishless crystal; it is not clouded by doubts or dullness. He enumerates a variety of methods to achieve this state of clarity. Pathos is the ability to connect with others using empathy. This helps the leader to connect with people, touch their hearts and inspire them. Clearly, one who is passionate and inspired to do their work is thousand times more effective than one who does the work just mechanically. Patanjali enunciates systematic methods to cultivate this power of pathos using four different ways to connect with people: friendliness, compassion, appreciation, and indifference. He provides guidance on when and in what context to use each of these four methods. In a larger context, every yogi is a leader. The word yoga refers to uniting in harmony. Whether a yogi unites the minds of millions of people towards a single cause, or they unite their own mind from a place of scattered awareness, the tenets of leadership are essential. Every yogi is a leader. Yoga—the art of uniting and bringing harmony in one's own body, breath, mind, and soul—calls for personal leadership through rigorous discipline. The various methods to discipline the mass of cells in the body include means to regulate the *prana* (energy) in the system, tame the raw power of the mind, and provide great leadership insights.

Ethos: the inner work

Mahatma Gandhi's famous words 'be the change you wish to see in the world', conveys a profound truth: the first step in leading others is to lead oneself. The great Mahatma himself was a shining example of this wisdom, inspiring and rallying the support of millions of people by personally living the lofty ideals, whether it was Satyagraha, spinning khadi in support of India's independence or leading a nonviolent revolution by fasting. So strong was his resolve that he stood by his ideals even during arduous times, such as when he was imprisoned or when he was subject to violence. By living his message, he infused it with extraordinary power; his life spoke louder than his words. Mahatma Gandhi himself had declared, 'My life is my message'. This captures the essence of ethos, the credibility that comes from living the principles of ethics and excellence.

The words of one who has cultivated ethos carry enormous weight. They have the power to deeply influence people. We behold the wisdom of such men and women with great respect and reverence; we see beauty in them and in their work. We refer to great teachers as gurus—literally meaning heavy, as their words carry extraordinary weight. Such a teacher is truly wise, not merely smart (Kaipa, 2013). In the Puranas, sacred writings containing legends and folklore on India, we come across many examples of kings who seek blessings of great sages, as the words of great ones have the power to manifest.

Maharishi Patanjali, revered as the father of yoga, refers to this secret power of great sages in his Yoga Sutras. In the second chapter of the Yoga Sutras, it is stated: *satya pratishtayam kriya phalasrayatvam* (for one who is established in truth, their vision become manifest) (Yoga Sutra, 2.36). Satyam is much more than merely speaking the truth; it refers to the core ethical value of integrity. A leader can claim to be true to their ideals only by integrating them into their own lives and by living them. In fact, they breathe life into the ideals by living them. What they think, say and do are in perfect harmony. In addition to gaining the power to manifest a vision as stated by Patanjali, living a life of satyam accrues credibility. Others trust the words and actions of the leader once the credibility is firmly established.

An incident from the life of the great Ramakrishna Paramahamsa sheds light on the value of practicing what we preach, in order to gain credibility. One day, a mother and her young son approached Sri Ramakrishna Paramahamsa. The mother complained about her son eating excessive amounts of sugar. She tried all tricks to make him stop consuming sugar, including punishment. But her efforts were in vain. 'Can the Paramahamsa help me'? she pleaded. Sri Ramakrishna Paramahamsa patiently listened to the concerns of the mother. He thought for a while and asked her to come back after two weeks with her son.

The mother was back at the ashram after exactly two weeks, with her son in tow. The Paramahamsa looked him in the eye, and lovingly said the following words to him, 'Sugar is not good for your health, my dear child. Will you stop eating it for my sake?' The mother could sense a transformation in the boy; she knew that the boy was convinced. The Paramahamsa then turned to the mother and assured her that her son will no longer eat sugar. The mother was surprised. 'I have said the same words to my son, but it did not work! Besides, why did you not tell him the same words two weeks ago? We had to travel far to reach your ashram.' Sri Ramakrishna Paramahamsa said, 'I am sorry to make you travel twice. However, I used to eat sugar every day until two weeks ago. I wanted to stop eating sugar so that my words gain credibility.'

The story also reveals that the power of personal example is far superior than the threat of punishment. We can put this idea into practice in our own lives as a leader. Here are some examples:

- Before advising children to be truthful, practice truthfulness. This has more power than offering threat of punishment if they lie.
- If we wish for our near and dear ones to eat healthy and exercise every day, model that first and then encourage them to do the same. This has more power than constantly reminding them of the negative consequences of unhealthy lifestyle.
- Similarly, if we want our team members to excel in their work, be a role model of excellence and cultivate exceptional work ethic.
- If we want our friends to avoid gossip, refrain from gossiping; avoid mundane and trivial talk.

In short, living the highest, most excellent version of oneself builds ethos. Furthermore, ethos is slowly cultivated over time. There are no shortcuts, excuses or exceptions. Maharishi Patanjali describes how the ethos is accrued over time: *satu dheergha kaala nairantarya satkara sevito drdha bhoomih*, that is, practicing for a long period of time, without interruption, and with honor and respect, makes it [the virtue] firmly established (Yoga Sutra, 1.14). Once again, in the second chapter he states, *jaati desha kaala samayanavacchinna saarva bhauma mahavratam* (the codes of conduct become great vows when no exceptions are made at any time, place, event, or towards anyone) (Yoga Sutra, 2.31).

In the jargon of modern management, one can say that ethos builds personal branding. How others perceive us determines how much they respect our words. The Bhagavad Gita states:

> *Yadyadacharati sreshtah tattadeve tarojanah/Sa yatpramanam kurute lokastad anuvartate* (3.21)—whatever a great person does, others emulate; the great ones set the standards that others follow. The first step in leadership is therefore, self-transformation, which is just another name for self-leadership. If we are unable to lead oneself, what hope is there to lead another?

Personal transformation is easier said than done. Duryodhana, in the Mahabharata, exclaims to Krishna: *Janami dharman na cha me pravrttih janami adharmam na cha me nivrttih/Kenapi devena hrdi sthithena yatha niyuktosmi tatha karomi* (I know what is right [dharma] and what is wrong [adharma], but I am unable to follow dharma nor abstain from adharma. I am a helpless puppet of an invisible hand that I am forced to obey). Maharishi Patanjali calls this predicament *pramada*. He also provides the tools to bring us out of this predicament; the key is to cultivate personal ethics and a strong will to follow what is right. This can be achieved by practicing *yama*, *niyama* and *samyama*, as described by Patanjali in the Yoga Sutras.

Yama consists of adhering to ethical codes of conduct that promote harmony in relating with the society. These include ahimsa (nonviolence), *satya* (truthfulness), *astheya* (non-stealing), *brahmacharya* (living our highest version of our self), and *aparigraha* (non-hoarding).

Niyama comprises personal disciplines that lay strong foundation for personal growth. Niyama includes *soucha* (cleanliness), *samtosha* (contentment), *tapas* (willingness to step out of our comfort zone), *swadhyaya* (self-inspired study), and *Iswara pranidhana* (devotion to our chosen ideals).

Samyama consists of *antaranga sadhana* (internal practices) that allow expression of the full potential of the mind. Maharishi Patanjali describes *trayam ekatra samyamah* (three components) of samyama (Yoga Sutra, 3.4) namely, *dharana* (focus), *dhyana* (tranquility) and *samadhi* (mental equilibrium). A focused, one-pointed mind mobilizes all our mental energies into the singular task at hand. Just as water flows faster and with more force when directed into a narrow funnel, the flow of awareness gains enormous power when it is focused. A tranquil, meditative mind conserves precious mental energy that otherwise is dissipated in turbulent, unnecessary flow of thoughts. A tranquil mind, therefore, has access to higher quality of thoughts that can bring creative solutions to the problems we imagine we face. Higher-quality thoughts can also be intuitive and brilliant insights can be the seeds for the next groundbreaking idea that changes the world. Mental equipoise helps us remain centered amidst disharmony or even chaos in the surroundings.

Patanjali further explains several methods to cultivate these qualities of dharana, dhyana and samadhi. An example of a method to strengthen dharana, the power of focus, is the practice of breath regulation or pranayama (*dharanasu cha yogyata manasah*) which prepares the mind to focus (Yoga Sutra, 2.53). A method to bring samadhi is to practice the yoga of action, which Patanjali states, has the power to bring samadhi—*samadhi bhavanartha klesha tanu karanarthascha* (Yoga Sutra, 2.2). A tranquil, meditative mind (dhyana) can be achieved by removing the turbulence (rajas) in the mind and the body by practicing yoga postures—*asanena rajo hanti* (Satyadharma, 2003).

When the mind is concurrently focused, tranquil and in equilibrium at the same instant of time, this powerful state of awareness is called samyama. According to Maharishi Patanjali, samyama is the only virtue that is needed to invoke excellence in any activity. Indeed, when we look for common traits among all the great masters in any field, we find them to be endowed with these three qualities.

In short, yama and niyama establish the ethical basis, while samyama creates the foundation for excellence. Ethos is simply the powerful blend of ethics and excellence. When we live by these ideals, we have the potential to be shining role models and to inspire others.

Logos: clarity of perception and expression

Logos is the appeal to logic. Logos builds upon cogent, coherent and clear flow of ideas that convince the intellect. Before articulating these ideas to others, a leader must convince himself or herself first. In the Yoga Sutras, Maharishi Patanjali provides the analogy of a flawless crystal—*abhijaatasyeva mani* (Yoga Sutra, 1.41)—as a metaphor to capture the state of mind of a yogi. The Bhagavad Gita gives the analogy of a flame in a windless place that illuminates the intellect:

> *Yatha deepo nivatastho nengate sopamasmrta/Yogino yatha chittasya yunjato yogam atmanah.* (As a flame in a windless place does not flicker, the mind of a yogi is bright and steady.)
>
> (6.19)

Often times, the intellect is muddied and dulled by laziness or even stupor. One can think of this as a veil of darkness that envelops the brilliance of the intellect, thereby eclipsing it. This darkness, termed *tamas* in yoga, is like the dark smoke that clouds the inner light from shining forth. A well-known mantra from the Upanishads states *tamaso maa jyotirgamaya* (lead me from darkness to light) (Brhadaaranyaka Upanishad) (Nikhilananda, 1990). Another famous mantra from the Rig Veda—the Gayatri Mantra—seeks the blessings of the sun to illuminate the intellect. Yoga practices provide many methods to clear the tamas and allow the inner light of the intellect to shine forth. Patanjali says, *tatah ksheeyate prakasha avaranam* (the practice of pranayama removes the dark covering of *avarana*s [the tamas] and allows the inner light to shine forth) (Yoga Sutra, 2.52). Apart from strengthening the power of focus, pranayama occupies a special place in yoga as it has numerous profound benefits to offer.

As tamas is lifted and clarity dawns, the leader invokes the tremendous power of the intellect. He or she is able to use this power to prove the truth of their ideas and convince others of the same. The leader also builds the necessary skills to articulate the ideas in an eloquent manner. This is the power of logos; one can think of logos as a dispassionate way to establish the rightness of an idea, much like a mathematician who establishes the validity of a theorem by supplying a proof.

Pathos: the heart-to-heart connection

Although logos is dispassionate and appeals to the intellect, pathos ignites the passion by connecting with the heart. As every politician and salesman knows, convincing the intellect alone is inadequate. Unless we touch the other's heart, we cannot win their full support. A leader provides a space of harmony in which others are made to feel valued and appreciated. We see this in the Bhagavad Gita, where the friendship of Krishna and Arjuna creates a perfect space of harmony for the highest teachings to unfold. Furthermore, engaging our 'heart and soul' into the task at hand fuels the passion that profoundly elevates the quality of our work.

The first step towards connecting with people at this deeper level is to respect them. According to yoga, respecting another is achieved by acknowledging and honoring the divine presence in them. The Bhagavad Gita states, *Ishwarah sarva bhootanam hrd deshe Arjuna thishtati* (the divine resides in the heart of all beings) (18.61). When we acknowledge this divine presence in another, we elevate them in our eyes, we see them as precious beings that they are. We value them. They are not mere roll numbers or mere human resources to get some work done. Furthermore, a leader does not see another being as inferior. Each one is a divine being who is respected and appreciated, and their contribution is valued. The virtuous Lord Rama could see the divine presence even in a small squirrel.

The greeting 'namaste' captures this sentiment of respecting the divine presence in another. When we begin a dialogue with the greeting namaste, we prepare the interaction with a positive attitude. It makes the statement that although there may be differences of ideas or opinions, my respect for you is unshakeable. Maharishi Patanjali posits this as a powerful practice; to see the divine essence in everything, practice the skill of beholding the single [divine] essence in everything (*Tad pradishedartham eka tattva abhyasaha*) (Yoga Sutra, 1.32).

The art of seeing the divine presence requires practice. It is easy to respect and appreciate the divinity in others who are happy and doing good work. But what about those who are experiencing misery? Or those who make mistakes? In order to see the divine presence in them, we need to change the way we behold them in our eyes. Here, Patanjali offers the following remarkable wisdom, which reveals a profound secret to connect with another: *Maitri karuna mudita upekshanam sukha dukha punya apunya vishayanam Bhavanathaha chita prasadanam* (Be friendly to those who are happy; be compassionate to those who are sad, appreciate those who are doing good work, and overlook the mistakes of others) (Yoga Sutra, 1.33).

Patanjali classifies people into four types. He suggests four different ways to connect with them, depending on which type they belong to. The four types of people are: those who are happy, those who are sad, those who are doing good work, and those who commit mistakes. Towards the first category of *sukha* people, that is, who are happy, Patanjali suggests connecting with them through *maitri* (friendliness). If we are not careful, an opposite emotion, perhaps jealousy, may surface. However, jealousy disempowers us, and from this weakened position, we cannot see the divine in the other. By offering friendliness as Patanjali suggests, we too become happy because we are joyful to see our friend in a happy place. From this happy place, we see everything as beautiful and divine.

For the second category, the *dukha* people—those who are sad—Patanjali suggests *karuna* (compassion) to connect with them, as friendship alone is inadequate. This is because we become sad when we see a friend in distress. From a sad state of mind, we do not have the mental strength to help them overcome their misery. Therefore, Patanjali recommends compassion towards those who are suffering. Compassion helps us to be sensitive to their condition without being affected by the negative energy. As a compassionate person, we assist them to find relief. We do not judge them or condemn them for being in a negative place (or how they got there). We simply offer a helping hand, to pull them out of their predicament.

For the third category of people, those who are doing *punya* or good work, Patanjali suggests *mudita* (appreciation). If we are not careful, the ego may sneak up and assert itself by way of faultfinding. By appreciating them, not only do we encourage them in their good work, we allow ourselves to see the beauty in their work.

For the fourth category of people, those who are involved in *apunya* (commiting mistakes), Patanjali suggests *upeksha* (forgiveness), which is a way to look past their mistakes. In other words, Patanjali recommends that we do not focus on their mistakes and flaws but shine the spotlight instead on their hidden potential. A leader sees in others what they cannot yet see in themselves. A leader helps awaken and unleash the full potential that lies dormant in them. Using these four *bhavanas* (ways to connect) for the four types of people, as enunciated by Patanjali, the leader always remains connected with others and evokes their full potential.

Summary

The three virtues of inspirational leadership—namely, ethos, logos and pathos—make the leader highly influential. Ethos builds the power of credibility of the leader using the principles of ethics and excellence. Logos expresses the scientific and intellectual side of the leader that helps him or her appeal to other's intellect. Pathos awakens the artistic and compassionate side of the leader, where he or she sees beauty in others and values them.

As in all powerful combinations, the coming together of ethos, logos and pathos creates great synergy: the whole is far greater than the sum of its parts. In other words, the leader who embodies all three virtues has extraordinary power to transform others and transform the world. The wisdom and practices contained in the classic yoga scriptures such as the Patanjali Yoga Sutras and the Bhagavad Gita provide valuable tools to cultivate ethos, logos and pathos.

References

The Bhagavad Gita. Gorakhpur: The Gita Press, http://gitapress.org/e-books.htm (accessed on 14 January 2019).

Jnaneshvara, S. *Yoga Sutras of Patanjali*, http://swamij.com/yoga-sutras.htm (accessed on 14 January 2019).

Kaipa, P. 2013. *From Smart to Wise: Acting and Leading with Wisdom* (1st edition). San Francisco, CA: Jossey-Bass.

Nikhilananda, S. 1990. *Upanishads* (Vols. 1–3, 3rd edition). New York: Ramakrishna Vivekananda Center.

Satyadharma, S. 2003. *Yoga Choodamani Upanishad*. Munger, Bihar: Yoga Publications Trust.

5

KAUTILYA'S RAJARSHI

An ideal leader

Radhakrishnan Pillai

Ancient Indian thinkers have had postulated many theories regarding an 'ideal king'. There has been no uniform pattern in their behaviour. At times, a ruler undertook good work till he obtained a powerful position, but the moment the desired standing was achieved, he opted to overlook his responsibilities. Power corrupts and absolute power corrupts absolutely. In this chapter, we will see the making of the king as advocated by Kautilya and how the same concept of an 'ideal leader' can be put to practice in our generation. Restless is the head that wears the crown. The moment one gets into the chair, the personality of the leader gets affected. Work pressure and multitasking, might create so much pressure that the leader might not get enough time to think in the right direction and in a wise way. In India, one of the words for a wise thinker is *rishi* (seer). The raja (king) who is a wise person and thinks in the right direction is called a *rajarshi*. The king in ancient times used to be educated in a *gurukul* in the *guru-shishya-parampara*. According to this tradition, an *anvikshiki*[1] (the right thinking) learner is shaped into a leader using the four *vidyas*.[2] This means when he or she becomes a leader, he or she still maintains *vinaya*[3] (humility) and carries the power given to him with the attitude of doing a service. This is a high ideal brought out by Kautilya. But this is not impossible to achieve if one is inspired for a higher spiritual cause guided by the right teachers.

Srimanta Yogi

This unique word is used by Ramdas Swami[4] while describing Shivaji Maharaj. *Srimanta,* meaning rich, and *yogi,* being a spiritual person—a *srimantayogi* is a king who, despite having affluence and abundance, lives in a completely detached way. This is exactly the concept of a rajarshi given by Kautilya. The concept of a rajarshi comes in Book 1, Chapter 7, of *Arthashastra*. It is called *raja-rishi vrittam* (the life of a sage-like king). This sage-like king is supposed to have

Conquered the six internal enemies, have control over the senses, cultivate his intellect by association with elders, keep a watchful eye by means of spies, bring about security and well-being by energetic activity, maintain the observances of their special duties (by the praja) by carrying out his own duties, acquire discipline by receiving instruction in political science, attain popularity by association with what is of material advantage and maintain proper behaviour by doing what is beneficial.

(1.7.1)

Pleasures of life is not excluded in the life of a sage-like king. A sage-like king should not deprive himself of worldly pleasures. Material well-being is also to be achieved. However, Kautilya suggests that anything in excess is harmful. The king should enjoy sensual pleasures without compromising his spiritual goodness. Therefore, self-control needs to be enforced. Rajarshi is an ideal leader in any field or social institution and not necessarily restricted to a monarch king.

The six enemies

There is a complete chapter dedicated by Kautilya on *Arishadvargatyaga*, that is, how to eliminate the six enemies[5] under the topic of *indriya-jaya*[6] (control over the senses). 'Control over the senses, which is motivated by training in the sciences, should be secured by giving up lust, anger, greed, pride, arrogance, and fool hardiness' (1.6.1).

What does control over the senses mean? According to Kautilya, it indicates 'absence of improper indulgence in (the pleasures of) sound, touch, colour, taste, and smell by the senses of hearing, touch and sight, the tongue and the sense of smell, means control over the sense' (1.6.2). We have five sense organs (*indriyas*) and control over them (*jaya*) is to be achieved. These five sense organs have five different sensations namely, eyes (sight), ears (sound), tongue (taste), nose (smell), and skin (touch). The five sense organs help us to connect with the outside world of activities. The impulses from these senses help to gather information and the *buddhi* (the intellect) processes them and take decisions for further action.

For instance, when we hear the doorbell (sound), our intellect decides that there is someone at the door and we go and open it (action). But at the same time, any of these impulses not being carefully analysed and not under control can create a problem for us. When we get food to eat (taste), one may get carried away by the very presence of it. We should eat it, but over-indulgence can be bad for health. If one is having health problems, excess of the same food can become poison. Thus control over the senses needs to be maintained: 'the practice of this science gives such control' (1.6.2).

In a way Arthashastra itself implies indriyajaya. This book gives the complete framework of how an ideal king should behave. So once the king puts into practice the theories, ideas and suggestions given in this shastra, he or she automatically becomes an *indriyajayi*. The goal of Arthashastra is to train a king/leader to be an indriyajayi.

'For, the whole of this science means control over the senses' (1.6.3): once again, Kautiliya reiterates the same point. The prime and essential teaching of the science of Arthashastra, as written by Kautilya, is about control of senses. Kautiliya cautions: 'A king, behaving in a manner contrary to that, and hence having no control over his senses, quickly perishes, though he be ruler right up to the four ends of the earth' (1.6.4).

If one does not have control over the senses, he or she will get destroyed completely. Even if one has all the power of the world, one needs to possess self-control or all the power would get lost. Kautilya further gives many examples to drive across this point:

> For example, the Bhoja King, Dandakya by name, entertaining a sinful desire for a brahmin maiden, perished along with his kinsmen and kingdom; and (so did) Karala, king of the Videhas, Janamejaya using violence against brahmins, out of anger, likewise perished; and so did Talajangha, (using violence) against the Bhrgus. Aila, extorting money from the four varnas out of greed, perished; and so did Ajabindu of the Sauviras. Ravana, not restoring the wife of another through pride, perished and so did Duryodhana not returning a portion of the kingdom. Dambhodabhava, treating creatures with contempt out of arrogance, perished and so did Arjuna of the Haihayas. Vatapi, trying to assail Agastya, out of foolhardiness, perished; and so did the clan of Vrsnis trying to assail Dvaipayana. These and so many other kings, giving themselves up to the group of six enemies, perished with their kinsmen and kingdoms, being without control over the senses.
>
> (1.6.5–11)

Each of these above kings[7] and their great learning from history were used as an example by Kautilya and other teachers to drive the point of what happened in the past. For example, Kautilya sites Duryodhana who had to face self-destruction for not having self-control and being carried away by pride and refusing to return the portion of the kingdom because of the Pandavas.[8] Kautiliya reasoned out, 'Casting out the group of six enemies, Jamadagnaya, who had full control over the senses, as well as Ambarisa, the son of Nabhaga, enjoyed the earth for a long time' (1.6.12). The opposite is also true. Any king who had displayed self-control was successful and, in the end, ruled the whole earth for a long period of time.

This is seen in today's generation too, in which we find leaders of the corporate world tend to overindulge and destroy themselves and their organisations. Subroto Roy, an Indian businessman, founder and chairman of Sahara

India, was named among the 10 most powerful people in India (*India Today*, 2012) and the group was termed as the second-largest employer in India, after Indian Railways (*Time Magazine*). However, since March 2014, he has been serving a prison sentence in Tihar Jail.[9]

The Hollywood movie *Wall Street* (1987) is the story of stockbroker Gordon Gekko, who believed that 'greed is good' for an economy, as it pushes one to create more. Gordon does makes lot of money initially. But his philosophy is finally shattered when he is involved in a scam and has to go to jail.[10]

What a leader should not do

Arthashastra is not only a compilation of Kautilya's wisdom, but also contains practical insights into leadership, its development and application. There is some valuable information about the challenges of leadership, something that today's modern world is struggling to understand. Kautilya not only tells us what a leader should do but also what he or she should 'not' do.

Although the rajarshi is trained to follow certain things, he or she is also equally aware of what he or she is not supposed to do. Kautilya carefully makes sure that what is to be 'done' is equally important as what is 'not to be done'. Taking both these factors into consideration, the rajarshi governs his kingdom with supreme wisdom.

Reasons for dissatisfaction of the Praja[11]

In Book 7, Chapter 5, from verse 19 to 26, Kautilya outlines 21 things that a leader should avoid doing. We will study these elements, which can be applied not only by political leaders, but also to business leaders, heads of departments, project leaders, and community leaders, or even to the head of a family or leaders of any type of institution or organisation.

> For, by discarding the good and favouring the wicked, and by starting unrighteous injuries not current before, by discontinuing customary practices that are righteous by indulgence in impiety and suppressions of piety, and by doing acts that ought not to be done and by ruining rightful acts, and by not giving what ought to be given and securing what ought not to be given (to him), and by not punishing those deserving to be punished and punishing those not deserving to be punished, by seizing those who ought not to be seized and not arresting those who ought to be seized, and by doing harmful things and destroying beneficial things, and by failing to protect from thieves and by robbing them himself, by ruining human exertions, by spoiling the excellence of works done, by doing harm to principal men and by dishonouring those worthy of honour, and by opposing the elders, by partiality and falsehood, by

not requiting what is done and by not carrying out what is settled, through the negligence and indolence of the king and because of the destruction of well-being—(through these causes) decline, greed and disaffection are produced among the people.

(7.5.19–26)

Let us look into each of these things in detail (also see Pillai, 2010: 109).[12]

- Discarding the good and favouring the wicked: like the praja of the king, there are people who are reporting to him, or are dependent on him. They wait for his or her directions, which in itself has a direct effect on their lives. In the case of a company, it's the employees. In a department, they are his or her team members. In a family, they are the children and relatives. The first and foremost duty of the king (leader) is to keep the praja happy.
- Now, the first reason for Praja to become unhappy is when the king shows partiality by discarding the good and favouring the wicked. People come to the leader for justice. When they do not find a solution to their problems among themselves, they seek the leader's advice, direction and justice. If he favours the wicked and discards the right, this turns out to be a very serious problem.
- Let us consider a situation where the king or a leader has to take a decision in the matter of a dispute. It is necessary to listen to both sides of the dispute. But after the two sides have expressed their views, the leader should not hurry with the decision. If required, the leader should listen to them separately and get the facts. He will then get a better idea of what is right. At times of *dharmasankat* (conflicting situations), when one is not able to come to any decision, then the help of scriptures[13] and masters learned in the particular field needs to be taken. Use of wisdom is essential.
- After one has analysed the situation, the leader should announce the verdict without being carried away by emotions. Also, the reason behind the conclusion one has reached needs to be explained. The leader should be just. Even while punishing the wrong, one should give them an opportunity to learn and improve.
- Causing unrighteous injuries that had not existed earlier: A king should never misuse his or her power of punishment or *danda*. In every kingdom or nation, there are methods of punishing the wrongdoer. There are laws that are made for the welfare of the people. Never try to inflict serious injury that goes beyond the law. For example, any verbal or physical injury should be avoided even for a serious lapse or bad behaviour. Punishments within the right limit are always to be respected and honoured.
- One should not start any new form of penalty that was not practiced in the past. However, even if it has to be done, it should be discussed

and deliberated with experts. Only after following the right process of lawmaking should it be implemented. As we do in a modern democratic process, a bill is discussed in the lower and then the upper houses of parliament, before it becomes an act.

- Indulgence in impiety and suppression of piety: Impiety means sinful and immoral activities and criminalisation of a system. The king has to avoid them. Indulgence in such acts not only gives disrespect to him but also spoils the image of the complete nation. And what is holy and good (piety) has to be continued. Institutions are built on reputation. One's reputation goes before oneself.[14] We find many leaders who are hypocrites. They show a very ideal behaviour in front of their people, while in their private life it is conflicting. As it is said, 'The character of a man is what he is in the dark'.

- When leading a kingdom or running an institute, there are times when the leader comes across conflicting situations. Sensitive issues like money, people management, and more, become regular concerns. If he or she cannot differentiate between what to agree and what to disagree with, he will always be unable to move forward. The real wisdom is to choose between various appropriate options in front of us. To master this art, the leader has to learn from more experienced people, whom we call the men and women of wisdom.

- The well-known serenity prayer[15]—'God grant me the serenity to accept the things I cannot change, courage to change the things I can; and the wisdom to know the difference'—applies to the leader too.

- Doing acts that ought not to be done and ruining rightful acts: a king should not be immoral. He or she is the head of the state and has responsibilities towards the total well-being of his people. He is like a parent to his or her praja. According to Kautilya, an immoral king will be unable to provide total well-being. By using immoral ways, he or she might bring total disaster to him- or herself and the kingdom.

- Hitler was using his power in a destructive way. He had many good advisors who suggested the right way to manage a conflicting situation. But instead of taking their wise guidance, he created one of the biggest disasters known to mankind.[16]

- Not giving what ought to be given: what rightfully belongs to be praja should be given to them without delay. The king needs to give the welfare of the praja top priority. Facilities for good health, hospitals, education, and encouragement for trade and commerce, agriculture should be provided. He should also make sure there is no corruption in the system.

- Also, rewards and recognitions are important in any kingdom. Our country too has various awards of national importance given to the people who have contributed for national development. Bharat Ratna, Padma Vibhushan, Padma Bhushan, and Padma Sri are recognitions that give a moral boost to the people.

- Sometimes a pat on the back is enough to make a person inspired to do good work for the nation. Even taking the advice and implementing them is good enough reward for a teacher or a wise person. In this way, a kingdom becomes a very inspiring place to be in. Even in modern-day government organisations, we find the system of rewards and recognitions being introduced. 'As the employees should be punished for their wrong doings, they should be rewarded for their hard work', said Raghunath Anant Mashelkar.[17]

- Securing what ought to be given: when a person gets his or her due in time there is a sense of happiness. What are the basic requirements of the praja? Security, law and order, food, shelter, material progress, education, health, and opportunities for growth are just to list a few. When these are given there is a sense of happiness all around. In turn, the king also gets the due respect and admiration. Same is the case when Kautilya advices that one of the key responsibilities of a king is to ensure that his or her praja will be given in time and with dignity what is to be given.[18]

- Not punishing those deserving to be punished: Leadership is a very dynamic responsibility. It includes the right to give punishment. Those deserving punishment should be punished. That punishment has to be fair. Like rewards and recognition is essential, so also punishments are important for a kingdom or institution to sustain. Kautilya Arthashastra for this reason is also called *dandaniti*. If this is not practiced, the law of the jungle will take over the kingdom. 'The king severe with rod (punishment) becomes a terror. A king with mild rod is despised. The king just with the rod is honoured'.[19]

- When criminals take over a society and the running of it, citizens loose complete faith in their leaders and the government. Organised crime then becomes a way of life and a leader needs to emerge who can eliminate such crime and criminals.

- During the 1990s, the praja of Mumbai city was totally upset with the crime rates. People had lost faith in the system. The underworld had taken over the business community. The government had appointed D. Sivanandhan, as Joint Commissioner of Police, Crime Branch (1990), to take action to break the underworld nexus.[20] The government even introduced a new law, the Maharashtra Control of Organised Crime Act,[21] so that those criminals who had escaped using the loopholes in the law itself were eliminated within the law. Once the city was assured of its security, business activities prospered and once again there was a positive vibe among the prajas; today, we find its economy flourishing. If criminalisation of politics happens, people lose faith in the government and a state of anarchy sets in; this needs to be prevented.

- Punishing those not deserving to be punished: In good governance, right amount of fear is important. But the leader should not punish the ones who do not deserve to be punished. Many poor people, who do not have education and understanding of law are punished by the government. The tribal people and communities like Ramoshis and Paradhis were treated like criminals by British and were punished.

- A study conducted by *Times of India*[22] analysed data from interviews with 373 death row convicts over a 15-year period, has found that three-quarters of those given the death penalty belonged to backward classes, and 75 percent were from economically weaker sections. This shows that there is a disparity. Justice delayed is justice denied. The pending cases of film actors (like Salman Khan), politicians and ministers (Bhujbal), corporate chiefs (Vijay Mallaya), and terrorists (like Dawood) raise doubt in the mind of the people about 'good governance'.
- In the war movie *Troy*,[23] the army general comes to the king and tells, 'Sir, the army is under the fear that you may punish them'. He adds something very crucial: 'Fear can be constructive, if you can manage it well'.
- Men are managed by the fear of punishment. It is because of the fear of the police that the crime rate is controlled. It is because of the fear of losing a job that employees become productive. It is only because of the fear of punishment that children are controlled by teachers and parents. So, Kautilya advices the king to use fear but never misuse fear, especially in case of those individuals who do not deserve to be punished. The ability to let go of the nonculprits is to be practiced by a leader.
- Seizing those who ought not to be seized, and not arresting those who ought to be seized: controlling crime is an extremely vital function of a good administrator in any society. By not arresting criminals, the police not only support existing criminals, but also encourage new criminals. Unfortunately, we have been glamorising criminals in various Hollywood movies like *The Godfather* and even in Indian movies like *Vaatsav, Nayakan, Dayavan, Satya, Once Upon a Time in Mumbai*, and others. This is sending a wrong message to the youth of our nation.
- Therefore, while it is important to arrest and take necessary actions against the wrongdoers, it is also equally important to protect the poor and not punish or arrest them. There are petty crimes that are done and some out of sheer necessity. The classic book by Victor Hugo, *Les Miserables*,[24] brings this out in a dramatic manner. A man gets arrested for stealing a loaf of bread under unavoidable circumstances and is put into prison.[25]
- (Avoid) doing harmful things and destroying beneficial things: a leader should not do anything that would harm the praja or the organisation. Also, beneficial things should not be ruined as in, for example, destroying respected religious symbols. The leader has to be like a wall—a protection as well as a barrier. When an outsider tries to attack one's people, one needs to step in front of them and face the challenge. So a leader has to be present when the people require him or her.

- When things are working fine, the leader should give credit to others, when things go wrong, he or she should take responsibility, and take charge of the situation. Standing like a rock, he or she should inspire subordinates to overcome the problems. 'When the underworld had taken Mumbai city under their fear, I asked my policemen to take action and give results. I took the blame of what they did wrong. Thus, my men knew there is a leader who stands by them,' said D. Sivanandhan.[26]
- Failing to protect from thieves: a leader should protect subordinates from robbers or any other external factors that can erode the wealth of people, state, individuals, or employees of an organisation. People expect such protection to be provided by the government. The king is like the father in a family, and is supposed to look after subjects' safety and security. When that is not done, people lose faith is such a leader and government.
- Every single person in every corner of the kingdom, beginning with the first and ending with the last person, needs to be protected. There is a constant fear among people that their hard-earned money should be kept in safe custody. Today, banks play a major role when we deposit our money into those accounts. 'I have a major role to play as head of India's first bank—State Bank of India. To be a custodian of the money and their faith', said Arundhati Bhattacharya, Chairman, State Bank of India.[27]
- Robbing (people) him- or herself (the king): the illiterate man can steal a mango from a roadside tree, while an educated man can steal away the whole road. Similarly, a more powerful individual has more chances of misusing power and taking to robbing one's own organisation. The various scams that occur in the political field prove this fact. The Comptroller and Auditor General[28] is unfolding various scams like 2G spectrum, fodder, coal allocation, and more. An internal fraud report by Deloitte shows that 88 percent of internal frauds were done by the leaders themselves. It reads: 'Senior management identified as most susceptible to commit fraud, whereas external parties were least likely to commit fraud, as per survey respondents'.[29]
- Robbing does not mean just stealing money and other physical objects. Honour, dignity and gratitude can be stolen as well. If a person truly deserves it, then he or she should be rewarded and recognised. The people are the leader's greatest assets. He needs to pay them well and on time. It is only if the army is strong will it fight for you. A leader has to be a good fighter inspiring the whole group. Faye Wattleton said it beautifully: 'Whoever, is providing leadership needs to be fresh and thoughtful and as reflective as possible to make the very best fight'.[30]
- Ruining human exertions by spoiling the excellence of work done: institutions are built by the hard work and commitment of a group of people

who are ready to sacrifice everything for a higher purpose. Imagine the pain inflicted if someone does harm to such institutions of excellence. According to Kautilya, ignoring such work would be a leader's mistake, and stealing away other's work by the king would be completely unacceptable.

- J.R.D. Tata created Air India (formerly Tata Airlines) as a world class airline. It was one of the most admired airlines across the globe, known for its punctuality and professionalism. However, when the government decided to nationalise it, J.R.D. Tata felt as if his baby was taken away from his custody. The excellent work done by him was spoilt.
- Doing harm to principal men and dishonouring those worthy of honour: A society that does not respect elders and men of knowledge cannot survive for long. *Vriddha*, meaning elders, are respected across most Asian cultures. Even young professionals with high education are considered vriddhas. We find this pattern common in today's corporate world when, after completing their formal education in reputed institutions like the Indian Institute of Technology and the Indian Institute of Management, they move on to become young CEOs of companies. Such people also fall into the category of vriddhas by virtue of their professional excellence.
- In the same way, there are principal men in a kingdom: advisors to the king. These men with their wisdom guide the whole kingdom and help the king to discriminate between right and wrong. Such people should never be harmed. Kautilya's father himself was such a man dishonoured by Dhanananda. Such people should be given the due honour and respect; by doing so, the king also earns honour and respect.
- Opposing the elders: Elders have an advantage over the younger generation. This is due to their experiences they have in life. Always there is a generation gap when youngsters show a lack of respect towards the elders. Kautilya says, do not oppose the elders; listen to their opinion before taking any decision. Their advice comes from love, concern and a sense of well-being for others.
- In the Mahabharata, Duryodhana opposed his elders. When wise men like Bhishma and Viruda were opposed, their experience, wisdom and advice were not utilised. It took Duryodhana towards destruction. However, Yudhishtira respected Bhishma's advice to the Pandavas on the duties of a ruler, dharma and good governance.[31] The Pandavas thus had a long lasting happy and prosperous kingdom.
- Partiality and falsehood: *Satyameva Jayate, Nanritam*—truth alone prevails, not untruth, says the Mundaka Upanishad.[32] The same quote has been represented in the national emblem of India. Truth alone triumphs fully, never falsehood. A leader needs to understand that in spite of the circumstances and challenges faced, finally, in the long term, one will turn victorious if he or she is on the side of dharma.

- The challenge of choosing between *shreyas* (the path of good) and *preyas* (path of pleasure) will always be encountered by a leader. Kathopanisad explains this in detail.[33] In those situations one should refrain from falsehood.

- A leader should not be partial. He or she needs to judge the person on the right side and support the truth. Dhritarashtra, due to *putramoha* (attachment to his son), was clouded in his judgement and partial towards Pandavas. In spite of Viruda, guiding him towards dharma, through advice in Vidura Niti,[34] he did not listen, finally leading to Kurukshetra and the death of all his children. A king like Dhritarashtra, being impartial could have avoided the whole episode. Leaders should also not insist their kids to take up leadership roles. It might lead to the frustration of the people.

- Not requiting what is done: according to Kautilya, people who have done good work and have granted favours should not be forgotten. The leaders never do work in isolation. It is a team of advisors, experts and the praja who support him. Also his *mitras* (allies) form an essential part of the kingdom.[35] We all live in an interdependent society.

- Therefore, a rajarshi will always requite; that is, make appropriate return for the favour or service done to him. We live in a duty-bound society, in which it is an essential requirement to help each other. Even animals have been known to remember good deeds done to them and in return show compassion, love and affection to persons who have taken care of them.

- Not carrying out what is settled: discussions, debates and arguments should finally lead to a good conclusion. But what has been concluded has to be carried out. Kautilya here is pointing out that if the king has settled on a particular decision, it is essential for him to carry out that decision into implementation.

- Just making promises is not enough. If a government has agreed, given a contract to a particular contractor, and then turns back and reverses the contract, it sends a wrong message to the contractor. This is not a good sign of leadership in government. One needs to keep the promise made even at the cost of one's life, says Ramayana.[36]

- Negligence: a leader should never be careless. Even a small issue should not go unnoticed. Neglecting basic needs of farmers (the praja of our country) have led to huge suicides.[37] The prosperity and the well-being of the praja should never be disturbed. The primary reason why leaders tend to be negligent and indolent is lethargy. Without vision, greed takes over. Therefore, the leader has to be continuously and ever alert.

- One may initiate several new projects and various institutions or companies. But the secret of success is not just starting something new but making sure that the start-ups keep growing. For that to happen, one needs to review. If neglected, these projects start to fall apart. It is like having children. Just giving birth to children is not enough. We need to ensure they get education, care, love, and proper guidance so that they become ideal citizens of a nation.

- The Aditya Birla group, under the leadership of Kumar Mangalam Birla—who became chairman at the age of 26 because of the untimely death of his father, Aditya Vikram Bira—has grown from a USD $2 billion group to a USD $41 billion group (2012). They have a business review council;[38] they plan in such a way that none of the more than 100 group companies that they have is neglected. Each has been given a direction and vision to be achieved. This has made the Aditya Birla group, one of the biggest successful conglomerates of modern times.

- Indulgence of the king: a king is not devoid of pleasures of life. He is living in luxury. But excess becomes indulgence. Kautilya suggests everything in moderation for the king. Therefore, the concept of indriyajaya is recommended.[39] When someone is in a leadership position, the king automatically gets a part of royalty that comes along with it. But if the raja is not trained to keep himself in restrain, he will not become a rajarshi.

- When he died, Sardar Vallabhai Patel[40] had hardly any money in his personal bank account. He was among the most powerful politician after India got independence. Yet he never misused power. Even though he had to deal with the other kings of the princely states, he could organise a complete sovereign nation without getting drawn into the power game—a true rajarshi of modern times. Another great political leader who displayed the qualities of a rajarshi was Lal Bahadur Shastri,[41] who was a contrast among the other corrupt and self-centered political leaders.

- Destruction of well-being: well-being is the state of a person being comfortable, healthy or happy. To make sure every citizen achieves this is the primary duty of any leader or government. For this various welfare schemes are being introduced. These schemes are used in every field, from education to housing, sanitation, finance, health, and more. Some notable government schemes run in India include Sarva Shiksha Abhiyaan,[42] the National Rural Employment Guarantee Act (NAREGA),[43] Pradhan Mantri Jan Dhan Yojana,[44] Beti Bachao, Beti Padhao Yojana,[45] National skill development programmes, pension schemes, Providing Urban Amenities in Rural Areas, Primary health centres, housing schemes, and others. Such welfare schemes should be encouraged and not destroyed. If destroyed, the progress of a nation would be curbed. Well-being ensures overall prosperity. A king who opposes such ideas is bound to create a public outcry. Thus, by making citizens unhappy, the king destroys his own well-being and also that of others.

Notes

1 Cited from Kautilya Arthashastra (Kangle, 1972), Book 1, Chapter 2, Sutra 1.
2 The four vidyas for a king are *aanvikshiki, trai, vaarta,* and *dandaniti.*

3 *Vidya dadati vinayam* is a traditional adage, meaning 'knowledge gives humility'.

4 Ramdas Swami was a 17th-century Marathi philosopher. He wrote a letter to Shivaji, the Maratha king, as mentioned in his popular work in Marathi literature, describing him as a 'Srimanta Yogi'.

5 'Casting of the Six Enemies', Kautilya Arthashastra (Kangle, 1972), Book 1, Chapter 6, Section 3, Part 1.

6 'Control over the Senses', Section 3 Chapter 6, Part 1.

7 The details of these kings is given by R.P. Kangle (1972) in his commentary.

8 All of the above stories and their kings have been explained in detail by Kangle (1972).

9 Subrato Roy is currently serving a prison sentence for an 'investment scandal' for misusing the funds of his investors in various of his group projects.

10 *Wall Street* is a 1987 American drama film, directed and co-written by Oliver Stone.

11 The topic 'What a leader should not do' has been covered as a separate topic in Pillai (2010). What a leader should 'avoid' spans 10 chapters.

12 Pillai (2010: 109).

13 The Dharmashastras give guidance for taking better decisions.

14 As observed by Sandeep Karnik, IPS, during a police training program held at Jalna on 26 March 2009.

15 The serenity prayer by Reinhold Neibuhr, was an American theologian, ethicist, public intellectual, and commentator on politics and public affairs, and professor at Union Theological Seminary.

16 In the Second World War, about 5 million Jews were killed and about 60 million people lost their lives.

17 Padma Shri, Raghunath Anant Mashelkar, known for his contribution in scientific development in India and protection of intellectual property rights, had made this observation at the golden jubilee celebrations (2015) of the Indian Institute of Packaging, a Government of India undertaking.

18 A popular piece of dialogue by Peter Parker in the movie *Spiderman 3*, produced by Sony, Inc.

19 Kautilya Arthashastra, 1.4.8–10 (Kangle, 1972).

20 For more details on how D. Sivanandhan made Mumbai a safe city in the 1990s, see Chapter 1, Pillai and Sivanandhan (2014).

21 Maharashtra Control of Organised Crime Act of 1999 was a law enacted by Maharashtra, India, to combat organised crime and terrorism.

22 Indulekha Aravind, 'Here's Proof That Poor Get Gallows, Rich Mostly Escape', *Times of India*, 7 August 2016.

23 Based on Homer's *Iliad*, which narrates the story of the 10-year Trojan War, *Troy* is a 2004 American epic war film written by David Benioff and directed by Wolfgang Petersen.

24 *Les Miserables* (1862) is a French novel written by Victor Hugo. Movies and dramas have been made based on this book by various producers and directors.

25 This man, who is honest, commits the act of stealing because of continuous hunger in the family and unemployment in the country. He pleads to the judge to let him go. But the judge instead takes the decision of the rulebook that, big or small, a crime is still a crime. He is arrested and jailed for more than 20 years. Thus, from a noble man, a criminal is born.

26 In the movie *Chanakya Speaks*, produced by Shemaroo Entertainment Ltd, D. Sivanandhan mentions how he inspired his people while tackling organised crime in Mumbai in the 1990s.

27 She made this comment while addressing a group of CEOs at a two-day seminar on 'Spirituality and Corporate Culture' organised by Art of Living in May 2015.

28 The comptroller and auditor general of India is an authority, established by the Constitution of India under Article 148, who audits all receipts and expenditure of the Government of India and state governments, including those of bodies and authorities.

29 Deloitte India Fraud Survey Report, Edition 1, Dec 2014 (www.deloitte.com/in).

30 Faye Wattleton (b. 1943) is the first African-American and the youngest president ever elected to the Planned Parenthood Federation of America, and is also the second woman to hold the post.

31 The Shanti Parva (Book of Peace) is the 12th of the 18 books of Mahabharata. It has three subbooks and 366 chapters. It is the longest book among the 18 books of the Epic. The book is set after the war is over, the two sides have accepted peace, and Yudhisthira starts his rule of the Pandava kingdom.

32 Mundaka Upanishad, 3.1.6.

33 The Katha Upanishad II (I.2 and 3.): 'The good (sreyas) is one thing, the pleasant (preyas) is another. These two having different purposes, bind a man. Of these two, it is well for him who takes hold of the good; he who chooses the pleasant misses his end.'

34 The Mahabharata, Udyoga Parva, sections 33–41.

35 Saptana of Kautilya contains seven pillars: Swami, Amatya, Janapada, Durg, Kosha, Danda, and Mitra. These are essential for the kingdom.

36 A popular saying goes: *Raghukul reet sada chali aayi, pran jaaye par vachana jaahi* (Tulidas Ramayana, Aryan Kand).

37 In 2012, the National Crime Records Bureau of India reported 13,754 farmer suicides.

38 The Business Review Council of Aditya Birla group is headed by Dr. Bharat Singh (www.adityabirla.com).

39 Kautilya Arthashastra, 1.6.3.

40 Sardar Vallabhai Patel (1875–1950) was the deputy prime minister and first home minister of India.

41 Lal Bahadur Shastri (1904–66) was the second prime minister of India.

42 Sarva Shiksha Abhiyan is an Indian government programme aimed at the universalisation of elementary education 'in a time-bound manner', as mandated by the 86th amendment to the Constitution of India, making free and compulsory education to children of ages 6–14 (estimated to be 205 million in number in 2001) a fundamental right. The programme was pioneered by former Prime Minister Atal Bihari Vajpayee.

43 The National Rural Employment Guarantee Act 2005, later renamed the Mahatma Gandhi National Rural Employment Guarantee Act, is an Indian labour law and social security measure that aims to guarantee the 'right to work'. It aims to ensure livelihood security in rural areas by providing at least 100 days of wage employment in a financial year to every household whose adult members volunteer to do unskilled manual work. It is one of the important scheme being implemented by the government to achieve inclusive growth.

44 Pradhan Mantri Jan Dhan Yojana, Prime Minister's People Money Scheme, is a National Mission for Financial Inclusion to ensure access to financial services—namely, banking savings and deposit accounts, remittance, credit, insurance, and pension—in an affordable manner. This financial inclusion campaign was launched by the prime minister of India, on 28 August 2014.

45 Beti Bachao, Beti Padhao (save girl child, educate girl child) is a Government of India scheme that aims to generate awareness and improving the efficiency of welfare services meant for women. The scheme was initiated with an initial corpus of Rs 100 crore.

References

Kangle, R.O. 1972. *Kautiliya Arthashastra*. Mumbai: University of Mumbai and Moti-
lal Banarasidas.

Pillai, R. 2011. *Corporate Chanakya*. Mumbai: Jaico Publications.

Pillai, R. 2014. *Chanakya's 7 Secrets of Leadership*. Mumbai: Jaico Publications.

6

MANAGEMENT OF ECONOMY
AND LEADERSHIP

B.P. Mathur

We live in an interconnected world with a globalised economy and developments across the world inevitably effect our economic well-being in India. Currently, the global economy is facing an unprecedented crisis. The present ruling economic ideology, whose main protagonists are the western countries, is free markets with deregulation, liberalisation, privatisation and globalisation as its mantra. The practice of this ideology by USA and its allies, particularly from the 1980s onwards, led to the global economic meltdown of 2008. The trigger was caused by big banks doing unethical financial engineering and trading worthless securities and making huge profits, with their executives cornering astronomical salaries. In order to revive the economy, the government in these countries poured billions of dollars in the economy and turned to Keynesian prescription of state intervention to boost demand. Although the Western economies have somewhat recovered from the downturn, growth continues to be sluggish. Many of these countries are burdened with heavy public debt. Eurozone countries such as Italy, Greece, Spain, and Portugal are facing serious economic crisis with huge unemployment problems threatening social unrest.

Analysing the reason for the economic downturn, the Nobel prize-winning economist Joseph Stiglitz observed that in final analysis, it was due to moral deprivation, 'something has happened to our sense of values, when the end of making more money justifies the means, which in the US subprime crisis meant exploiting the poor and least-educated among us' (Stiglitz, 2012: xvii). Jeffery Sachs, another distinguished economist, says, 'Our greatest national illusion is that a healthy society can be organized around the single-minded pursuit of wealth. The ferocity of the quest for wealth throughout society has left Americans exhausted and deprived of the benefits of social trust, honesty and compassion' (Sachs, 2011: 9).

India embraced a new liberalised economic policy in 1991, reposing full faith in market economy, kowtowing West's economic ideology. Although this has helped faster economic growth, created an ambitious, well-to-do, upward mobile middle class, the fate of the majority has not improved. There is widespread poverty, unemployment, illiteracy, and deprivation in society, with the majority of the population barely able to make two ends meet and for whom life is a daily grind.

It is now well recognised that the free market economy model creates serious socioeconomic problems, such as rising inequality in society, a culture of consumerism, and high levels of unemployment, and is severely detrimental to ecology. Britain's exit from the European Union and nomination of Trump as the Republican presidential candidate were indications of people's dissatisfaction and disapproval with current economic policies.

For the last several years, thinkers and intellectuals all over the world are groping in the dark, to figure out the 'right economic model' as both the socialist and free-market economic systems have failed. Eminent historian Eric Hobswam observes,

> Since the 1980s it has been evident that the socialists, Marxist or otherwise, were left without their traditional alternative to capitalism, at least unless or until they rethought what they meant by 'socialism' and abandoned the presumption that the (manual) working class would necessarily be the chief agent of social transformation. But the believers in the 1973–2008 reductio ad absurdum of market society were also left helpless. A systematic alternative system may not be on the horizon, but the possibility of a disintegration, even a collapse, of the existing system is no longer to be ruled out. Neither side knows what would or could happen in that case.
>
> (Hobsbawm, 2011: 418)

It may be worth noting that the idea of free markets and globalisation is not the same thing as the Indian philosophical concept of *vasudhaiva kutumbakam*. Globalisation is the outcome of the West's industrial and technological civilisation, which has led to the flourishing of world trade and commerce. Its nature is materialistic and consumerist and its motivating force is profiteering and self-interest. It results into cutthroat competition, rivalry and conflict. On the other hand, *vasudhaiva kutumbakam* is essentially a cultural and spiritual concept. It looks towards the whole world as one family with love, harmony, cooperation, and mutual support as the basic ingredients. It rules out unlimited consumerism. Its philosophy is rooted in self-imposed control, equitable sharing of resources, and taking care of every member of society.

Can India's ancient wisdom and knowledge provide an answer to the problem which the world is facing today? What kind of leadership can usher in a prosperous world, without losing its ethical and moral moorings, so that every human being is able to lead a satisfying and fulfilling life?

Rajarshi leadership

Rajarshi leadership combines the vision of a raja/leader with the wisdom of a rishi/philosopher; a leadership which focuses on material pursuits, with spiritual insights firmly rooted in ethics and morality. Leadership is essentially conceiving a vision, communicating and persuading others to share that vision, and putting together skilled people to accomplish the vision in terms of definable goals and measurable outcomes. Thus, leadership is making things happen and getting things done. Leaders possess holistic vision and pursue excellence. On the other hand, rishi-vision views life in terms of its spiritual dimension, which gives rise to noble values such as truth, beauty, love, service and sacrifice. It is a combination of these two visions that constitutes Rajarshi leadership. This has been expressed beautifully in the Bhagavad Gita, in its last shloka, summing up its message as: *Yatra yog'esvarah Krasno yatra Partho dhanur-dharah/tatra srir vijayo bhutir dhruv nitir matir mama* (Wherever there is Krishna, the Lord of Yoga, and Arjuna, the man of action, there is wealth, success, steady growth, and justice) (Ch 18:78).

Wealth and India's cultural heritage

India's ancient philosophy has deeply reflected on human beings' purpose on planet earth and recognised four goals of life called *pursharth-arth*: wealth, *kama*, or worldly pleasures; *dharma*, or righteous living; and *moksha*, or salvation. These goals reconcile worldly pursuits with spiritual goals. The doctrine recognises that every human being has multiple goals, which, if pursued, bring meaning and purpose to one's life. Although moksha is the ultimate goal of a person who has fulfilled his or her worldly responsibilities, a normal human being regularly pursues three other goals: *arth*, *kama*, and *dharma*, in what is known as *trivarga*. The doctrine of trivarga says that while it is perfectly desirable to engage in livelihood to make money, and enjoy pleasures of life and recreational activities, they must be within the boundary of dharma. Dharma is that which sustains progress and welfare of the world and embraces every type of righteous conduct on the part of the individual as well as the state.

Western philosophers such as Max Weber and Albert Schweitzer have expressed a view that Hinduism as well as Eastern philosophies are life-negating, take the mundane world as an illusion and feel that the purpose of human life is to seek liberation from the world and unite with the Supreme Reality. Because of this philosophical outlook, they have neglected life in this world, which is responsible for their lack of economic development and backwardness. Weber has developed a theory of cultural roots of capitalism and emphasised that Protestant ethics, more particularly its Calvinist version has been responsible for developing a work culture and attitude towards life which is responsible for the success and prosperity of Western societies. The conclusion that Indian philosophy is life-negating, unfair and an incorrect understanding of its broad dimension. Historian A.L. Basham observed,

> In ancient India, her people enjoyed life, passionately delighting both in the things of the senses and the things of the spirit. . . . The average Indian, though he might pay lip service to the ascetic and respect his ideals, did not find life a vale of tears from which to escape at all costs; rather he was willing to accept world as he found it, and to extract what happiness he could from it. . . . India was a cheerful land, whose people, each finding a niche in a complex and slowly evolving system, reached a higher level of kindliness and gentleness in their mutual relationships than any other nation of the antiquity.
>
> (Basham, 2003: 9)

It would be instructive to look at our ancient scriptures such as the Mahabharata and Kautilya's philosophy to understand Indian cultural outlook towards life, money and wealth.

Mahabharata and material prosperity

Mahabharata discusses two general attitudes to arth, radically opposed to each other. On the one hand, wealth is regarded as the first condition not only of a happy and dignified family life but also of a stable social order. On the other hand, wealth, when accumulated, gives rise to further desire for it, therefore causing a lack of happiness and peace and being destructive for spiritual life. Mahabharata balances these two opposite viewpoints. After the great war, with enormous destruction and bloodshed, Yudhishthira is overcome with remorse, he doesn't want to rule and renounces everything. He is dissuaded by his brothers, Draupadi and Krishna, and given a long sermon by Bhishma lying on his deathbed (Shanti-parva) (Badrinath, 2007: 9).[1] Arjuna argued for material prosperity, as evident from the following stanzas:

> From increased wealth flow all the good works, as do the rivers from the mountains.
>
> (Shanti-parva, 8.16)

> On wealth depends the rise of a family, and on wealth depends the rise of dharma; for him who has no wealth, there is happiness neither in this world nor in the next.
>
> (Shanti-parva, 8.22)

To a question from Yudhishthira about what the attitude towards money should be, Bhisma takes a very balanced position and explains that there are context in which it is legitimate to regard wealth as a primary factor in life, and material prosperity as of great importance in life. However, there are context in which craving for wealth would lead to misery and unhappiness.

> Given money a person masters this world as well as the next, and gains access to truth and dharma. With no money, his life is no life at all.
>
> (Shanti, 130.43)

> The loss of money and property is for a man a great misfortune, greater than even death; for they, money and wealth, are also the means to his fulfilling his desires and dharma as well.
>
> (Udyog, 72.27)

Commenting on the evil effects of money, Bhisma says that 'striving for money is certainly not conducive to happiness. When obtained one is overcome with the desire to protect it' (Shanti, 177.26); 'greed for money is suffering' (Shanti, 177.37); and 'I grieve for those who regard money as everything' (Shanti, 104.8).

> The ways of making money are the ways that produce mental obsession, miserliness, arrogance, pride, fear anxiety. For human beings these are money related pain and suffering.
>
> (Vana, 2.42)

> Accumulated wealth like beauty, youth, health, and company of dear ones is transitory.
>
> (Vana, 2.47)

Mahabharata aims at self-control by individuals. The aim is to prevent the necessity of wealth turning into greed and greed into lawlessness. Wealth should be earned through dharma.

> Only that wealth is truly wealth that has been earned in the ways of dharma. What has been collected through adharma to others is a wealth damned. One should not, in one's greed for money, abandon what is universally right and good.
>
> (Shanti, 292.19)

State and money

Mahabharata makes a distinction between the individual and the state with regard to money. Although an individual should have a balanced approach towards money, the state's (king's) coffers should be full for a kingdom to be powerful and strong. In fact, it is the dharma of the king to have an overflowing treasury.

> The strength of a king is based on treasury; army is based on treasury; the social order is based on army; and the people are based on dharma.
>
> (Shanti, 130.35)

> The king whose treasury is empty is treated by indifference even by the common man; nobody is satisfied with the little he gives, and none is eager to work for him.
>
> (Shanti, 133.6)

> Let the king fill the treasury: having filled protect it: protecting it, increase it; for in all ages that is the dharma of the king.
>
> (Shanti, 133.1–2)

Kautilya and wealth

Kautilya, who flourished around 300 BC, had forcefully underlined the importance of wealth both in personal life, as well as statecraft. As illustrated in *Chankyasutra, Sukhasya mulam dharma/Dharmsya mulamartha, Arthasya mulam rajyam* (Dharma or righteousness is the root of happiness, Wealth is the root of dharma; The state is the root of wealth) (Subramaniam, 2000: 21).

> Kautilya elaborates in great detail the importance of wealth for leading a comfortable life.
> All virtues are ever dependent on wealth, wealth captures pleasures, everything is dependent on wealth. Wealth enriches and enhances life.
> The rich are ever happy, the poor ever sad, happiness and sorrow are divided among the rich and poor.
>
> (ibid., 97–8)

Kautilya was the first political theorist to realise that accumulation of wealth is the key to the power and authority exercised by the state.[2]

> All state activities depend first on the treasury. Therefore a King should devote its best attention to it.
>
> (Arthshastra, 2.8.1.2)

> A king with depleted treasury eats into the very vitality of the citizens and the country.
>
> (2.1.16)

From kosa (wealth) comes the power of the danda (Government). With the treasury and the army (kosa – danda) the earth is acquired with the treasury as the ornament.

(2.12.37)

Kautilya advocates an activist state taking part in manufacturing and trading, thus augmenting economic prosperity. While emphasising on the need for wealth collection, Kautilya underlines the principle of equity in taxation.

Leadership is character and moral conduct

The cornerstone of ancient Indian thought was moral behaviour of the rulers, which also influenced individual morality. Indian theorists stressed upon the prime necessity for the ruler and his ministers of conquering personal desires for pleasure and power. This is true even for modern times, as character and acting without selfish motive is the most important attribute of a leader. General Mathew B. Ridgway, hero of the Second World War, says, 'character stands for self-discipline, loyalty, readiness to accept responsibility, and a willingness to accept mistakes. It stands for selflessness, modesty, humility, willingness to sacrifice when necessary and, in my opinion, faith in God'. Motivational guru Stephen Covey emphasises that a leader's most important characteristic is to adhere to principles and maintain self-discipline.

The highest manifestation of ancient Indian culture is reflected in the Ramayana which presents an idealistic picture of *dharamrajya*: a universal empire based on righteousness. According to the Ramayana, a ruler must have ideal conduct, unimpeachable in every respect, as people not only follow the leader, but society believes that evils and mishaps among the people are caused by the wrongdoings of the ruler. Rama is an embodiment of righteousness, renunciation and noble virtues. He is described as 'one who laid down the rules of good conduct for all people, by precept and practice'. Rama, as an ideal ruler was an embodiment of dharma in all its aspects, presenting himself as a dutiful son, an affectionate brother, a loving husband, and a stern and relentless ruler. He is an ideal example of Rajarshi, a royal sage who combined political statesmanship with philosophical wisdom.

The Mahabharata exhorts the king again and again that discipline of dharma is the discipline of the king. A king who tries to discipline his subjects without disciplining himself will become an object of ridicule. 'When the king has conquered his own self, he has conquered his enemies too. The king who remains defeated by his own self, how can he be victorious against enemies' (Shanti, 69.4, cited in Badrinath, 2007: 433).

Bhishma propounds 36 self-disciplines that a king should cultivate diligently, such as securing wealth without cruelty, fearlessness, avoiding self-praise, giving up arrogance, serving the elders, seeking material prosperity, etc. (ibid., 430–38). A state is founded on the trust of the people and this can be secured by truth and justice.

> For the kings, no means are far more effective than truth, no wealth greater than truth. For it is upon the trust of people that the state is founded; when that trust is destroyed, because of the untruthfulness of the king, the state is destroyed too.
>
> (Shanti, 56.17)

> Freeing yourself from likes and dislikes, and keeping preferences, anger, greed and vanity far away, treat all being with a sense of equality.
>
> (Shanti, 59.104)

Kautilya underlined five duties of the king: punishment of the wicked, rewarding the righteous, development of state revenues by just means, impartiality in granting favours, and protection of the state (Subramaniam, 2000: 88).

The Arthashastra emphasises that Rule of Law alone guarantees security of life and welfare of people and is dependent on the self-discipline of the king (Rangarajan, 1992: 144–9). Self-control is exercised by giving up lust, anger, greed, conceit, arrogance, foolhardiness, and living according to the shastras. A king who has no self-control and gives himself to excessive indulgence in pleasures will perish. The Arthashastra prescribes a detailed code of conduct for the king. When in court he shall not make petitioners wait at the door, but attend to them promptly himself. When the king makes himself inaccessible to his people and is seen only by those near him, wrong decisions are bound to be made; the people will become angry and may go over to the enemy (Arth, 1.19.26–28). The welfare and protection of the people is the main function of the state/king: 'in the happiness of his subjects lies the king's happiness; in their welfare his welfare. He shall not consider as good that pleases him but treat as beneficial to him whatever pleases his subjects' (Arth, 1.19.34).

An ideal king—rajarshi—is one who a) has self-control, having conquered the inimical temptations of the senses; b) cultivates the intellect by association with the elders; c) keeps his or her eyes open through spies; d) is ever active in promoting the security and welfare of the people; e) ensures the observance of dharma by the people, by authority and by example; f) improves his or her own discipline by continuing learning in all branches of knowledge, and g) endears him- or herself to the people by enriching them and doing good to them (Arth, 1.7.1–8).

Current global economic order – the missing ethical compass

Free-market economy, known as capitalism, is the current dominant ideology of the world. Its principal characteristics are materialistic values, consumer society and giant corporations with their huge production apparatus. It is driven by the powerful urge to earn profits, invest, innovate, and grow economy in an exponential manner. Its success is measured by continuous growth of GDP, which means more and more production and consumption of goods and services, irrespective of its social or economic value. In the past, this system has undoubtedly brought a great deal of prosperity and economic betterment to the world, particularly to Western countries, its chief protagonist. The basic philosophy of this system is 'economism': a belief that man is principally driven by economic factors and ignores his psychological and spiritual dimension. Its values are materialistic, considers earning money and accumulating wealth as summum bonum of life, and has no compunction in saying 'greed is good'. Because of a lack of ethical and humanistic values, the free-market system has caused great damage and suffering to humanity across the world, as discussed here.

Environmental degradation

The vast expansion of human economic activity is proving disastrous to environment sustainability. Think tanks such as the Club of Rome have been pointing out that, for the past many years, the earth is already in an overshoot phase and its capacity to absorb exploitation of depletable natural resources has already exceeded. Its most visible impact is climate change because of emission of carbon dioxide and other gases, as a result of extraordinary growth in fossil fuel use for energy. Environmental crusader and former US Vice President Al Gore says that violent impact of human civilization on earth's ecosystem has created a worldwide eco-crisis that threatens the habitability of the world and calls for massive changes in human behaviour and thinking. Mahatma Gandhi was against Western-style development and exhorted people to reduce consumption" 'the Earth provides enough to provide every one's need, but not for their greed'.

Economic inequality

The experience of USA and other Western countries demonstrates a disturbing pattern of growing income and wealth disparity during the past three decades. In the USA until 1980, the top 10 percent earned 35 percent of all income, while the bottom 90 percent shared 65 percent of income. By 2010, however, the numbers changed: the bottom 90 percent's share fell to 52 percent and the top 10 percent's rose to 48 percent, with almost all gains going to top 1 percent and their share increased to more than 20 percent. Despite considerable increase in productivity of workers, their share of wages has not increased and billions in profits have been transferred to the rich upper class. Thomas Piketty, a young French economist, has made an insightful study of the existing economic disparity in developed countries. The owners of capital get disproportionate share of the national pie and have virtually become rentiers. This has led to concentration of wealth in the hands of a few, a phenomenon that is incompatible with meritocracy and the principles of social justice of a democratic society.

The situation in India related to disparity of income and wealth is worse. Thirty percent of the population lives below the poverty line and another 40 to 50 percent at the margin, barely eking out a living. The Arjun Sengupta Commission (2009) had noted that 830 million Indians are poor and vulnerable, living on less than Rs 20 a day, and have experienced hardly any improvement since 1990. The principal beneficiary of the economic growth has been the middle- and higher-income group, numbering 230 million. The skewed distribution of economic development is evident by the growing number of billionaires in India. It is estimated that India has more than 100 billionaires and their combined wealth is equivalent to one-quarter of the country's GDP.

Consumerism

Disparity of wealth, with a large part being cornered by a privileged minority, is leading to consumerism. Consumerism is a cultural pattern that leads people to find meaning, contentment and acceptance primarily through consumption of goods and services. The World Value Survey and other studies of rich societies show that increase in income is not leading to a happier life. Affluence creates its afflictions, such as addiction to shopping and gambling, obesity, eating disorders, depression, mental illness, and loss of social trust. In a highly researched study, two British epidemiologists, Richard Wilkinson and Kate Pickett, argue that greater inequality tears into human psyche, creating anxiety, distrust and an array of mental and physical ailments. Striving for self-worth through material wealth is a zero-sum game in which the constant need for betterment and approval only serves to entrench people in an almost neurotic spiral of consumption.

The present crisis in global economy is largely due to selfishness and lack of morality on the part of the people who control the levers of economic power and are leaders of business and industry. Do Indian wisdom and tradition have some solution to offer to meet the challenges facing the economic policy makers and leadership today?

Dispersed leadership and excellence

According to Indian wisdom a leader is one whose actions are motivated by public good: *lokasangraha*. The Gita says: *lokasangrahamevapi sampansyan karmakartum arhasi* (a leader sets aside his personal motives and works for public good) (3.20). A person who dedicates his or her life energy for the pursuit of public good and public well-being can be called a rishi

90

or transcendental leader. Mahatma Gandhi was the best representative of rajarshi leadership. He won the heart of millions of Indians and led the country to attain the cherished goal of freedom. Because of our value system, India has a tradition of producing transcendental leaders such as Lal Bahadur Shastri and A.P.J. Abdul Kalam, who led spartan lives and dedicated themselves to the service of the nation. A transcendental leader has very few wants and leads the life of a renunciate. Dr. S. Radhakrishnan, India's philosopher statesman, speaking on the occasion of the adoption of India's national flag in the House, on 14 August 1947, observed, *Sarve tyage rajadharmesu drsta—Rajdharma* embodies all forms of renunciation. 'All Philosophers must be kings. Our leaders must be disinterested. They must be dedicated spirits. They must be people who are imbued with the spirit of renunciation' (Radhakrishnan, 2007: 181–2).

A transcendental leader creates institutions, nurtures them and develops leaders to run them. In today's world, the old hierarchical model of leadership is outmoded. Problems are so complex, change is rapid and information flow is so massive, that no single individual can grasp the entire situation. Top leaders cannot make the system work, without the help of many others throughout the society. Therefore, we should perceive leadership in terms of think tanks, idea creators, scientists, university professors, business and industry leaders, nongovernmental organisations (NGOs), and others. It is going to be a collective process rather than an individual enterprise. Motivational author John Gardner says,

> Leadership in our society is dispersed to an extraordinary degree. Despite the lavish media attention to high-level leaders, we are not wholly dependent on leadership at the top. We are dependent on leaders who function at many levels and in all segments in the society— business, government, organised labour, agriculture, the professions, the minority communities, the arts, the universities, social agencies, and so on. . . . If it weren't for this wide dispersal of leadership our kind of society couldn't function. . . . Our top leaders have a crucial role in helping us to achieve a sense of direction, to aid us in sifting priorities and clarifying values. . . . There is a continuous dialogue up and down the scale among the various level of leadership, and those below have a good deal to do what goes on above.
>
> (1984: 135–6)

In a high-performance society, people expect one another to be of high standards as well. High-performing sports teams, musicians, business and industrial organisations, educational institutions, and scientific establishments inspire their members to great heights of personal performance. Individual excellence is imperative in every human endeavour. A plane may crash because the designer was incompetent or because the mechanic responsible for maintenance was incompetent. A society cannot achieve greatness unless individuals at many levels of ability accept the need for high standards. We need excellent doctors, engineers, primary school teachers, mechanics, and excellent businessmen. The standard of our society depends upon all-pervasive striving for good performance. Good leadership is a natural outcome of society which rewards merit and excellence.

N.R. Narayana Murthy, Founder and Chairman Emeritus, Infosys, asserts that a company, an institution or a nation can achieve success only on the basis of a long journey of aspiration, hard work, commitment, focus, hope, confidence, humility, and sacrifice:

> To rally people to commit to such regime that is grueling yet rewarding in the end requires great leaders – change agents – who have the courage to dream big and stand up to their beliefs, who have the power of creating a grand vision, and who can articulate that vision to large mass of followers. These leaders have to create trust in their followers through leadership by example, instill hope and confidence in them about the future, make them feel enthusiastic and proud about their being part of the journey, and convert the vision into reality through hard work and excellence in execution.
>
> (Narayana Murthy, 2009: xxiii)

The Bhagavad Gita extolls the virtue of dedicated work and excellence in all human endeavour. *Karmanayevadikaraste ma phalesu kadachana* (II. 47) and *yogah karmasu kaushalam* (Do your work with utmost dedication, excel in it and move beyond desire-prompted selfish action) (II.47). Rajarshi leadership inspires everyone in society to be excellent and be a high performer.

Rajarshi leadership: the answer

Today, the world is caught in strife, intolerance and violence. The problem is due to human selfishness and materialistic values, where money plays a dominant role, reducing humans to a commodity. India's ancient philosophy gave primacy to the spiritual dimension of life and emphasised that earning wealth and enjoyment of worldly pleasures while legitimate, should be within the bonds of dharma. Our ancient scriptures exhort that we should do selfless service and work for the welfare of humanity. Swami Vivekananda had said that the national ideals of India are *sewa* and *tyag*—service and renunciation. This is expressed in the ancient prayer—*Loka samastha sukhino bhavantu*— may the entire universe enjoy peace and plenty. It is only a Rajarshi mode of leadership, which can find lasting solutions to economic as well as social and political problems, which the world is currently facing.

Notes

1 All the shlokas are cited from this book. (The numbering of all verses are from Gita Press, Gorakhpur edition.)
2 The reference to *Arthashastra* verses are cited from Rangarajan (1992: 253).

References

Badrinath, C. 2007. *The Mahabharata*. Hyderabad: Orient Longman.

Basham, A.L. 2003. *The Wonder That Was India*. New Delhi: Rupa & Co.

Gardner, J.W. 1984. *Excellence*. Bombay: Vakils, Feffer and Simons.

Hobsbawm, E. 2011. *How to Change the World: Tales of Marx and Marxism*. London: Little Brown.

Narayana Murthy, N.R. 2009. *A Better India: A Better World*. New Delhi: Penguin Books.

Radhakrishnan, S. 2007. 'The Dawn of Freedom', in R. Mukharji (ed.), *Great Speeches of Modern India*. New Delhi: Random House.

Rangarajan, L.N. 1992. *Kautilya Arthshastra*. New Delhi: Penguin Books.

Sachs, J. 2011. *The Price of Civilization-Economics and Ethics after the Fall*. London: The Bodley Head.

Stiglitz, J.E. 2012. *The Price of Inequality*. London: Allen Lane.

Subramaniam, V.K. 2000. *Maxim of Chanakya*. New Delhi: Abhinav Publications.

7

ADMINISTRATION AND RAJARSHI LEADERSHIP

Anuradha Balaram

Introduction

Administration is derived from the Latin word *administrare* which means to manage the affairs of people. Administration, therefore, refers to a group of people, who are responsible for managing common resources for a well-defined purpose, usually the welfare of all concerned. Hence, public interest should be put before self-interest in administration. In this chapter, administration refers to the government sector.[1] Focusing on the role of bureaucracy, this chapter argues that effective administration involves an alignment of values, a high level of synergy and commitment to these values represented by both politicians and bureaucrats.

Before we go further, it is necessary to understand who a rajarshi is. A rajarshi is one who is a fine blend of a king (who, through action, aims for external glorious achievements such as honour, effective task fulfilment, recognition, material and physical well-being of people under his or her governance, and so on) and a sage (who aims for deep spiritual attainment through detachment, control of senses, unselfishness, connectedness with the universe, and so on). Administration, unlike leadership, is not confined to one individual. In fact, it is many-headed or hydra-like, and unless complete commitment to the right values is ingrained at every level, accountability of the system becomes suspect. If an administrator has to be a rajarshi or to faithfully follow the vision of a rajarshi, then she[2] would have to have the necessary power, authority and knowledge to execute the complex task at hand. At the same time, she needs to be righteous, morally sound and committed to certain lofty ideals. A visionary rajarshi at the helm of affairs alone will not be effective, since like-minded rajarshis are required at various levels of administration in order to take the vision forward. In India, to initiate effective administration for the people's benefit, rajarshis are required at the central, state, municipal, and panchayat levels. They are also required in departments involved in policy making, implementation, regulatory, service-providing, and in advisory think tanks. Needless to say, this requires an idealistic mindset of all concerned, a deeply ingrained value system in the society at large, an evolution in the quality of the human beings involved, a great commitment towards the public cause, and considerable coordination and cooperation to be effective.

The basic premise of this chapter is that the values of those in power as well as the society at large have a major impact on administrative organisations. Hence, when administration is not effective, mere administrative reforms are only part of the answer. What is required is a well-entrenched value system in society, which will demand such values from those who manage their affairs or serve them. The objective of this chapter is to see what elements are required to put together an organisation of skilled and committed people within a government set-up so that there is seamless execution of the vision of an enlightened leader—a rajarshi at the helm.

The chapter raises the following key questions:

- What are the key features of a rajarshi administration? Can an entire administrative system (politicians as well as government servants) have such traits or is it enough if the leader has these traits?
- Have there been any models in history worth emulating today?
- Is good governance akin to rajarshi administration?
- Has Indian administration lived up to the values enshrined in the constitution?
- If we want to have a more wisdom based and ethical administration at all levels of government, what needs to be done?

The approach to this chapter is not that of a scholarly treatise, but rather that of an ordinary citizen struggling to understand why most administrators have let go of lofty ideals and have settled for short-time tangible gains. An effort is made to go back in time and look at periods in India and elsewhere when, as historians and writers have given us to understand, administration was at its best. Different schools of thought, which have influenced governance and public administration, are discussed. The idea is to understand the basic values and philosophical ideals, which have had an impact on administration during different time periods and identify some best practices and value systems, which could perhaps guide us today. Contemporary literature on recent efforts to reform public administration, ethics in public administration, principles of good governance, and more have also been studied to see whether any attempt has been made to create an enlightened administration based on a sound value system. Indian constitutional values, which form the bedrock of Indian administration, are scrutinized to see whether (and why) there is a significant gap between its spirit and its execution in day-to-day administration.

Administration and value systems
of select ancient societies

In tribal societies, at the dawn of so-called 'civilization', individualism was not given precedence over the tribe. Hence, there was far less possibility for individual greed to surface and the tribe remained cohesive and well-administered according to their relatively simpler needs. Even children were considered common to the tribe and mothers would nurse any child who needed sustenance, not just the one they had given birth to. Paternity was also not given undue emphasis and the tribe behaved as an extended family. Living in the present and being in harmony with nature, these values ensured that there was no need for a large administrative set-up. As societies became more complex, traits like individual property rights, protection, preservation of one's own bloodline, and competitiveness for nature's bounty emerged, leading to a greater consciousness of 'Mine' and 'Thine'. Administration became more complex, from a tribal chieftain to a king and his coterie of ministers, to the various forms of government that we know of today.

Various ancient civilizations have had a profound influence on present-day administration. Some of these are outlined here.

Indus valley civilization (3000 BC–1500 BC)

This ancient urban civilization had a highly developed administrative system that effectively and systematically planned towns with buildings, efficient transport, effective drainage, flourishing trade, and so on. It is evident that the Harappan people were highly disciplined and aware of their civic duties. Unfortunately, not much is known of the values underlying this society and whether common people were exploited by the administration or not.

Egyptian civilization (3100 BC–332 BC)

Characterized by highly efficient agricultural practices and remarkable technical achievements, as shown by the construction of pyramids, sphinxes and other massive public works, the pharaohs, who were considered to be the connection between Egyptians and gods, showed tremendous administrative skills. Egyptian people believed in complete obedience to the pharaoh (since he was divine), valued hygiene and aesthetics highly, and had a firm belief in the afterlife, when they would have to answer for their actions in this life. They believed in Maat—a value system—which emphasized truth, balance, order, law, and morality. The common people were in fear of the pharaoh and there is evidence of exploitation of labour.

Mesopotamian civilisation (3100 BC–539 BC)

The ancient Sumerians and Babylonians had a complex urban administrative set-up. The Babylonian king, Hammurabi was most famous for his inscriptions of strict laws on stone in public places so that all citizens were aware of the expected moral code and knew the penalties of misconduct.

Ancient Greek civilisation (800 BC–AD 600)

Greek philosophers like Socrates (470 BC–399 BC), believed in human excellence and valued the moral worth of the individual. In his *Republic*, Plato (428–348 BC) discussed the most fundamental principles for the conduct of human life. He delved deeply into the nature and value of justice and the other virtues, both from individual and from the society's points of view. Plato discussed four key virtues: wisdom, courage, temperance, and justice. His concept of the 'philosopher–king' is very similar to the rajarshi concept. Plato believed that the rulers or guardians of the society were gifted with superior natures and therefore had no need for wealth or other external rewards. Rulers should not own private property. Instead, they should live and eat together at government expense, and should earn no salary greater than necessary to supply their most basic needs. Under this regime, he believed that no one will have any underhand motive for seeking a position of leadership, and those who are chosen to be guardians will govern solely from a concern to seek the welfare of the state in what is best for all of its citizens.

Another great Greek philosopher, Aristotle (384 BC–322 BC) believed in a happy life for citizens. In order to live a happy life, people must have good judgement to select certain core values, such as endurance, self-mastery and fairness. They should then make rules, which will help them to live up to these values. Good character comes from practice and habit. This will help people to reach morally correct decisions when faced with difficult choices. He emphasized the central role of motives in decision-making and in taking action. All actions should be performed in moderation so that there is a balance in life. Administrators should have the practical wisdom to know what is best for people and human behaviour needs to be controlled in a way that there is happiness for the community.

Ancient Chinese civilisation (2100 BC–221 BC)

The ancient Chinese developed a vast, complex and highly centralized bureaucratic state. Although there were many schools of Chinese thought, Legalism evolved as a branch of Chinese philosophy that was concerned primarily with administration and the rule by law. This was totally unlike the earlier Confucian system, which laid great emphasis on individual and family virtues. Under Legalism, the state need not concern itself with moral or philosophical questions. Shen Buhai and Han Fei, who developed this system, did not refer to divine authority or ethics. A legal code was developed and this applied equally to the ruler and the subjects. Personal charisma of the ruler no longer was important. Through a system of rewards and penalties, ministers were kept under control. The laws were well-known to the public and equally applicable to all citizens. For the Legalists, the correct political order could be based on the measurement or statistical result of any programme. Therefore, no dispute was considered necessary. Present-day Communism in China is strongly influenced by these ideals.

Roman school of thought

Cicero (106 BC–43 BC) was a lawyer and political thinker who had a far-reaching influence in Europe during the Renaissance and the French revolution and also in the USA during the Declaration of Independence.[3] Cicero questioned the established moral value of the time and wrote extensively about liberty, humanism, and individual success. He spoke about statecraft and political action and encouraged pride and courage over religious faith. He preferred a republican form of government to a monarchy and did not appear to be concerned about the poor and the vulnerable. Cicero did not encourage democratic thought. Friedrich Engels, a German philosopher (AD 1820–95), referred to him as 'the most contemptible scoundrel in history' for opposing land and class reforms.

Islamic administration and fundamental principles

Public administration in Islam is based on certain fundamental beliefs found in the Holy Koran. Accordingly it is emphasized that human beings must achieve moral perfection, as they are answerable for their deeds in the life hereafter (after life). Dereliction of duty is not only a crime in law, it is also a sin in Islam. Anybody in administration who is put in a position of trust will have to be worthy in the eyes of Allah. Like other systems, Islam provides legal checks and social strictures in order to make administrative accountability possible. The Shariah Law is derived from the Koran and all higher-level administrative positions are to be filled with ideologically committed persons. In fact, technical skill and knowledge take a secondary position to Islamic values. The dignity of the human being is valued highly and decent labour standards, scope for employee's skill development as well as self-esteem is to be provided by the employers. Legal, social and moral accountability need to go hand in hand. Persons in authority are to be respected and obeyed but obedience to the written word of Allah takes precedence.

Therefore, in the ancient world, the need for high morals influenced some societies (Islamic); charismatic leadership along with strong belief in afterlife influenced others (Egyptian); and the Rule of Law took firm ground as well (Babylonian, Chinese). There was also a slow shift from monarchies to republics and a greater reliance on human effort than on religion (Greek, Roman).

Values and administration in ancient India[4]

In ancient India, administration was supposed to have a moral basis (dharma) and kings relied on brahmins (purohits) for wise counsel. From early childhood, kings were exposed to spiritual ideas. Throughout, pursuit of wealth by the powerful was considered acceptable only through fair means and that too when it is shared with others. Young Rama was taught by Sage Vasishta to ask himself the question 'Who am I' and to seek the Truth through contemplation, dispassion and an understanding of the oneness of the universe. Bhishma, on his deathbed, taught Prince Yudhistra the need for a king to be vigilant, disciplined, balanced, controlled, and impartial. King Janaka was a fully realized soul who did not identify with worldly pleasures. Arjuna was taught by Lord Krishna about the need for detached action. There are many examples throughout Vedic literature that show that kings were taught spiritual values to help them to govern righteously.

Chanakya (350 BC–275 BC) pointed out that, in the absence of government, people behave like fish, with the strong devouring the weak; hence the necessity for the state to protect the citizens and enhance their welfare. The king should be diplomatic, should communicate effectively with subjects and should be well accepted by them. However, he emphasized on the need for occasional subordination of ethical principles when absolutely necessary. In fact, Chanakya was practical and in many ways differed from the high moral code considered advisable to administrators preceding him. He gave primacy to the success and prestige of the king and believed there were occasions when the end justifies the means. He specified qualifying standards for appointment of ministers. These qualities are: power of concentration, character, thinking capability, communication skills, and observation and vigilance.

Thiruvallurvar, in his classic Tamil verses, *Thirukural*, says that a leader should have complete awareness, courage, and generosity and should be aware of what is happening at all times. He should have a balance between the ability to punish the offenders as well as be merciful by nature. Thiruvalluvar advocated that a leader should consult his ministers and other wise men. In fact, he advocated top administrators to listen to bitter criticism and not turn away from it. Keeping officials informed about ongoing activities is important so that they have the larger picture in their vision. However, he cautions that disclosure of certain critical assignments before completion could lead to problems. Selection of subordinates should be done after due diligence and after weighing the merits and demerits. Once selected, independence in functioning should be given. He says that there should be no expectation for services rendered—like the clouds, which provide rain without expecting any return from the earth.

In the Panchatantra, Vishnusarman states that a king should behave like a gardener and motivate and encourage his subjects with recognition and rewards as a gardener waters his garden so that it bears fruit. He is also expected to manage his subjects like a cowherd. The king should treat all subjects like his sons. The king should also be aware of the world around him and not blindly follow the advice of those around him lest he be misguided. He should be able to distinguish between well-wishers and those who surround him for personal gain. Vishnusarman says that unless an administrator recognises and appreciates the qualities of others, he will not get good advisers. He believed that the image of the king in the eyes of the people was very important.

For Emperor Ashoka (304 BC–232 BC), with his code of dhamma, administration was based on very high human values, viz. tolerance to all, nonviolence towards man and beast, protecting the environment by planting trees, preventing ostentatious expenditure during ceremonies, conquering hearts through meaningful communication, not through war and so on. He propounded his value system by setting up edicts and pillars all over his vast monarchy. Ashoka introduced the following values into his society by actively promoting them in all spheres including administration (see Table 7.1):

Table 7.1 The Right Values: Dhamma

	Right Values	*Brief description*
1	Right View	Understanding what causes stress and trying to reduce it
2	Right Resolve	Having no ill will towards others
3	Right Speech	Truthfulness, using words that include others rather than distance them, soothing speech, meaningful speech
4	Right Action	Abstaining from taking life and other people's properties
5	Right Livelihood	Honest earning
6	Right Effort	Hard work, persistence and building up skills
7	Right Mindfulness	Putting aside greed and misery
8	Right Concentration	Focusing on the Right Values

Source: Author

Hence, in ancient India, the king was expected to set the moral tone for the subjects to follow and through charisma and personal example, the king was expected to ensure a righteous administration.

Modern views on administration

Several ideas in the modern world have made a significant influence in our present-day administration.

Western school of thought and liberal administration

Western countries were much influenced by classical liberalism, which advocated civil liberties for individuals and representative democracies governed by a Rule of Law. Economic freedom and accumulation of private property was encouraged. Government had to be minimum and the 'invisible hand' or Natural Law would take care of the society. In the late 19th century, classical liberalism developed into neoclassical liberalism, which argued for government to be as small as possible to allow individuals the opportunity to act freely. Classical liberals believed that utility was the foundation for public policies. Utility, which emphasises the happiness of individuals, became the central ethical value of all liberalism. Although utilitarianism inspired wide-ranging reforms, it became primarily a justification for laissez-faire economics.[5]

Weberian[6] model and rationalism

Modern administration has long been influenced by Max Weber, who advocated that ideal administration is one which is rational, technically efficient, follows strict hierarchy and subordination, and is based on well-established rules. For several years and in many parts of the world, including India, the Weberian model was adopted, but this model was by no means an ideal one for developing countries like India. This is mainly because an impersonal, mechanical, rational system can at best be efficient and accountable but not empathetic to the needs of the citizens. The functional boundaries between the politician (who made the policy) and the bureaucrat (who implemented the policy) became fuzzy as more civil servants colluded with their political masters, either for gain or from fear of losing their privileged positions. Rules were interpreted according to the people involved and were not uniform to all. Mediocrity, inertia, apathy, lack of specialization, and so on among the administrators resulted in bureaupathology[7] and in an anti-bureaucratic stance. Under no stretch of imagination could this form of government be considered 'rajarshi' as the human touch was missing and people felt alienated from the administrative machine. Consequently, in the last two decades of the 20th century, the more developed countries experimented with 'New Public Management' as an alternative to the Weberian model.

Welfare state

Here the state plays a key role in the protection and promotion of the economic and social well-being of its citizens. It is based on the principles of equality of opportunity, equitable distribution of wealth and public responsibility for those unable to avail themselves of the minimal provisions for a good life. Social insurance against unemployment, subsidies for the vulnerable, public provision of health and education services and high taxation are features of such governments.

An extreme form of a welfare state is the trusteeship concept advocated by Gandhiji, which was motivated by a genuine concern for the poor and called for 'Ram Rajya' in which everyone was equal and there were neither those who governed nor who were governed. Property was to be voluntarily surrendered by those who had it and the people who managed it were to seek upliftment through service rather than acquisition of material wealth or power. This was grounded on the philosophy of *aparigraha* (nonpossession). It called for a considerable change in the mindset of people at all levels and education had to be reoriented completely to make the younger generation appreciate this idea and accept it as a way of life. Although this was an ideal situation (and notwithstanding the Bhoodhan Movement), it appeared to be impractical in the medium term, although efforts were made to instill these values in the young minds, with continuous re-enforcement every now and then.

Good governance and effective administration

The Worldwide Governance Indicators, compiled by the World Bank, measures and ranks countries on the basis of certain indicators, as depicted in Table 7.2.

Scandinavian and Nordic countries are among the best-governed countries because they rank high in all the above indicators. The Nordic people have a great love for nature, maintain their physical well-being through sport, are logical and scientific in their reasoning, and work hard for high material comforts. Even urban people have ties with small farming communities and with the fisherfolk as they value nature and the pristine environment highly. They value care, trust, punctuality, honesty in public life, and simplicity; the affluent generally dress, eat and travel in the same style as the prosperous middle classes. Most public documents and public servants can

Table 7.2 Indicators of Good Governance[8]

	Indicator	Measures
1	Voice and Accountability	Democracy, freedom of expression, freedom of association, and a free media.
2	Political Stability	Absence of violence/terrorism
3	Government Effectiveness	Quality of civil service, independence from political pressures, quality and implementation of public policies
4	Regulatory Quality	Sound implementation of policies by various government institutions as well as promotion of private sector development
5	Rule of Law	Quality of contract enforcement, property rights, the police, the courts, as well as the likelihood of crime and violence.
6	Control of Corruption	The extent to which public power is exercised for private gain, including both petty and grand forms of corruption, as well as 'capture' of the state by elites and private interests.

Source: https://info.worldbank.org/governance/wgi/#home, accessed 5 May, 2019.

be easily accessed by people. Women have a significant role in politics and administration. The Nordics have managed to blend in their welfare state, the principles of equality and socialism from the east with freedom and market forces from the west.

New Zealand is another country, apart from Scandinavian countries, which has earned a reputation for good governance. New Zealand has very little corruption because people endorse integrity as a value. New Zealand believes in government openness, civic activism and social trust, with strong transparency and accountability mechanism in place, allowing citizens to monitor their politicians and hold them accountable for their actions and decisions.

Though Singapore is extremely well-governed, it cannot be considered a model for rajarshi administration and leadership because it has an authoritative government and there is low priority on listening to the voice of the people. Dissent or opposition to government policy is usually crushed.

Bhutan, though not a leading economic power, has managed to give the world a wonderful model of governance by adhering to Buddhist values. Unlike other countries, Bhutan aspires to maximize its Gross National Happiness and not its GDP. Bhutan defines happiness as a product of harmonious living where tradition and nature are valued. Bhutan recognizes its people as the country's greatest asset. The traditional system of redressing grievances (where every citizen has access to the king) helps to bring about impartiality in administration. Since all citizens of the country believe in the Buddhist concept of karma, they do not accept mechanical following of rules and procedures as adequate, rather they expect duties to be discharged with consciousness, responsibility and by following the highest moral codes.

New public management

In the past few decades, many countries have been disillusioned by the poor performance of their governments and have consciously reduced the size of the public sector because of a deep conviction that private sector is more efficient and can deliver many public services more effectively. These governments (the UK, New Zealand, Australia, and several other countries, including India, to some extent) introduced hands-on professional management in public services, set out explicit standards and measures of performance, encouraged greater competition in the public sector, and insisted on more discipline in resource use. Taxpayers had to be assured that the services provided are 'value for money' and citizens were treated as clients, who usually paid for services rendered by the government.[9] Greater reliance on the market forces, decentralization of decision-making, better service orientation, and a more managerial approach to administration (that is, rules are important but some flexibility and discretion is allowed) are elements of this new system. Since the focus of new public management is efficiency in resource allocation, there is a considerable reduction in subsidies and grants. Welfare measures are very carefully calibrated and kept to the bare minimum. In developing countries like India, where there are large sections of the population are vulnerable, adoption of this style of public management needs to be done cautiously.[10]

Public value paradigm

Just as the shareholder's return is the basis for corporate decision-making, Mark H. Moore, a Harvard professor, coined the term Public Value to give prominence to what the citizen values in government decision making. Participatory Democracy and Sustainable Development are the main pillars of this type of governance. For example, a village school may not be economically justified, as the number of children going to the school is small compared to the cost of maintaining the school, yet the local people may decide that the social outcome of maintaining the school warrants public expenditure on this school. This paradigm is useful to guide civil servants towards the achievement of economic and social outcomes by ensuring that public interest is always kept in sight. Adaptability and flexibility are key virtues, ensured through continuous evaluation. Efficiency needs to be judged according to broader goals, including society's well-being, sustainability and accountability. Hence, processes (trust, consensus, collaboration, transparency, and others) are as important as outcomes. Results are less important than relationships in this form of governance. Hence, in this form of administration, there will be less reliance on markets (compared to New Public Management) and more on empathy of the administrators (unlike in the Weberian system). Stakeholder involvement by citizens at all levels of decision making will be facilitated and ensured by the administrators.

Values enshrined in the Indian constitution

The Preamble, the Fundamental Rights and Duties clearly bring out certain core values and the philosophical basis for our Constitution. The main values enshrined in the Constitution and how they reflect the values practiced by the Indian society, are outlined here:

Sovereignty, unity and integrity

At the time of independence, it was very important for us to ensure complete political freedom and not be aligned to any superpower. However, we did lean more towards the socialistic philosophy of the USSR than the capitalist philosophy of the USA and Great Britain. Since we were not self-sufficient in technology, we relied, to a great extent, on the USSR for our initial development. Nevertheless, we projected an independent non-aligned stance in various international forums and were not constrained by the views of other countries. This we continue to do in international forums like the World Trade Organization and G-20. We protect our borders from external aggression, for which we have a committed armed force. However, the sovereignty of our nation is under threat. Jammu and Kashmir still remains a state where sections of the largely Muslim population do not accept themselves as Indians. China has laid claim to Arunachal Pradesh.

India today consists of 29 states and 7 Union Territories. We would like to believe that we are a co-operative federalism, with a strong union government and strong states. The federal system is India is undergoing strain on account of the perception by some state governments that the union government is encroaching into their turf through various fiscal policies and developmental schemes, without adequate consultation or consensus of the state governments. There is a wide variation in the resources and capabilities of different states and they vary greatly in their dependence on the union for their well-being.

It is the people's duty to uphold the sovereignty, unity and integrity of India. In reality, the people of India, do not always think of themselves as Indians, rather they have a greater allegiance to their language, caste or religion. This is because India is composed of many diverse people who have been administratively brought together at the time of independence. Swami Vivekananda's solution to the problem of diversity in India was to awaken the spirituality that lies dormant in all Indians, which he considered the lifeblood of the nation. He advocated us to think that 'the soil of India is my highest heaven, the good of India is my good' instead of building divisive walls between religions, castes, regions, and groups.

Socialism and socioeconomic justice

Socialism envisages a classless society where there is minimum inequality of income and wealth among people. India was strongly influenced by the Soviet Union and its socialistic ideals. The Constitution has recognised that vulnerable sectors of the society, who have long faced exploitation, need to be given preferential treatment when it comes to education and employment. However, despite socialism being a main feature of our Constitution, and concerted efforts by central planners to ensure that India has 'growth with equity' there is evidence that inequalities in income and wealth distribution are widening in the last two decades and efforts to really help the poor and vulnerable seem to be more hype than real. Distribution of wealth often seems to be into the pockets of those who are supposed to be a mere channel in the process. Sri Aurobindo's words become more relevant in this context, as he suggested: 'Do not look up to men because of their riches or allow yourself to be impressed by the show, the power or the influence. . . . Any perturbation of mind with regard to money and its use, any claim, any grudging is a sure index of some imperfection or bondage'.

Secularism

Secularism ensures freedom of religion to all citizens and prohibits discrimination on the grounds of religion. In recent times, religion has become an important public issue that divides rather than a private issue that promotes harmony and oneness in the minds of the individual. Communal riots, religious fundamentalism and deep insecurity of religious minorities have increased. People need to be educated about the difference between spirituality and religious dogmatism.[11]

Democracy and republican character

The government derives its authority from the will of the people. As elected representatives of the people, politicians are accountable to the people of India. India is governed by persuasion, not coercion. India is not a monarchy, yet there is no doubt that Indians seem to be in awe of powerful political persons or other influential persons (including actors and godmen) merely because of their charismatic presence.

Liberty

Essential individual rights such as freedom of thought, expression, belief, faith, and worship are respected. These are Western values, which we have adopted, but the civic sense, orderliness and community spirit of Western nations, which ensure that these rights do not adversely affect the community, do not seem to have been adopted by Indians with equal fervor.

Equality

Our constitution assures every citizen of equality of status and equality before the law. When it comes to equality of opportunity, India's commitment to incorporate the scheduled castes, tribes, backward classes, and others within the mainstream through reservations has caused deep bitterness among the forward classes, who resent the fact that they have limited seats to compete for in public educational institutions and public sector employment.

Fraternity and human dignity

Swami Vivekananda's comment, 'all Indians are my brothers and sisters', seems to be remembered by very few people. The spirit of common brotherhood that he advocated has not really been accepted by a pluralistic society like ours. The human dignity of women, children, the marginalised poor, tribes, scheduled castes, the differently abled, transgender people, and so on are not adequately protected, despite there being government organisations to protect their interests. Deeply entrenched prejudices have ensured that even though temple doors have been opened, untouchability has been eradicated and so on, caste- and class-consciousness are firmly rooted in the minds of most people, affecting the way they live.

Unfortunately, despite the noble intentions of the makers of the Indian Constitution, the spirit of the Constitution has not been upheld satisfactorily. One reason for this could be that the Constitution was based more on Western values and less on our ancient value system. As a result, the institutions that were created to perform administrative functions did not conform to the culture and values of the people it was meant to serve. Indians have not been able to overcome religious, caste and linguistic affiliations to consider themselves as truly Indian.

Performance of the Indian administration

A quick look at the various arms of government as envisaged by the Constitution, and their actual delivery as given later in the chapter, gives an idea about the divergence in the value systems of the founders of our Constitution and the people of India, who have to uphold these values.

Legislature

Nani Palkhivala, a highly reputed lawyer, has drawn our attention to the fact that it is a pity that we trust our parliamentarians to steer our country, without specifying any basic qualification or training for them. We allow people with questionable integrity and even criminal records to represent us in parliament and legislative assemblies. The very term 'parliamentary behaviour', which was once meant to indicate polished and tactful speech and polite mannerisms, has now been understood as shouting, booing, thumping, throwing things, and so on. As a result, although considerable public money is spent, hardly any worthwhile deliberations[12] are undertaken in parliament. Even budgets are often passed without discussion. The executive, over time, has set up several non-elected regulatory bodies, which determine how the country should function. These bodies are not accountable to the legislature, thus weakening the primal role of legislature in a democracy.

Some of the major problems noticed in Indian administration are the short-term mindset of most political parties who spend the first year in power undoing all the schemes or programmes started by the earlier government. This leaves the ordinary citizen confused as welfare schemes are discontinued—housing schemes, for example, are starved of funds midway, priorities are changed and new schemes are started instead of ensuring continuity to old ones.

The considerable apathy of the educated and better informed citizens of the country results in the poor being induced to vote for leaders, who promise them some relief. Elected governments often make decisions based on 'electoral compulsions' and not on what is in the nation's best interest.

There is a lack of common ideology among various layers of government and the formation of weak, ineffective coalitions coupled with power struggles between the union and the states (a collapse of federal spirit), leads to a weak and ineffective administration. Lack of role models or enlightened statesmen, criminalisation of politics and corruption at all levels add to the problem.

Executive

The cabinet ministers, ministers of states and bureaucrats are responsible for ensuring that policies are effectively implemented. Lan Pritchett of Harvard University has called India a flailing state, in which the elite institutions at the national (and in some states) level remain sound and functional but in which its head is no longer reliably connected via nerves and sinews to its own limbs. Indian administrators are individually known for their superior intelligence and capability, but collectively they have not been able to deliver good administration to the people. One reason could be that India inherited its administrative institutions as a colonial legacy, of which the primary purpose was not developmental or service provision. Rather it was set up to maintain order and to ensure steady revenue. As a result, the Weberian bureaucracy we inherited did not emerge from the local soil and there is little effort made to understand the local values and create local institutions, which connect well with people. Although the 73rd and 74th Amendments to the Constitution promote local government institutions, only very few states—such as Kerala—have had considerable success with empowering panchayats and urban local bodies to act decisively on behalf of the people. In Kerala, a state with the best practices in decentralised decision-making, there has been adequate transfer of funds and functions to local government institutions, but panchayat presidents have no control over the government servants who are posted to implement their decisions—these functionaries report to hierarchical civil service and not to elected representatives. Local government representatives therefore have little control over implementation.

Despite the Right to Information Act being in place, the average citizen is confused by a plethora of conflicting rules and procedures and shudders at the thought of dealing with a government organisation. Government servants are usually not service minded and the name 'public servant' is a misnomer. Projects are designed without adequate stakeholder involvement and often lead to resistance from the public; this is especially so when it comes to land acquisition for development purposes. The contractor–government nexus is quite common and public interest is sacrificed.

There has been a progressive deterioration of public services. Even people who can ill afford it are moving away from public health and educational institutions, because of the apathy towards government-run schools and hospitals. There is evidence that many people in critical government services (even in police or revenue departments) are recruited after collecting huge sums from them before they join service—this ensures that they feel no guilt or shame when they use their official position to amass huge unearned wealth. Corruption, speed money, misuse of official position, and the like are considered the norm rather than an aberration. As a result, several organizations are dysfunctional and no longer serve any public purpose.

Judiciary

Justice is so delayed that it might as well be denied. Cases are filed for frivolous reasons and without adequate investigation clogging the system. Crimes seem to be on the rise but the conviction rate seems to be low. Newspapers are full of terrorist activities, politically driven communal violence, crimes against women and vulnerable communities, biased investigation, and gross inefficiency of the entire system, resulting in loss of confidence on the part of the public in the state's ability to protect their rights. Further, there are increasing reports that judges are themselves corruptible. The Malimath Committee[13] pointed out that although it is important to ensure that no innocent person is punished, this should not paralyse the system to such an extent that even those who are obviously guilty get away. Lawyers are often a law unto themselves and free legal aid is grossly inadequate.

Influential groups

Administration needs to be monitored by influential civil society groups. However, the media in India today is more interested in sensationalising rather than the accurate reporting of facts. Economic crimes, though punishable, are condoned by the general public and a tainted politician or civil servant is not boycotted by society. Trade unions seem to be more concerned about petty power struggles rather than the long-term interest of the employees.

In short, despite high values being enshrined in our Constitution, we, Indians, have not respected these ideals adequately, either because we do not relate to them or because our value systems have degenerated over time. Hence, this becomes all the more reason for us to cultivate a rajarshi model of administration.

Creating the right environment for rajarshi leadership and virtuous administration

There have been several rajarshi leaders in the Indian administrative set-up. However, most of them are known only to those whom they've worked with.

This is primarily because a good administrator (at least in the Weberian sense) is supposed to be 'faceless' and a systems person, not one who flaunts his or her own image. Among politicians, however, there are more people who have left a mark on the sands of time. None is so endearing to the present generation as our earlier President, Dr. Abdul Kalam, who kept his values intact throughout his tenure as a scientist and an administrator. He not only showed how these values can be streamlined into administration, but also took on the role of a mentor for future generations. The main values Dr. Abdul Kalam stood for are honesty, self-awareness, self-discipline, faith in goodness, deep kindness, patriotism, secularism, co-operative teamwork, continuous knowledge seeking, total involvement in the chosen mission, and other such universal values which he demonstrated in his life. Manik Sarkar, the Chief Minister of Tripura, is yet another example of a selfless leader of his people, who donates his entire salary and lives on a subsistence wage of Rs 5,000 per month. In my personal experience, I have found that spiritual growth in an administrator helps him/her to serve without bias and to use appropriate words, expressions, gestures, and actions that encourage people to bring out the best in themselves. Such administrators are able to identify change agents, who will assist in the task of creating a positive atmosphere in the organization.

For administration to function effectively under rajarshi leadership, the following elements are critical:

- The values of the leader and the administration at all levels must be well aligned. It was Aristotle who pointed out that the aim of worthy administrations is to continually ensure that citizens and civil servants inculcate virtue in everything they do. For this every individual should know what is good for mankind as a whole, since no individual can be unaffected by his actions. This calls for moral literacy—awareness of what virtue is, understanding the interconnectedness of life on earth, introspection and enquiry about things in life. This can only happen if the education system in the country endorses certain universal values, which become ingrained in society from childhood onwards. Value-based education which inculcates a sense of honour in each individual to bring out his/her infinite potential rather than resort to base qualities will go a long way in bringing about a convergence of universal values like compassion, striving for excellence, selfless service, and so on. Since many moral dilemmas require careful reasoning, spiritual content has to be part of induction and in-service training programmes for administrators. Humane and virtuous outcomes—not merely material outcomes—should be the goal of administration. Wise mentorship of retired professionals should be streamlined seamlessly. This will enable access to experiential richness, greater empathy and interpersonal insight. The accumulated spiritual wisdom developed over centuries of human experience must be kept in mind through education and training at all levels and through public discourses. Individual rights must be upheld but there should be a balance between own interest and public interest. Only when the societal values are strong will there be limited conflict on fundamental values between the politicians, the bureaucrats and between different interest groups.

- There should be adequate growth and development in the society. Unless basic needs are satisfied well beyond subsistence level, citizens will not be able to dwell on values—either their own or that of the administration. The USA, China, Korea, Taiwan, and most other countries first had to reach a high income level before they could orient their bureaucracy to be less corrupt and ensure effective punishment for the corrupt; China, for example, sentences corrupt officials to death.
- Local institutions with a clear understanding of local values should be set up and strengthened to deliver what the people value most. Access, transparency and accountability should be ensured so that administration is humane, fair and has integrity.
- Throughout history and till very recent times, women did not play an important role in administration. Now, however, feminine qualities such as compassion, building rather than destroying, willingness to seek consensus, and deep understanding of people are being given great importance in administration. If the world is to be considered a home and every person a family member, then increasingly such feminine qualities need to find voice in administration.

Conclusion

In earlier periods, administration and leadership were combined in a single entity: the king, who would be advised by a set of ministers and priests. However, he usually ruled either through personal charisma, divine authority bestowed on him by the society or with the help of a clearly defined moral code. Whenever the king was himself enlightened, spiritually inclined and genuinely concerned about his subjects, he surrounded himself with wise counselors and ministers and the outcome was the physical, mental and moral well-being of the people. In later times, however, leadership and administration grew apart, with a well-entrenched bureaucracy often reducing the power of the politicians (people's leaders) to mere nominal heads. From the time Weber's bureaucratic system took a stronghold all over the world, leadership and administration took separate identities and often had conflicting goals.

Based on my own personal experience and discussions with fellow administrators, I have come to the conclusion that in today's India, neither the Weberian model nor New Public Management will work well. The former is too mechanical, rule-bound and distant to appeal to the people. The latter focuses more on efficiency and cost cutting, with too much reliance on the private sector to provide public services (with, of course, regulatory oversight by government) and this too can only tackle part of the problem at best. Indians do not need a minimum government, but a responsive government. Therefore, the Public Value paradigm is the way forward, but it will require considerable change in the mindset of the administrators. At all levels of administration, we need people with rajasic qualities (dynamism, ability to take risks, confidence, personal charisma, and more); tamasic qualities like sloth and apathy should be rooted out with proper selection, mentoring and continuous training. Rajasic qualities must be moderated with rishi-like insights into what really matters for the society to be happy and to achieve the full potential of the community without harming the environment. The administrator should focus on building relationships with all concerned stakeholders. Administration at present tends to rely on rules and technology and is not always aligned to the values of the leader (or ruling party). In fact, the values the ruling party stands for is often not clear to the electorate. Citizens do not insist on being governed by those with impeccable values. Unless core values are determined by the people and insisted upon from politicians and administration who represent and serve them, rajarshi leadership and administration will remain out of reach.

Administration is usually fuelled by powerful interest groups and not by a strong moral code. It is the social fabric that matters for people-centred administration to be effective, not mere administrative reforms. Governance cannot improve without setting up appropriate institutional arrangements to engender and even incentivize better conduct by all concerned. The leverage point of change comes from other dimensions of society and hence only a society with a well-defined and accepted value system will ensure a continuing stream of rajarshi statesmen and virtuous administrators. In India, there is a real need to awaken the spirituality inherent in all the citizens. Regardless of the religion that an individual believes in, some universal values such as respect and consideration for humanity, care for Mother Earth and Nature, acceptance of different ways of thinking and living, belief in interconnectedness of all, an attitude of gratitude, and the like, have to be instilled in all members of the society. Only then will India be able to become a world leader again both in material wealth and in highly evolved philosophical reasoning.

Notes

1 Only civil administration has been taken on board in this chapter, although military administration is also adaptable to a rajarshi set-up, under enlightened leadership.
2 'She' and 'he' are used interchangeably throughout the article to mean a person.
3 This is because many of his letters were read widely after the 14th century AD and deeply influenced European and American political thought.

4 Indian treatises like Ramayana, Mahabharata, Bhagavad Gita, Buddha Charitha, Arthashastra, Panchatantra, Manusmriti, Thirkural, Shukra Niti, Kadambari, Raja Tarangini, and Hitopadesh deal with the underlying need for ethics in governance.
5 A greater reliance on the market and less on the state.
6 Max Weber (21 April 1864–14 June 1920) was a German sociologist, philosopher, jurist, and political economist whose ideas profoundly influenced social theory and social research.
7 Term used by Victor Thompson for all negative aspects of Weberian bureaucracies.
8 India, unfortunately, does not rank among the best-governed countries; see https://info.worldbank.org/governance/wgi/#home, accessed 5 May, 2019.
9 For example, toll roads.
10 Government has to ensure that vulnerable sections of the population have access to basic necessities. There is a fear that large private corporations could influence governments in such a way that public interest may be at risk.
11 Religion focuses on a particular path to reach god and often excludes people who follow another path or religion. Spirituality helps people realise the essential oneness in all creation and tends to elevate the seeker to a harmonious being.
12 Question hour is usually a meaningless exercise and serves little purpose.
13 Malimath Committee Report on the Criminal Justice System, 2003.

8

CULTURAL ENTREPRENEURSHIP AS INCLUSIVE LEADERSHIP

Successes, perspectives and future directions

Deepti Navaratna

Culture as a resource: from promotion to sustainability

Culture is often studied as the product of sociopolitical underpinnings, class—caste dynamics, gender inequalities and societal prerogatives. Culture has been thought as a relic of the past, rarely studied as an active agent in shaping the current, especially economy and entrepreneurship. The impact of culture on economics remains an uncomfortable topic, as culture is an untidy parameter to be included in scientific predictions that economic analyses endeavor to understand. The conventional attitude to investment into culture has been that of 'preservation', 'archival', 'conservation'. The Government of India has a Ministry dedicated to the promotion of culture, whose self-appraisal reads:

> The mandate of the Ministry of Culture revolves around the functions like preservation and conservation of our cultural heritage and promotion of all forms of art and culture, both tangible and intangible. The Ministry's task is to develop and sustain ways and means through which the creative and aesthetic sensibilities of the people remain active and dynamic. In order to achieve these objectives, the Ministry undertakes various activities that flow from subjects allocated under the Govt. of India's Allocation of Business Rules.

Culture is a strong vector in the everyday life of an Indian, given India's long and diverse heritage. Deen Dayal Upadhyaya, thinker and sociologist, proposed that it is only through culture that true nationhood could be built: '"Bharatiyata" (nationhood of Bharat) can manifest itself not through politics but through culture. If we have anything that we can teach the world, it is the feeling of cultural tolerance and a life dedicated to duty'. Despite such a heightened awareness about the strong role of culture in shaping individual and national identities, India has yet to fully harness its largest resource of tangible and intangible civilisational knowledge into contemporary strength.

Support to entrepreneurship development conventionally has been routed through schemes and programmes of ministries, which either serve to enrich the manufacturing base and efficiency and align policies that favor indigenous industry (Ministry of Culture, Government of India, n.d.). Well-ramified hierarchical structures of power and stakeholders operate in conjunction with national bodies to transform spaces in which the entrepreneur operates. The presence of a dedicated Ministry for Textiles under the Government of India speaks volumes of India's long-standing expertise in textiles. The preamble for the ministry reads:

> Realising the vast potential for creation of employment opportunities in the agricultural, industrial, organised, and decentralised sectors and rural and urban areas, particularly for women and the disadvantaged; acknowledging the tremendous impetus provided by the Textile Policy of 1985 to the economy, resulting over these years in compounded annual growth rates of 7.13 per cent in cloth production, 3.6 per cent in the per capita availability of fabrics; and 13.32 per cent in the export of textiles; raising the share of textiles to 13 per cent of value added domestic manufacturing of the country; and to one third of the export earnings of the country.
>
> (Ministry of Textiles, n.d.)

However, such a detailed quantification of market size and target generation has been lacking in assessment of creative industries that fall under the umbrella of arts other than film music, media and entertainment. The relatively newly formed Ministry of Micro, Small & Medium Enterprises primarily incentivises state government initiatives and supplements efforts through its schemes and policy agendas. Here again, the structures of deployment include public-sector enterprises, autonomous bodies, boards, institutes of small business and entrepreneurship development, and grass-roots level societies that interact and shape entrepreneurial outcomes. Often a governing body such as the National Board for Micro, Small and Medium Enterprises is put in place to review existing policies and make recommendations to the Government for future formulations (MSME Annual Report, n.d.). Such large structures more or less manage and regulate the economic environment by the following functions:

- Assisting with know-how to manufacture or produce product, augment technology and modernise infrastructure
- Providing seed money to buy infrastructural facilities or human resources for services
- Creating industry- and enterprise-wise quality control protocols and quality certification

- Generating capital, either financial or social
- Creating awareness about modern management thinking; fundamentals about managing a business beyond simple account or financial management
- Accruing appropriate training facilities for leadership
- Initiating thought leadership and support for branding, product placement, design intervention, and packaging
- Designing welfare schemes for artisans and workers
- Developing measures to promote capacity building and empowerment of the units and their collectives

The most apparent disadvantage in such a multiorganisational and well-intentioned system is that the path from data analytics to assessment to policy making and policy to implementation is complicated by several layers of information loss, delays and slow turn-around times. It also is well known that such large structures of governance could be slower in responding to rapid changes, making pre-emptive grass-roots level strategy and emergent responses slow for the entrepreneur. Overall in such a power hierarchy, the entrepreneurial environment, which in today's world is rapidly changing, makes it difficult to predict and manage change to the advantage of the entrepreneur. In addition, the entrepreneur in such models is far separated from the other stakeholders both for quick across-the-board-informational exchange and analysis. Often entrepreneur and social stakeholders are separated from managers and from policy makers both in space and time. Although technology has made it easier to collapse such time–space constraints, technology is only as smart as the way in which the curated information is used and entrepreneurial decisions are only as intelligent as the larger heterogeneous collective of stakeholders, context and time. Another complicating factor is that cogent integration of information into action-oriented leads for policies or implementation is difficult, especially if impacts and implementation are assessed across multiple economic sectors with intrinsically different priorities. The Ministry of Culture's Annual Report has sparsely quantified data on size, volume or growth statistics of culture-based arts based industries, which are not overlapping with other ministries (Ministry of Culture, Government of India, n.d.). There are no recognised organisations, whose job is to research the sector and inform on characteristics of the sector. The Ministry of Textiles, in addition to many advisory bodies, has a number of research organisations, such as the South India Textile Research Organisation or the Bombay Textile Research Association, doing this job. With both ministries having overlapping mandates, in handlooms, indigenous textiles and cultural services in arts, the research data available is fragmented and makes it difficult to study the impact on the sector or even identify its long-term characteristics. However, government policies and initiatives are not completely without impact or success. According to a recent Federation of

Indian Chambers of Commerce and Industry (FICCI) report, such policies are synergising well with the Indian Media & Entertainment (M&E) industry, both directly and indirectly (KPMG India, n.d.).

Indian culture as a hotbed for entrepreneurship

From the time of the Silk Route to present times, cultural products have significantly contributed to India's growing economy before its contemporary recognition of being a cultural entrepreneurship-driven process. Post-independence, India's film and food industries have matured into world-class enterprises. According to a KPMG survey, India's recorded music business will nearly double over the next five years, bringing in an annual income of Rs 18.9B (US $300M) in 2019—possibly making it one of the world's top ten music markets by value. KPMG's figures place India's music industry value for 2014 at Rs 9.8B ($155M) (Ingham, 2015).

According to a 2017 FCCI report, despite a sluggish global economy, the M&E industry in 2016 was able to sustain a healthy growth on the back of strong economic fundamentals and steady growth in domestic consumption coupled with growing contribution of rural markets across key segments (KPMG India, n.d.).

India's history is testament to many successful innovations within and of culture. Art springs from individual enterprise and creativity and consuming art within communities is as old as human societies. The birth of Natyashastra, the primordial text of arts, as elucidated in its early chapters, itself was an entrepreneurial effort, in which the essence of the four vedas were reimagined to be broadcast in a fifth veda, the Natya Veda. Natyashastra drew upon the cultural products, imaginations, philosophies from its era and opened up the possibility of theatre being the medium through which vedic knowledge could be propagated. Cultural entrepreneurship has always been practiced even at tribal and aboriginal cultures of India. Ritual folk traditions continue to be reinvented as performative traditions to suit the needs of the day. Temples of South India were veritable institutions promoting and harbouring various forms of cultural entrepreneurship as well. Indian classical music from the Natyashastra to the present is an impressive case study in engineering and marketing sound with carefully curated raga grammar. The history of Carnatic music traces the very many transformations brought about by its migration from the Hindu temple to the court to the performance concert hall today.

Despite this long history of entrepreneurship, the state of the culture sector, museums, cultural archives, and libraries housing cultural artifacts remain poor. Indian museums remain poorly curated and local art galleries remain fraught with infrastructure, leadership and revenue generation issues. State and national agencies promoting culture often relegate themselves to sponsoring performances, giving lump sum grants to artists for specific projects or fund large festivals celebrating Indian culture. Although it is an important part of the culture mandate, none of this kind of 'granting' ends up empowering cultural institutes or artists to achieve some self-reliance in generating revenue for the future. 'It is a habitual thought—it is okay to be continually dependent on state and national funds for sponsorship of cultural events and activities, very few organisations think beyond the next large festival or extravaganza', says the founder of an Indian Classical dance organisation in Chennai. It is often difficult to change the thinking on this dependency, as it is assumed that culture ought to be promoted as a national interest. 'Patronage' is thus a double-edged sword, and even as history is testimony to the fate of arts, which solely depended on royal or community patronage, cultural enterprises are still fraught with this old mindset.

The wave of change in this matter has started with cultural agencies and autonomous bodies working under the ministries. Efforts to monetise on cultural resources and diversify strategies on revenue generation are slowly trickling into mandates. Conventionally regarded as give-out agencies where profit is taboo, sustainability and utilisation of facilities is being incentivised. 'We have been told to focus on collaborative projects and productions, where investment is distributed and revenue is generated to offset spending', remarked the Director of a museum of repute in New Delhi.

Another underserved and underutilised sector in culture are archives and digital libraries. Developing sustainable digital libraries in India will greatly augment the cause of culture and economy. The current challenges of digital preservation have moved from mere preservation, creating access in a world of short shelf life of technology, instability in the media used, internet-based sharing, and national copyright guidelines on source material. Ability to provide access to multiple users at once, remote access and availability of cultural data in multiple formats are possible today because of digitisation. India is one of the largest repositories of manuscripts in the world—not surprisingly, given its longstanding culture of knowledge systems. The Indira Gandhi National Centre for Arts (IGNCA) and, later, National Mission for Manuscripts has digitised more than 400,000 ancient Indian manuscripts (Gaur, n.d.). The National Archives of India is the custodian of the records of enduring value of the Government of India. It is the biggest archival repository in South Asia. It has a vast corpus of records, namely, public records, private papers, oriental records, cartographic records, and microfilms, which constitute an invaluable source of information for scholars, administrators and users of archives (www.nationalarchives.nic.in/; Gautam, 2007). Despite a staggering amount of data present in such archives, complications with ownership rights, permission rights and access rights do not allow open access to these collections.

Another ongoing issue is loss of large resources and migration of such repositories outside of India in ethnographic collections across the world. Dr. Ramesh Gaur at Jawaharlal Nehru University discusses about the need of the hour:

An approach on preservation of its physical resources was never discussed. In similar way, the concepts of digital preservation have been introduced in India very lately, i.e., sometime in year 2008 only. A good beginning was made with the launch of National Digital Preservation Programme (NDPP) of India. However, due to lack of continuity of the programme, still we are far from having a proper National Digital Preservation Programme in place. There are number of issues and challenges to overcome to various barriers to access and preservation of Indian cultural heritage resources. There are number of individual efforts, but we are still looking for a successful collaborative model. I have a fear that if something is not being done sooner, we may lose, the digitised material currently lying in DVDs and File Savers. What we need right now, a comprehensive National Digital Preservation Programme.

(Gaur, 2010)

IGNCA, SNA and other national museums have painstakingly documented and curated several forms of art, artifacts, tangible, and intangible heritages. 'The core issues preventing monetising such resources along the lines of what is done in the West are: bad archive design, poor knowledge retrieval and visualisation parameters, not keeping up with technological advances and general dis-spirit about facilitating access', observed a professor of Information Design at the National Institute for Design, Bangalore. 'It is rather difficult to locate manuscripts, official records, gazettes, informational interviews in one place. Researchers in Art History and Culture often spend a lot of time travelling to different archives just to find out if certain manuscripts are available', said a senior scholar and researcher with more than 30 internationally acclaimed books to her credit. Cultural archives are rarely seen as revenue-generating mechanisms, seldom curated to link it to cultural tourism or attract international scholarship to use its facilities. Here again, a model needs to be devised where the consumers of cultural resources, creators, managers, and preservation policy makers have to be brought together.

Culture and economics: an uncomfortable nexus

Culture is defined as a tangible and intangible body of symbols, language, beliefs, and values that are shared by members of a society. The tangible and material aspects of culture include the society's objects, tools and technologies, apparel, culinary objects, civilisational symbols, and artifacts. The intangible or nonmaterial culture includes the shared values, beliefs, language, and creative traditions of art. Culture and society are thus inextricably related to each other. Human evolution has been heavily influenced by not just the genetics of humanity but also the complexities and challenges that social living created. The social brain hypothesis proposed by British anthropologist Robin Dunbar, propounds that human intelligence evolved primarily to facilitate success in negotiating and managing survival reproduction in large and complex social groups (Dunbar, 1998). When sociological structures of society and culture were defined, the boundaries of each were governed by race, ethnicity, geography, regional, and community-based characteristics. In today's world, where capital and investment can cross national boundaries easily, it is thought that the potential to economically thrive is equal across the globe. Yet mindsets, cultures and attitudes towards growth affect economic outcomes, even in a world where maps are dissolving.

The branch of cultural economics today thus is dedicated to studying relationships between culture and economic issues, analysing how preferences and behaviours are shared through social capital and social networks. The branches of neuroscience, education and cultural anthropology are keen on understanding how learning and social cognition is innately linked to cultural conditioning. It is now widely accepted that practice within a culture can either augment or shape human cognition significantly affecting behaviour, beliefs and finally, human experience. Cultural economics differs from traditional attitudes of economics in attributing causality to consumer decisions. This difference is especially important in the context of understanding the issues fostering cultural entrepreneurship. Although a traditional economist takes into account the product-based and extrinsic factors, a cultural economist places the decision making process in the context of cultural value-symbol-belief plexus. This is one reason why the academic study of cultural economics has moved from economics to an interdisciplinary field including sociology and anthropology. This places the entrepreneurial activity of a cultural entrepreneur in the web of complex interrelationships that could strongly dictate even macroeconomics.

It is still the general presupposition that in today's globalised world, the factors dictating economic growth are the same across the globe – be it the African nations or the Caucasian cultures or the South Asian nations. The universal laws of supply and demand, maximisation of profit and pricing are supposed to apply equally across ethnicities, human behaviour and pervading culture which are thought to be symptomatically contributing to economic successes. As early as 1776, Adam Smith in his classic *Wealth of Nations* emphasised that self-interest contributes to public interest in a reciprocal way (Smith, 1904). He points out that self-interest includes monetary, social, emotional, and spiritual needs, which we organise as cultural values today. John Stuart Mill argues that men are driven by cultural values and needs and that such drives could be greater than just achieving financial success (Mill, 1990). Other social scientists have studied how intrinsically ethics contribute to economic growth, as in the case of Max Weber, who studied how institutions of religion can augment human productivity. He studied Protestant work ethic that regarded creation of wealth as a duty and attributed their success to such a cultural underpinning (Weber, 1930). Luigi Guiso et al. (n.d.) offer suggestions as to how value systems interact with economic development processes. David Landes (1999) in his *The Wealth and Poverty of Nations* concludes that national economies are eventually shaped by cultural factors and attitudes. Cultural desirabilities, tolerance to thrift, impetus on hard work, tenacity, honesty, and tolerance matter in the long run. Cultural attitudes can influence market dynamics and resist global changes. The print sector in India continues to survive and thrive amidst digital media, on the back of small-town, regional and rural markets (KPMG India, n.d.). Radio industry and its reach in India is still rather large, despite the internet boom, broadcasting away to the growing urban and rural consumers.

In the Indian milieu, entrepreneurship is affected by our larger beliefs in individual enterprise and variance, the power we attribute to social structures and capital, and the tolerance we show to unconventional work–life paths. These attitudes are different from industrialised European societies in which individual variance is better tolerated and social power structures allow out-lier behaviour to a larger extent. This is extremely relevant in the case of social and cultural entrepreneurship where an individual delicately and sufficiently disrupts social status quo towards transformative change. Acceptance of such a change is critical to the entrepreneur's success, the drive to take such risks definitely rests on an individual's assessments of how an idea will be received and, finally, on what he or she thinks adds value to society. Courtney Martin and Lisa Witter argue that 'cultural entrepreneurship is different than social entrepreneurship because it is primarily focused on reimagining social roles and motivating new behaviours'. In a published case study, 'Cultural Symbol-ism and Entrepreneurial Brand: The Indian Context', Ramesh Kumar, Jagan-nath Janakiraman and Shankar Sethuramalingam examine the relationships between 'self-concept' and symbolic behaviour of consumers, and how such remote social thinking affects brand acceptability and success (Sethuramal-ingam, n.d.). Hence, a very powerful entrepreneurial idea, despite successful implementation and meaningful innovation, may fail to create impact and sustain any initial success. Another key issue is of timing. Digital media today, which was considered to be an auxiliary distribution platform across subsec-tors has emerged to be a dominant factor in domestic revenue generation. In such a scenario, failure to respond quickly with digital strategies is failure to survive in a changing landscape. Companies and start-ups have to respond with innovative business and branding models in a changed mindset quickly or another wave of change is upon them.

Some 'meta-social' entrepreneurship models seek to develop sustainable change by investing in changemakers than in the process. 'Rather than giv-ing philanthropy away, we invest it in companies and change makers', reads the vision of the Acumen Fund (www.acumen.org). Many successful models of inclusive leadership across the globe have realised that sometimes the solution to local issues is going 'glocal'. Building allies for the entrepreneur through cross-sector, cross-domain partnerships enable sustainable change making which has yielded more sustainable results. The Ashoka Fellowship, for example, realises the importance of creating a global community in which partnerships are forged across sectors— community of Fellows and young changemakers—to learn and drive social innovation (www.india.ashoka.org). The Awesome Foundation (www.theawesomefoundation.org) 'forwards the interest of awesome in the universe, 1000$ at a time'. This model puts investors, creators and innovators in the same space to make decisions together. More importantly, there is shared social responsibility invested at the start of the idea. Such models of inclusive leadership in the culture sector, share risk amongst all levels of investors, managers, catalysts, and consumers—whether they are investing time, money or social capital.

Another angle to truly understand cultural entrepreneurship in India is to fully distinguish what the cultural entrepreneur does differently than the social entrepreneur. Another important aspect is to appreciate the motivations of investors, managers and 'supporters' of cultural products. This will likely yield a lot of insight into the nature of what will succeed as a successful model for inclusive leadership. A cultural entrepreneur is likely to work with cultural bodies of knowledge and disrupt value systems and beliefs long held about the use of this knowledge. For example, for a long time, several folk music performances in Shaivaite temples were only performed as rituals in temple premises. Their performative and cultural value was never imagined until an artist–entrepreneur decided to place it in a global festival of traditional dance or endeavors to market it to nontraditional audiences outside the temple. Here the entrepreneur is both educating the community about what other value the ritual-based performance could have, which in turn could create both creative capital, visibility and social status for the community in the larger social framework. This is what drives artists to paint in the Kerala Mural style on different media for different end users, such as tea coasters, lampshades, sarees, etc. Many traditional puppeteers have decided to choose contemporary themes for play, so that people across multicultural spaces can appreciate the finesse and beauty of traditional puppetry. Artists innovate with themes, medium, language, music, lighting, aesthetics, curative styles, context, spaces, and places to find newer meanings and value for their products. Such entrepreneurs already have stakeholders in the communities who have co-created and share this knowledge. They are likely to invest in the entrepreneur only if they cognizant of the conjoined stake they hold with the entrepreneur. Imminently, they are most likely to invest in models where they are 'at the table'. Despite a large amount of 'support' given to classical music from government, the classical music ecosystem is largely still run by private enthusiasts, connoisseurs and artists who persist despite the labour, management and finance-intensive process of art presentation. The Founder and Director of a 30-year-old institution presenting Indian classical dance and music to Bengaluru audiences concurs: 'In my experience, my success at running this organisation has largely depended on my ability to suggest and convince a small but stable community of music/dance lovers of why sustenance of sampradaya is important. Only those who see personal value in the process invest.' However, India is one of those fortunate nations in the world where cultural consumption is not regulated by public sector or the governmental infringements. The strength of the Indian cultural sector is indeed its social capital, which supercedes intellectual capital. This needs to be harnessed effectively to convert and increase cultural consumption within India.

Brief review of study of cultural industries across the globe

Across the globe, impact assessment or measurement of the contribution of culture-based industries have been sparse until recently. Generating long-term multivariate data strong enough to substantiate observed phenomena has suffered from poor methodologies for analysis. Inherent difficulties in measuring ramified economic effects still exist. Much like in India, globally, the traditional perception was that investment in the cultural sector should be government-driven to ensure public well-being and as a means to foster the spirit of the people governed. Even today, measuring the contribution of cultural industries to national GDP is difficult as it is scattered across services and communications sectors.

Ernst and Young, in association with UNESCO and International Confederation of Authors and Composers Societies analysed 11 creative and cultural industry sectors globally (The Cultural and Creative Industries (CCI) Study, n.d.). Against a combined generated $2,250 billion in revenues (3 percent of the world GDP), television generated $477 billion, newspapers and magazines $354 billion, and visual arts $391 billion. It was reported that revenue from these sectors were higher than the entire GDP of India ($1,900 billion). Creative industries generated 29.5 million jobs, which employ about 1 per cent of the world's active population. The top three employers are visual arts (6.73M), books (3.67M) and music (3.98M). More importantly, the CCI sectors were inclusive and diverse when it came to the demographic it hired, including young, old or middle-aged men and women of all backgrounds. In Europe, people employed were typically 15–29 years older than any other sector (The Cultural and Creative Industries Study, n.d.). According to the same study, creative industries have more women in the workforce than conventional work sectors. The study pointed out as to how boosting cultural infrastructure can catalyse all other urban economies in a city. The construction of the Guggenheim Museum led to the creation of more than 1,000 full-time jobs, and tourist visits have since multiplied eightfold, according to the report.

Cultural entrepreneurship as a culturally negotiated process: implications for inclusive leadership

Cultural entrepreneurship as a practice is a unique kind of social entrepreneurship. An entrepreneur creates a product or experience of value within a culture. Since the success of the entrepreneurial activity is inextricably linked to value systems, symbolic meanings and desirability dictated by pervading cultural thought, consumerism in such a domain is far harder to predict than most entrepreneurial activities, especially in the wake of digitisation, globalisation and intercultural syncretism. Cultural entrepreneurship draws heavily on anthropological knowledge embedded within cultures, indigenous technologies and traditional knowledge systems. In such a complex dynamic, the cultural entrepreneur is placed in an interdisciplinary co-operative plexus of stakeholders within and beyond his or her individual reach. This underscores the need for evolving indigenous models of inclusive leadership, which are culturally viable and sustainable in changing global economies and yet successfully manage to convert social capital to entrepreneurial success. Cultural entrepreneurship has conventionally been imagined as a person-centric process. However, we live in an era where the insulations of local culture and consumerism are being rapidly regulated by complex set of global factors such as digitisation, globalisation, interculturalism, and bottom-up social mobilities. This has transformed the cultural entrepreneurship process from an individual-focused paradigm to an inter–co-operative model of working with human, technological, financial, and social capital.

To fully understand the complexities that face cultural entrepreneurship today, a detailed understanding of the kinds of leadership, structures of power, institutions, processes, and factors governing success is important. This is significant to locate the entrepreneur in both the domain of entrepreneurship and society to rethink cultural leadership as inclusive dynamic. India's history of cultural patronage has moved from kings, statehood to nationhood to self-driven creative economies. Although the Indian budget dedicates a good amount of budget towards fostering cultural activities for artists, institutions, museums, and others, a detailed study into impact assessment of its various schemes and funding in longitudinally is missing. More importantly, an impetus on empowering creative economies of the country as revenue-generating agencies is needed. Monetising cultural resources, tangible and otherwise to lead the wave of converting cultural capital into entrepreneurial capital is required. Attracting subsidiary and feeder capital to generate economic traction requires diversified yet sustainable strategies in the culture sector.

Several different people at different capacities and levels of the culture sector practice cultural leadership. Largely, there are the leaders, managers of cultural institutions that promote art and the makers of culture themselves. Senior leaders and directors of government-funded cultural institutions and policy-making bodies regulate and advise governmental priorities. Producers, manufacturers, innovators, artists, and entrepreneurs who populate small-scale industries are actually involved in the product creation. NGOs, advisory boards, private enterprises, production houses, and organisations operate intermediately between them. At each level of this ecosystem, there are distinctive challenges, promises and issues. A larger question is how to regulate this multitiered web of independent and interdependent entities to accentuate growth and sustainability for the entrepreneur. What kind of leadership is most effective? What could be the structure of such a leadership platform in reality? Should macro policymaking only be government-driven? Should decision-making be vested with one body? How can consumer and market analytics be curated into strategy? How can efficiency of implementation of such policies be increased? How can synergy be created between grass-roots–level culture producers, cultural catalysts and national policy making? How can the rapidly changing ground realities for the entrepreneur be studied, researched and curated into effective policy prescriptions?

Cultural entrepreneurship has always been a socially negotiated process, where value creation was augmented by culturally driven realities. Culturally driven opportunities made entrepreneurs of many traditional art forms while relegating some to oblivion. In many streams of cultural entrepreneurship research, there is a tendency to view culture as a direct deterrent to entrepreneurial enterprise, the nonhomogeneity of tastes, geographically situated local economies and consumerism are often thought of as 'constraints' for large-scale expansion of such endeavors. Aldrich and Fiol (1994) in fact, counter this notion by stating that 'founders who utilise encompassing symbolic language and behaviours will gain competitive legitimacy more quickly than others'. Ellmeier (2003) observes that cultural entrepreneurship is a practice with no 'real' capital or sans capital, referring to tangible capital which may not be required to spin a worthy idea. However, the contribution of intangible capital, knowledge bodies, social networks, status, reputation, hereditary trade knowledge cannot be ruled out. Fine (as reviewed by Sabatini, 2003), speaks of how the entrepreneur concept has academically moved to sociology from a dominant economics perspective. Mokyr (2013) highlights the role of cultural entrepreneurs as agents of transformative change who coordinate and navigate cultural beliefs and attitudes to create a change for all.

Lounsbury and Glynn (2001) propose a model of cultural entrepreneurship. The authors categorise entrepreneurial capital into resource capital and institutional- or industry-level capital. Although resource capital is important for success, industry-level determinants could prove to be equally potent predictors of outcomes. The degree of acceptance of a cultural product, larger industry norms regulated by sectors and governmental regulations and overall industry infrastructure affect entrepreneurial processes. A recent study examined Indian cultural entrepreneurs and identified seven aspects that facilitate sustainable practices: a) cultural value creation, b) intrinsic motivation, c) external recognition, d) minimised risk, e) contextual understanding, f) innovation and learning, g) perseverance and ethical standards and social networks (Sardana, 2015). One can clearly see that success in cultural entrepreneurship outcomes are dictated by extrinsic factors such as access to social networks, using innovation to survive rough market conditions, to consolidate on existing markets and to place your brand. It is not a solitary journey of an intrinsically motivated and informed entrepreneur, but a coordinated series of strategies and policymaking by stakeholders at several levels.

The importance of cultural industries to national economy and generation of creative capital needs no underscoring. In India, research into efficacy of creative industries is still sparse and available data are scattered across multiple sources and are difficult to analyse qualitatively. Dedicated research into specific sectors is definitely the need of the hour. In highly contextually separated domains with the cultural industry, large hierarchical models in which the investor–consumer or investor–manager—entrepreneur–manufacturer divide is multirung and segregated, maybe too sluggish to impact and implement. A collective framework of shared investment chaperoned by risk management that can liaison with necessary power and policy structures could more likely succeed in the Indian context.

References

Aldrich, H. and C. Fiol. 1994. 'Fools Rush in? The Institutional Context of Industry Creation', *The Academy of Management Review*, 19(4): 645–70, www.jstor.org/stable/258740 (accessed on 4 January 2018).

The Cultural and Creative Industries Study. n.d. www.worldcreative.org/ (accessed on 4 January 2018).

Dunbar, R.I.M. 1998. 'The Social Brain Hypothesis', *Evolutionary Anthropology*, 6: 178–90. doi:10.1002/(SICI)1520-6505(1998)6:5<178::AID-EVAN5>3.0.CO;2-8

Ellmeier, A. 2003. 'Cultural Entrepreneurialism: On the Changing Relationship between the Arts, Culture and Employment', *International Journal of Cultural Policy*, 9(1): 3–16.

Gaur, R.C. 2010. 'Facilitating Access to Indian Cultural Heritage: Copyright, Permission Rights and Ownership Issues vis-à-vis IGNCA Collections', in T. Ashraf, J. Sharma and P. Gulati (eds.), *Developing Sustainable Digital Libraries: Socio-Technical Perspectives*, pp. 235–51. Hershey, PA: IGI Global. doi:10.4018/978-1-61520-767-1.ch013

Gaur, R.C. n.d. 'Digital Preservation of Indian Cultural Heritage: Issues and Challenges', www.dpconline.org/blog/idpd/digital-preservation-of-indian-cultural-heritage (accessed on 4 January 2018).

Gautam, M. 2007. 'Electronic Records Management: Challenges and Issues: A Case Study, National Archives of India', *Atlanti*, 17(1–2): 63–73, Trieste.

Guiso, L., P. Sapienza and L. Zingales. n.d. 'Does Culture Affect Economic Outcomes?', www.aeaweb.org/articles?id=10.1257%2Fjep.20.2.23 (accessed on 4 January 2018).

Ingham, T. 2015. 'India's Music Business Will Almost Double in Value by 2019: KPMG', www.musicbusinessworldwide.com/indias-music-business-will-double-by-2019-kpmg/ (accessed on 4 January 2018).

KPMG India: FICCI Media and Entertainment Report 2017. n.d. https://home. kpmg.com/in/en/home/events/2017/03/kpmg-india-ficci-media-entertainment-report-2017.html (accessed on 4 January 2018).

Landes, D. 1999. *The Wealth and Poverty of Nations: Why Some Are So Rich and Some So Poor.* New York: W.W. Norton & Company.

Lounsbury, M. and M.A. Glynn. 2001. 'Cultural Entrepreneurship: Stories, Legitimacy, and the Acquisition of Resources', *Strategic Management Journal*, 22: 545–64. doi:10.1002/smj.188

Mill, J.S. 1990. *Essays on Politics and Culture.* Gloucester, MA: Peter Smith Pub Inc (1 January).

Ministry of Culture, Government of India. n.d. *Annual Reports*, www.india.gov.in/annual-reports-ministry-culture (accessed on 4 January 2018).

Ministry of Textiles, GoI. n.d. http://texmin.nic.in/ (accessed on 4 January 2018).

Mokyr, J. 2013. 'Cultural Entrepreneurs and the Origins of Modern Economic Growth', *Scandinavian Economic History Review*, 61(1): 1–33.

MSME. n.d. *Annual Report*, http://msme.gov.in/relatedlinks/annual-report-ministry-micro-small-and-medium-enterprises (accessed on 4 January 2018).

Sabatini, F. 2003. 'Ben Fine (2001) *Social Capital versus Social Theory: Political Economy and Social Science at the Turn of the Millennium*', *Review of Social Capital versus Social Theory by Ben Fine, Economic Notes*, 32: 403–8. doi:10.1111/1468-0300.00120

Sardana, D. 2015. 'What Facilitates Cultural Entrepreneurship? A Study of Indian Cultural Entrepreneurs', *Journal of Creative Behaviour* doi:10.1002/jocb.131

Sethuramalingam, R.K. n.d. 'Cultural Symbolism and an Entrepreneurial Brand: The Indian Context', https://hbr.org/product/cultural-symbolism-and-an-entrepreneurial-brand-the-indian-context/IMB489-PDF-ENG (accessed on 4 January 2018).

Smith, A. 1904. *An Inquiry into the Nature and Causes of the Wealth of Nations.* E. Cannan (ed.). Library of Economics and Liberty, www.econlib.org/library/Smith/smWN.html (accessed on 4 January 2018).

Weber, M. 1930. *The Protestant Ethic and the Spirit of Capitalism* (originally published 1905). London and Boston: Unwin Hyman.

9

FEMINISM AND INCLUSIVE LEADERSHIP

Bridging tradition and modernity from an Indic perspective

Srividya Ramasubramanian

The feminist perspective

Feminism is an interdisciplinary approach that includes several social movements, political activism and ideological orientations that focus on equality and equity for all peoples, particularly based on gender and sexual identity and expression. There is a common pursuit of social, political, legal, economic, and cultural equality through collaborative sharing of power, authority and resources. It focuses on identifying and making visible social inequalities and injustices to work toward a more just, inclusive, fair, equitable, and compassionate community. It aims to understand power relations, gender inequalities and sexuality by providing critical insights into social and political relations. Feminist theory examines gender inequalities in terms of their social roles and everyday lived experiences from a variety of disciplinary perspectives.

The primary goal of feminism is to undermine and dismantle patriarchy, which is a social system in which men are seen as authority figures and leaders, either in the family, industry, government, law, education, sports, or other social institutions. Such societies are often oppressive to women by positioning them in subordinate roles. Arguably, women can also act as agents of oppression in patriarchal societies because of their socialisation within the culture of male dominance, just as men can be victims of the patriarchal system, especially when it comes to traditional gender roles that become more binding than liberating. Radical feminism rejects patriarchy entirely and suggests that separation is the only viable solution, whereas other feminists work within the existing system to find ways to challenge, resist and counter patriarchy. Thus, critically examining the social mechanisms that characterise patriarchy as the norm and shedding light on the ways in which it manifests itself in everyday life is an essential aspect of feminist scholarship, including feminist leadership.

128

Conventional patriarchal leadership

Traditional conceptions of leadership in general, including rajarshi leadership, sees the individual as a leader (mostly male), as a visionary who motivates followers to share their goals, as one with heroic superhuman attributes, as a decisive decision maker, as an embodiment of virtue and character, and as one who inspires and directs others' behaviours and actions toward a visionary goal. This notion of leadership places emphasis on the charismatic leader and how they are able to inspire others to follow their vision. Such conceptualisations of leadership continue to follow conventional notions of leadership embedded in patriarchal and militaristic ideas of authority. Such a leader is by definition hierarchical, competitive and spectacular rather than inclusive and participatory. He/she does not value emotionality, relationships and collaborative processes.

Patriarchal leadership has taken the form of entrepreneurial leadership and transactional leadership (Aviolo, 1994). These modes of leadership emerged from the rise of neoliberal capitalist markets (Blackmore, 2013; Blackmore and Sachs, 2012). Entrepreneurial and visionary leadership is especially focused on having entrepreneurial vision, communicating this vision charismatically with followers, and building a team to manage resources effectively to achieve this vision. However, such discourses of visionary entrepreneurial traditions of what it means to be a rajarshi are challenged as being gendered, masculine, patriarchal, and culturally biased. Leadership discourses associated with such patriarchal forms of leadership have focused on investing in executive power with the leader, with a focus on acquiring skills relating to financial investment, innovation and strategic marketing. There is not much emphasis on emotional literacy, distribution of power, politics and social justice included within this traditional notion of leadership. In fact, the feminine aspects of leadership are looked down upon with contempt by patriarchal leadership styles.

Workplaces are specific contexts within which ideas of power and respect become rooted in dominance, violence and authority. Traditional notions about leadership are inextricably linked with patriarchal social and cultural structures. Patriarchal leadership is a traditional, hypermasculine and militaristic style of leadership. Here, the emphasis is on gaining power over others, rather than sharing power with others. Domination, aggression, authority, and hierarchy are important aspects of patriarchal leadership. In this approach, followers are motivated by leaders using a command-and-control approach that fuels competition to increase productivity. These types of leaders are more concerned about their own ego inflation through acquisition of property and profits through any means, including force and unethical tactics, rather than work towards the common good of society or the organization as a whole.

129

In patriarchal forms of leadership, masculine traits are glorified as ideal and desirable qualities of good leaders, while feminine qualities are undervalued and underemphasised. The hypermasculine leadership style emphasises competition, authoritarianism, obedience of subordinates, productivity, and greed, rather than meaningfulness, fulfilment, authentic happiness, and the human potential. Hierarchies, divisions of labour and organisational structures are created that reinforce stereotypical conceptions of gender, race and social class. It is important to point out that masculine qualities per se are not inherently negative or unhelpful in being a good leader. Masculine qualities such as rationality, logic, reason, strength, focus, discipline, and order are to be nurtured even within feminist organisations. However, when these traits manifest as violence, aggression, arrogance, and callousness, they are likely to become counterproductive to having healthy and productive workplaces. In fact, patriarchal forms of leadership essentialise and dehumanise men as much as they deny women their humanity by narrowly associating men with only masculine traits.

Historically, great leaders were equated with successful kings and commanders-in-chief who conquered territory and subjugated enemies through bloody wars. Even in mythological contexts, heroes were often depicted as bloodthirsty, violent, aggressive, and power-hungry. Within Indic contexts, epics such as the Mahabharata and Ramayana, as well as shastras such as Arthashastra, provide leadership lessons on war tactics, strategies to maximise damage on enemies and ways to conquer by violent means. Although there are exceptions—role-model leaders such as Rabindranath Tagore and Mahatma Gandhi, who were compassionate, caring, just, and inclusive—traditional leadership discourses do not necessarily focus on such people who played a transformative role in their societies through sacrifice, humility and nonviolent means. Even if they do include a broader definition of leadership beyond the royal and nobility, most of these narratives elaborate on the lives of transformative male leaders from elite classes without including female leaders and leaders from other classes of society.

Examining patriarchal leadership through the lenses of gender

Sandra Bem (1993) discusses how dominant discourses in patriarchal societies are characterised by three 'lenses of gender': androcentrism, gender polarisation and biological essentialism.

Androcentrism is a male-centred approach that privileges male experiences as the norm and as superior to female-lived experiences. The extent to which leadership studies privilege the male leadership approach as the norm and as superior, such discourses can be considered androcentric. For example, if leadership is implicitly assumed to be about power, authority, and profit maximisation, such ideas privilege androcentric, male-centred understandings of what it means to be a good leader.

The second lens of gender focuses on gender polarisation, which is the narrative that highlights the differences between genders, rather than similarities. For instance, by linking masculine traits purely with male leaders and feminine traits purely with female subordinates, we engage in gender polarisation. Leadership discourses often distinguish women CEOs from male ones by suggesting that they lead from their heart and emphasise on ethics of care and compassion, as compared to their male counterparts. However, such discourses further aggravate the gender divide by promoting ideas that gender identity is binary and associated rigidly with the embodiment of physical sex. By repeatedly pairing women with feminine characteristics and men with masculine characteristics, they leave little room to see the interconnectedness and fluidity of gender and sexual identity.

Third, biological essentialism is when discourses in society ignore the social construction of gender, and in our particular context the social construction of leadership, while overemphasising biological factors for gender polarisation. In other words, when we believe that men are inherently superior to women in terms of leadership qualities because of their biology, we are engaging in a biologically essentialist argument by ignoring the social, cultural and political environments that shape leadership.

Three approaches to leadership: traits, skills and styles

Although patriarchal forms of leadership focus on leadership traits, more recent literature centres on leadership as a process that is collaborative and team-oriented (Chin, 2004). Existing research elaborates at least three approaches to leadership studies: trait-based, competency-based and style-based. The trait-based approach places emphasis on leadership as an innate trait that some individuals are born with. These characteristics tend to be masculine traits such as dominance and confidence. Much of this literature on trait-based leadership has typically evolved from analyses of 'great men', rather than examining the leadership practices of both men and women. In other words, masculine traits were implicitly associated within the mental model of what it means to be a good leader.

The competency-based approach emphasises on the competencies and skillsets of the leader. This skills-oriented approach moves away from the more biologically essentialist trait-based approach by seeing leadership as a skill that can be nurtured and developed. Skills such as communication, interpersonal relations, creating a vision, and being self-aware are some examples of competencies that can be developed in good leaders. From a feminist perspective, this approach focuses on collaboration and interpersonal connectedness. Feminist leaders tend to be much more collaborative in their approach to teams (Chin, 2004).

The third approach focuses on leadership styles based on how leaders behave and what they do rather than what they are skilled at. This process-oriented approach distinguishes between task-oriented behaviours versus relationship-oriented behaviours. Task orientation focuses on achieving the goal, while relationship orientation emphasises building stronger relationships with other team members. The latter orientation is associated more closely with feminist leadership, where the leader is positioned to make other team members feel welcomed, accepted and listened to rather than focusing merely on profit maximisation and task accomplishment.

Transactional leadership places greater emphasis on control and directedness. In contrast, transformative leadership is about being an agent of change (Tichy and Devanna, 1986). A transformative leader is a visionary leader who sets a compelling vision for the organisation and works with all stakeholders to guide them towards the larger mission. However, feminist leadership styles go beyond transformational and transactional styles of leadership, both of which focus more on task orientation rather than relationship orientation. Feminist leadership focuses on the process rather than the goals. The means are as important as the ends. The emphasis shifts from 'what leaders do' to 'how they do what they do'.

Feminist leadership as an alternative to patriarchal leadership

Feminist leadership is not simply about numerical representation of women in leadership positions or gender differences in ascribed leadership traits. It is an inclusive leadership ethic that can be embraced and practiced by all genders. It goes well beyond simply focusing on women and leadership, and also addresses political agendas such as anti-sexism, anti-racism and anti-xenophobia. It is a collective distributed leadership practice that works within a democratic framework to allocate power and resources in socially just ways, rather than delegate work, risk and responsibility to subordinates (Blackmore, 2013). The feminist leadership approach critiques reductionist binaries of man/woman, mind/body, rationality/emotionality, objective/subjective, and private/public. Whereas patriarchal modes of leadership dehumanise and stereotype both men and women in narrow ways by associating them with masculine and feminine traits, feminist leadership allows all genders to explore the full human potential while challenging patriarchy. This approach shifts from a patriarchal neoliberal capitalist outlook that emphasises on power, competition, conquest, and greed to one that revolves around a sense of individual and collective agency derived from cooperation, collaboration, compassion and care.

Feminist leadership focuses on subverting and questioning this traditional masculine notion of power and in doing so, often embraces feminine qualities as an alternative. It focuses on empathy, compassion, listening, purpose, joy, intuition, creativity, beauty, inclusion, trust, harmony, and care. To be clear, people of all genders can be feminist leaders. Feminist scholarship is not about saying that women are better leaders simply because they are women. Nor is it about explaining how women lead differently than men. The main emphasis is about examining what power looks like, how it is distributed and how it functions within organisations. Feminist leadership is inclusive, participatory, collaborative, and horizontal.

Feminist leadership is not about inheriting innate leadership traits, but about demystifying the notion of leadership as something that everyone can build upon with the right kind of support and nurturing environment. In fact, it goes beyond skill development and trait formation. The approach is built around providing access to opportunities, resources and decision-making in ways that can transform not just the individuals, but also their organisations and communities. Feminist transformational leadership is concerned with bringing about positive social change, including and especially focusing on gender equality. Such a transformation is possible through increased self-efficacy and self-confidence, consciousness-raising about inequalities and social injustices, and internalisation of feminist principles and ideals (Kark, 2004).

Feminist leadership styles focus on collaboration and the process itself, rather than the outcomes. This means the ways by which the objectives are carried out is as important as the goals themselves. Consensus-building and creating a nurturing environment are valued by feminist leaders in decision making. The relationship between leaders and the rest of the team is much more egalitarian and collaborative. These styles have also been referred to as 'distributed leadership' and 'shared leadership'. In this model, greater attention is paid to community-building and collective identity rather than on task completion per se. There is greater attention paid to power dynamics and on affirming the individuals in the team. Such an approach is also called 'relational leadership', where interpersonal relationships and individual strengths are affirmed with the goal of building trusting relationships. Rather than fear and competition, the emphasis is on self-expression, collaboration, participation, and self-care in an inclusive, nurturing and welcoming environment. In contrast to visionary leadership, where the vision is built by the leader for the entire organisation, feminist leadership is consultative, collaborative and consensus-oriented.

Feminist leadership is political in nature. This form of leadership is informed by the feminist agenda of social justice and equity. Its agenda is not just to include feminine traits in its scope and to include women in leadership positions. Although not all feminist leaders would see themselves as activists, they share a common theme of working towards making unjust practices and social inequalities visible. Feminist leadership is informed and inspired by facilitating the development of more holistic and inclusive communities. Power is a central theme that feminist leadership is concerned with. The ways in which power can be used and abused are of concern. Feminists distinguish

133

between powers used to control others versus powers used to enable individuals to express their potential. Facilitative power is one that validates, recognises and enables those who typically do not get support and feedback to bring out the best in themselves. Feminist leaders, therefore, work to dismantle structures, policies and social attitudes that hinder such progress through empowerment of the oppressed. Taken-for-granted notions of power have to be analysed constantly to ensure that power is being used to enable rather than inhibit justice towards those who are typically repressed within organisations. Feminist leadership involves taking risks and making personal sacrifices as one works towards a transformative agenda.

Feminist leadership is informed by an ethic of care and compassion. Respect, nurturing, care, and empathy are an important part of feminist leadership. The emphasis is on creating a welcoming and caring environment. Anti-violence is an important aspect of feminist leadership, where creating safe spaces for individuals to freely express themselves and genuinely care for one another is of the utmost importance. Although patriarchal approaches undervalue and under-recognise caregivers, feminist leadership sees care as a guiding philosophy. However, it is important to understand that feminist leaders do not stop by simply empathising and expressing compassion towards those who are oppressed. Rather, they work toward disrupting these hierarchies in ways that will uplift those who are otherwise neglected and repressed.

Decentring and decolonising feminist leadership

Several grassroots and indigenous feminist movements in the Global South and in otherwise marginalised communities have challenged and resisted what they see as mainstream: Western, privileged and white feminist voices. They call for not only dismantling gender inequalities, but also simultaneously paying attention to other systems of oppression and privilege. There is a need for a broader emancipatory agenda that addresses issues of discrimination and lack of equity based on gender, sexuality, race, ethnicity, social class, and the like. That is, feminist leadership should be inclusive in ways that challenge and resist hegemonic styles, including Western colonial agendas. Feminist leaders are motivated by ideals such as fairness, equity and justice, in terms of issues relating to gender, sexual identity, race, ethnicity, social class, and the like. There is a desire to include marginalised voices and bring them to the centre of the conversation. Therefore, feminist leadership literature and discourse should also pay attention to ways in which it should be more inclusive of varied life experiences shaped by race, ethnicity, nationality, and social class, and how it is defined, enacted and practiced.

Although feminist leadership proposes to be about inclusion, participation, and respect for differences, the energies are primarily directed towards men and patriarchy, without much regard for power and politics involved even in the practice of the feminist leader's use of their own power. Unfortunately, this has meant competition and dominance of Western and Eurocentric forms of feminism that are seen as progressive, liberal and modern. Indigenous, non-Western and ethnic forms of feminism are still sometimes 'othered' and framed as not truly feminist. For example, much of the recorded history of feminism and modern feminist movements is in English and documented within Eurocentric/Western contexts, making them inaccessible to several feminists in other parts of the world.

Postcolonial feminists argue that although feminist movements have been predominantly led by Western middle-class, white women in North America and Europe, there are alternative notions of feminism, including postcolonial feminism, Third World feminism and transnational feminism that are more inclusive. If feminist leadership is described more broadly, as those who can lead their communities towards equity, well-being, peace, and prosperity for all, then such a definition would include several community organisers from around the world who resist patriarchy and other modes of oppression in ways that value local sentiments and cultural sensitivities. They raise the consciousness of their community by bringing attention to and making visible injustices, especially those relating to gender inequalities.

Some would argue that feminist leadership itself is an oxymoron, given that feminists seek to break down binaries between leader and follower and other hierarchical structures. In other words, given that leadership has been traditionally defined in masculine patriarchal ways, some feminists reject leadership itself as a concept to aspire for. Similarly, some feminist leaders from non-Western, non-White, non–middle class backgrounds reject feminism as a term since they perceive it to be elitist and therefore, contrary to feminist principles of equity and inclusion.

In our particular context of feminist leadership within Indic traditions, there has been very little written and published as formal scholarship. However, there are several grassroots movements that could fit broadly within the feminist ideology, even if they do not coincide with the modern feminist movements in North America and Europe. Certainly, the ideas of social justice, inclusive structures, and non-oppressive emancipatory politics were central to the Indian freedom movement from colonial occupation. However, even prior to the Indian freedom movement, there are several ideas and concepts from Indo-dharmic philosophies and histories that are relevant to the feminist leadership literature. The feminist leadership literature has, to our knowledge, never been connected to Hinduism and Indo-dharmic concepts such as Shakti and Bhakti. This chapter attempts to de-centre and decolonise the traditional patriarchal Western ideas of leadership by examining them through Indic feminist ideas.

Feminist spirituality and the Indo-dharmic perspective

Feminist theology examines religious texts, rituals, traditions, and organisations from a feminist perspective. They seek to interpret, critique and resist male-dominated representations of God, of religious authority figures and leaders, and beliefs related to gender roles. Feminist theology has typically been limited to the study of major Abrahamic traditions such as Christianity, Islam and Judaism. They have, for instance, questioned how the Bible presents women as morally deficient or inferior to men, worked on fighting for equal rights for Muslim women, and sought to open up new opportunities for Jewish women to be leaders within Jewish traditions.

Atheist feminists have called for the rejection of theology by arguing that religions around the world have been oppressive toward women. Feminists in general have rightfully been suspicious of religious institutions, which have, more often than not, sought to control women's bodies, sexualities and desires. Patriarchal religion has successfully used mass media through popular film, television and others to present a very narrow masculine notion about what spirituality is and has connected it to organised religion. However, spirituality is a much more personal experience with higher power and allows everyone to investigate and experiment with what is meaningful and sacred to them.

There are several feminist-affirming spiritual traditions that people are routinely accessing and practicing. This can be better captured through the term, 'feminist spirituality'. One can argue that separating feminism and social justice from spirituality has further alienated those whose everyday lives do not separate the sacred from the secular. By relegating spirituality to local customs and traditions of 'other' cultures, white Western feminists have taken a cultural relativist approach that treats spirituality as 'unfeminist'. It ignores the fact that most women around the world relate to ideas of their bodies, their behaviours and their beliefs, including ideas about social justice, through the lens of spirituality.

Feminist spirituality creates a space in which value and respect for feminine aspects of divinity are affirmed and restored. Finding ways to liberate those marginalised in society from oppression is an essential part of a feminist spiritual quest. The fight for justice and freedom for all is a spiritual feminist practice. A feminist spiritual vision includes the fulfilment of the whole human potential as part of the spiritual life. It focuses on affirming life and fostering ways in which love, justice, freedom, and peace can be sustainable in societies. Reclaiming spirituality as an integral part of feminism is itself a feminist political act of decolonising the divine. It recognises that social and political transformation are integrally linked with spiritual transformation. In fact, it can be argued that spirituality is a central aspect for political and social justice activism. The false dichotomy between the spiritual and political is counterproductive.

Spirituality is a much-contested term and is a complex construct. Ramasubramanian (2014) distinguishes theistic from nontheistic spirituality. Nontheistic spirituality encompasses such topics as meaningfulness, belongingness, service, and purpose. The focus is on positive values such as appreciation, wisdom and altruism. Theistic spirituality also includes such virtues, but furthermore, it focuses on the sacred, the transcendental and connectedness with a higher force or power. These are further divided into Abrahamic (Judeo–Christian–Islamic) and Indo-dharmic (Hinduism, Buddhism, Sikhism, Jainism, and others). Indo-dharmic spiritual traditions have long emphasised the idea of dharma or ethical principles as determined by several contextual factors such as the place, time, and occupation or social class of the individual. Although Abrahamic traditions see what is revealed in their scriptures as gospel truth, Indo-dharmic traditions place less emphasis on texts, scriptural knowledge and religious authority.

Literature on Indo-dharmic feminist traditions is scarce. In particular, this chapter focuses on Hindu perceptions of the divine feminine form. They influence, shape and inform Hindu expressions of female power, authority and agency. Several Hindu rituals and concepts such as *sati, pativrata* and *jauhar* have been rejected as patriarchal and misogynistic by feminist scholars. However, Indo-dharmic religions also offer a variety of imagery and discourses around the goddess or the feminine divine, which have the potential to challenge and resist the notion of these religious traditions as androcentric and patriarchal. There are also examples of several women feminist leaders within Hinduism over its history and several men and women who have adhered to feminist principles. It is therefore important to examine alternative constructions and understandings of the feminine from within Hindu mythological traditions that offer a feminist philosophical interpretation.

This chapter calls for the examination of Indic ideas such as Shakti and Bhakti through feminist lenses. The purpose is not to valorise ancient Hindu ideas as legitimate, nor to celebrate the current situation for women in India, which is rather abysmal in terms of gender inequalities. The goal is to investigate the extent to which such concepts can inspire and empower feminist leaders toward social justice, inclusion, collaboration, courage, strength, and community-building. In contrast, if these principles further serve towards alienating, demeaning and devaluing feminine traits, skills, and styles of feminist leadership, they are to be rejected or at least re-imagined. Hence, we recognise, as a whole, that religion, spirituality or Indo-dharmic traditions, per se, are neither feminist nor patriarchal. These concepts are dynamic and context-sensitive. For instance, if dominant Hindu narratives seek to suppress non-Hindu, non-Brahmanical, non–middle class, indigenous, folk traditions of feminist leadership, then they are once again using power and privilege to exclude rather than include, which takes them away from the feminist ideal.

Feminist leadership, the Shakti principle and femininity

Although patriarchy, violence, dominance, and aggression continue to be dominant themes in the imagery and practice of Hinduism, it also places emphasis on the feminine divine or Shakti. These ideas of Shakti inform and shape expressions of authority, power and agency. Therefore, from a feminist leadership context, it is important to examine ways in which the social construction of the Goddess or Shakti principle resists patriarchy and offers an alternative form of meaning-making that has potential for empowering women and underprivileged groups in society.

Pintchman and Sherma (2011) offer several such an alternative and more pluralistic understanding of Hindu goddesses that reclaim their dignity, status and agency, thus bestowing similar dignity and respect to those who might not traditionally be seen as deserving of them. They bring to light the practice of Shakti worship in the form of Kali, especially in northeastern India, as a way to recognise the capacity of women to attain spiritual enlightenment through practicing an ethic of care and inclusion towards marginalised women. It is important to continuously and critically assess the ways in which Hindu principles such as Shakti might either help or hinder feminist ideals.

Feminist leadership that takes Shakti principles into consideration is a powerful alternative to traditionally hypermasculine leadership styles that have undervalued, ignored and demeaned feminine qualities in leadership. Such a style deliberately and purposefully integrates both masculine and feminine qualities with consciousness and awareness to restore balance and bring harmony to our lives. Given that leadership has been historically defined within patriarchal and hypermasculine cultures, the balance needs to be tilted toward nurturing greater self-awareness and self-mastery to lead a wholesome, harmonious and peaceful life, while serving others in inclusive ways. Shakti leadership has been described eloquently by Bhat and Sisodia (2016) as a form of conscious and self-aware leadership style that is contrasted with paternal, egocentric leadership.

The Shakti principle refers to the primordial energy that is creative, regenerative, sustainable, and restorative. It is power that comes from an infinite timeless source that manifests thoughts and ideas into various forms in reality. Shakti is not an inanimate and lifeless force. Rather it is a living, intelligent and conscious power. It is associated with feminine qualities such as compassion, cooperation, empathy, and care. It is important to clarify that both men and women have access to Shakti and the power of the feminine represented through this principle. In fact, the purpose of human life is to overcome dualities, including between the feminine and the masculine, by integrating them to generate non-dualistic synergies.

From the Indo-dharmic perspective, Shakti is a latent, primal, evolutionary force that is locked up within us and has to be untapped and channeled into productive, creative and meaningful ways. In contrast, Shiva is seen as the eternal, unchanging, pure consciousness. While Shakti represents the ever-changing dynamic energy, Shiva represents the constant consciousness that forms the substratum of the universe. Shakti represents variety and diversity, while Shiva represents oneness. The two cannot exist without the other. The focus of yoga is the union of Shakti with Shiva, which complement one another as the whole. When these two principles merge, there is synergy, creativity, meaning, and order.

Shakti is also representative of wealth, prosperity and consumption. From the viewpoint of Shakti philosophy, power is not a negative term but something that is welcomed and valued. However, power and privilege are shared with people, rather than being used to dominate or oppress. Although it might seem contradictory that the Shakti principle on the one hand stands for an ethics of care and on the other hand seeks to generate wealth, this contradiction is resolved through ideas such as conscious capitalism (Bhat and Sisodia, 2016). Conscious capitalism emphasises meaningful solutions to real-world problems, in order to enable others to blossom to their full potential. It values a culture of caring, love, transparency, and accountability. It reimagines leadership as selfless and purpose-driven.

According to tantric tradition of Hinduism, Shakti can be further divided into *Iccha Shakti, Jnana Shakti* and *Kriya Shakti*. Iccha Shakti is willpower and the creative desire to express and experience our wholeness. Jnana Shakti is the power of knowledge and wisdom that guides sentient beings to make intelligent choices to align mind, body and spirit. Kriya Shakti is the physical and material energy that manifests as abundance and wealth through meaningful action. Applying these ideas to feminist leadership, it is important to find ways to nurture creativity, wisdom, intuition, and positive action.

These aspects of Shakti manifests into the goddess or the Divine Mother through many forms of imagery such as those associated with Durga, Kali, Lakshmi, Saraswathi, Sita, and Radha. It is beyond the scope of this chapter to examine the myths, folklores, and narratives that present these complex goddesses in multiple ways, as strong and vulnerable, compassionate and ruthless, ugly and beautiful, and dominant and subservient. Within patriarchal, Brahmanical, hierarchical, and Sanskritised interpretations of Shakti, she is often presented as domesticated, subservient, flawlessly beautiful, and sexually objectified. On the other hand, folk, vernacular, and indigenous traditions often embrace other aspects of the same goddess imagery to present her as dark, bloodthirsty, sexually free, independent, and dominant. This is not to suggest that there are no exceptions or contradictions that complicate the understanding and interpretation of Shakti across these traditions. In fact, the meaning-making process of Shakti or the feminine divine principle in Hinduism has shifted with time, being influenced by Vedic heritage, medieval history, and more contemporary understanding of what it means to be a woman in society.

When Shakti principles coexist with Shiva principles, power is no longer a source of ego enhancement, corruption, manipulation, oppression, subordination, violence, and greed. Instead, feminist leadership that integrates these principles leads to distributed power, purposeful living, and emancipation of the powerless. Here, the leader becomes a transformative agent of social change in creating a prosperous, peaceful, and purposeful life for everyone within the organisation and society in a harmonious way. Not only does a feminist leader share power with others, but he/she also helps others to empower themselves by encouraging others to get in touch with their own intelligence, wisdom, and creative energies. Feminist leaders focus on using this energy for the greater common good rather than their own self-interest.

Inclusive leadership and the Bhakti tradition

Feminist perspectives on the rajarshi model of leadership takes an intersectional approach that recognises that leadership is not a standardised norm but is instead situated within specific contexts such as gender, race, ethnicity, class, nationality, religion, age, sexual orientation, and culture. Such differences are seen as socially constituted through structures, processes and cultures within organisations. Therefore, it includes feminine, indigenous and culture-centred approaches to leadership. This approach re-envisions the rajarshi model as an inclusive leadership that focuses on purpose, meaning and fulfilment, rather than on productivity, efficiency and metrics. It is about a relational practice built on trust, respect and empathy, working towards a shared purpose of social justice in an ethical, principled manner. Feminist leadership is informed by the politics of difference so that diversity and pluralism are embraced through exploration of zones of discomfort and deep forms of listening to marginalised voices.

The Indo-dharmic concept of Bhakti evokes similar ideas of love, care, inclusion, social justice, and pluralism. Chackalackal describes Bhakti in this manner:

> Bhakti, according to the Indian tradition, is a loving devotion and it includes a total self-surrender; a readiness on the part of the Bhakti to let go oneself into the bountifulness of the divine, motivated by sheer love. It is not a mere intellectual exercise to attain theoretical knowledge about the ultimate reality; far more, it is an attempt to know and experience reality by a commitment in love, which ultimately, turns out to be loving devotion culminating in total self-surrender.
>
> (2004: 274–5)

The practice and attitudes of those in the Bhakti path differs in many ways from that of jnana or the path of knowledge. In the Bhakti path, the self is seen as an instrument of the divine, but in jnana yoga, the self is seen as expanding all around to include the divine universal consciousness. Greater self-efficacy and locus of control are emphasised in the rational,

140

problem-solving approach of jnana yoga, while greater emotional intelligence and emotion-focused strategies to cope with adversity are emphasised in bhakti yoga.

The Bhakti movement can be thought of as one of the first feminist movements in India and started around the 8th–9th century CE. The radical saint leader Ramanuja of the 11th–12th century CE marked an important period of the Bhakti movement, when he converted several so-called lower-caste devotees into Brahmanism. The movement then spread to several other parts of India. It was in the 13th century that the Bhakti movement took off in other parts of India (Jones, 2009). Some scholars include the satyagraha or non–co-operation movement of Mahatma Gandhi as part of the Bhakti movement. Others contend that Bhakti continues to be a lived practice, such as the *vaarakari* tradition that is still practiced actively in Maharashtra (Jones, 2009).

The Bhakti movement was much more than a devotional, spiritual movement. It was also a political and social movement that emphasised love, equality, progress, and social egalitarianism (Burchett, 2009). In fact, considering its emphasis on gender and caste equality, scholars refer to it as a 'democratic doctrine which consolidates all people without distinction of caste, community, nationality or sex' (Raghavan, 1966: 32). According to Omvedt and Patankar (2003: 277), it is a radical movement 'bringing together women and men of low caste to proclaim equality and reject Brahmanic ritualism'. Similarly, Mokashi-Punekar and Ramanathan (2005: 123–4) describe it as a 'deeply spiritual and democratising movement' that is characteristically 'revolutionary in spirit'.

With its emphasis on gender equality, nonviolence, tolerance, diversity, subjective experiences, and freedom from oppressive familial patriarchy (including marriage and procreation), Bhakti was more a social reform movement rather than a purely spiritual or theist movement. This inclusive spiritual movement focused on acceptance, love and inclusion, but also on courage, renunciation of luxuries and strength. Traditional gender, caste, class restrictions were shunned and questioned vociferously by many Bhakti yogis. The movement focused on the sensual, erotic, emotional, and devotional, and thus stood in stark contrast to the orthodox, patriarchal and hierarchal Brahmanical ritualistic worship of medieval times.

The Bhakti movement allowed for the religious and spiritual aspirations of lower castes and women to be accommodated in ways that orthodox Brahmanical Hinduism had not done so in the past. In terms of caste/religious inclusivity, Chokhamela of Maharashtra, Nandanaar of Tamil Nadu and Kabirdaas of North India were some of the first saint composers from lower castes whose works became central to the literary tradition of India. The movement was also a reaction to the intellectualism and philosophical emphasis on Sanskrit Vedic culture. Similarly, Brahmanical ritualism was a dominant force during this era, emphasising orthodoxy, Sanskrit scriptures and strict rituals, which were not affordable or accessible to the largely illiterate and poor masses of people. Yet it is to be noted that there were only few Bhakti saints who were from lower castes and women.

Apart from challenging rigid caste hierarchies, the movement also questioned patriarchal notions of what it means to be a man and a woman. Unlike Vedic India, in which women enjoyed such privileges as choosing their partner, chanting hymns and more, in medieval India, there was a deterioration of women's rights (polygamy, sati, dowry, pardah, and jauhar). In particular, widows were not treated well and were expected to commit sati. Even today, patriarchy is the dominant mode of leadership and everyday life in most parts of India, where gender inequalities and social injustices based on gender, class, caste, religion, and ethnicity are rampant. There is little tolerance or acceptance of the blurring of gender roles, for instance, even in contemporary India. In terms of gender fluidity, for instance, Bhakti poets such as Tirumankai Aazhvaar, a male Vaishnavaite poet, writes about the erotic love of a *talaivi* (heroine) for her Lord, from the perspective of a woman (Venkatesan, 2010), which reversed traditional gender roles. Similarly, Akka Mahadevi from Karnataka rejected social norms by giving up her wealth, security and status as a queen to become a wandering, naked saint, thus resisting the ways in which gender roles and sexual oppression were imposed on her by embracing radical or *Veera Shaivism*. It was a radical step during those times to challenge gender norms and caste/class hierarchies.

Drawing from these principles of the Bhakti movement, Indic notions of rajarshi leadership would recognise and value pluralism, inclusion, emotional intelligence, compassionate care, and social justice. By shunning hierarchies and divides, such leadership would be transformational so that the emphasis is not on the fulfilment of personal ambitions of the leader, but on sharing power with others within the organisation. Moreover, such leadership would value and nurture the emotional, spiritual and ethical aspects of the individual, the organisation and the collective society as a whole. Relational leadership that operates from an ethic of care can draw inspiration and instances from the Bhakti movement to be not just inclusive, but also to value emotionality and emotional intelligence. At the same time, related ideas of servant leadership of the Bhakti saints have to be questioned and challenged as there is a danger of segregating caregiving as exclusively a woman's job. Also, one should be wary of misinterpretation of the ethic of care as giving up one's one individual freedom and desires. It is important that self-care and freedom of the feminist leader's own rights are kept central to the conversations when it comes to servant leadership rather than seeing this as an opportunity to mistreat and discriminate against feminist leaders.

Feminist leadership in practice

So far we have examined what feminism is, how feminist leadership is conceptualised and how Hindu ideas such as Shakti and Bhakti help reconceptualise rajarshi models of leadership as a more inclusive and transformative feminist leadership. Now, let us look at ways in which feminist leadership can be practiced within organisations. Work environments have become toxic with stressful organisational cultures that are emotionally taxing and mentally exhausting for workers. The key question to ask ourselves as feminist leaders is 'how do we lead our organisation with soul?' The goal is to create workspaces that are nurturing, meaningful and creative, while being productive. Patriarchal workplaces are toxic in nature and are rooted in power, authority, respect, and domination. Rather than foster competition, insecurity, inflexibility, and hierarchies, a feminist workplace fosters collaboration, cooperation, trust, and equity. Feminist leadership is about nurturing both masculine and feminine qualities. In particular, it is about embracing, accepting and fostering feminine qualities such as intuition, openness, empathy, concern, and compassion.

Although these principles are excellent in theory, there can be several challenges in practicing feminist leadership. First of all, many people do not distinguish between feminism and the feminine. Also, feminist leaders need not be women, but can be of all genders. Feminism is not about women's leadership styles. It is about subverting, challenging and resisting patriarchal leadership that emphasises hypermasculine traits, while devaluing and demeaning feminine qualities.

Another challenge is that feminist values and principles are not widely endorsed across organisations. Therefore, feminist leaders find it difficult to gain legitimacy as leaders, especially if they have to stay authentic. Authenticity is being self-aware and aligning one's behaviours with one's values. It is about acting on one's beliefs and following through on behaviours that resonate with one's ideological and political orientation as feminists. Authentic leadership places emphasis on interacting transparently and honestly with others, with trust and other positive emotions such as hope and optimism. However, when working in a patriarchal hypermasculine hegemonic work environment, it becomes difficult to stay authentic and true to one's principles while also gaining legitimacy as a leader.

A related obstacle is one of tokenism. Feminist leaders often represent a minority within organisations, which are traditionally masculinised and patriarchal spaces. Power dynamics, gender role expectations and lack of attempts to incorporate diversity (through intersectionalities of gender, race, ethnicity, sexual orientation, and more) serve as added stressors. Feminist leaders often find themselves to be alone, lacking mentorship and support from those that they can trust. They are also heavily scrutinised, especially if they are seen as not representative of the typical leaders. They, therefore, become hypervisible and could experience high levels of performance anxiety because of added scrutiny of their speech, appearance and behaviours.

Another issue is that feminist leaders, especially women and minority leaders, are more harshly examined than others in terms of both their personal and professional lives. Feminist leadership seeks to break down binaries and barriers such as masculine/feminine, powerful/powerless, haves/have-nots, and even public/private. A feminist leader stands with and in truth with transparency and honesty. There is little difference between their public persona and private realms in terms of their politics. What happens within their family and other aspects of their lives are also equally important as compared to what happens at their workplace. Although patriarchal leadership often draws a sharp line between their public and private lives, compartmentalising the two, feminist leadership makes the personal also political. Therefore, issues such as family leave, wage gaps, domestic violence, and a healthy work–life balance are relevant for a wholesome, complete life experience and are significant to the feminist leader.

Rao and Kelleher (2000) talk about working with power and recognising that power can come from many different stakeholders to enable transformative change. They also urge the feminist leader to focus on the dialogic process and the need to have a holistic vision beyond simply advocating for one's position. Politics is an integral part of feminist leadership. It is about changing the idea of what power looks like in organisations, who has power, and what this power is used for. It is about making power visible through greater transparency and accountability. It is about democratisation of the process of leadership training, development, and selection so that leadership is based on virtues such as wisdom and compassion rather than based on seniority and other such indicators of authority. Power has to be, therefore, legitimate and earned for, with the respect and love of co-workers. The feminist leader has to be self-aware and reflect constantly about the ways in which our personal values, attitudes, and behaviours might be complicit with systems of oppression that we are trying to break through. Structures, spaces and processes are needed to be in place for true collaboration and dialogue.

The ethic of care is central to practicing feminist leadership from a Bhakti framework, which values and recognises the importance of self-care, altruism and compassionate communication with others in the organisation. Drawing from the Bhakti movement principles of breaking barriers and hierarchies, such feminist leadership should be one that is horizontal and nonhierarchical. Yet, if this principle is taken to its extreme, there is the danger of burnout and martyrdom of feminist leaders who sacrifice their own ambitions, goals, health, and well-being trying to serve the larger goal and purpose. More recently, feminists have included radical self-care as an integral part of feminist principles, suggesting that taking care of one's own self is itself a political act.

Creating an organisation that values inclusion, diversity, and respect for differences is an essential aspect of feminist leadership. The approach is collaborative and participatory. It focuses on building trust and nurturing a welcoming environment by affirming individuals as they are and helping them seek their full human potential. In practice, feminist leaders also have to be cautious to not make all decisions only through consensus-building, consultations and collaboration. Realistically, collaboration and co-creation can mean that a lot of resources such as time and energy are needed to understand various perspectives before making decisions. At times, effective feminist leaders have to exert authority, especially during emergencies and crises, by acting in a decisive manner. Therefore, the leadership style should be situational and context-driven, so that feminist leaders can respond thoughtfully depending on the needs of the situation. A delicate balance has to be struck for feminist leaders between leading from the heart and leading based on the context.

Conclusion

In conclusion, this chapter draws on Indo-dharmic spiritual traditions and Hindu concepts of the Shakti (the feminine aspect of divinity) and Bhakti movement (a spiritual and social movement that sought to break caste, gender and other hierarchies to reduce social inequalities). These concepts help us challenge traditional patriarchal conceptions of rajarshi leadership as a single charismatic visionary leader with masculine traits such as dominance, aggression and discipline. It opens up the space to reimagine modern ideas of rajarshi leadership in the new millennium as feminist leadership that is nonhierarchical, relational, inclusive, and embraces emotionality, care, collaboration, and respect as the essential core principles. The purpose of rajarshi leadership from a feminist critical lens, drawing on Shakti and Bhakti, is not self-aggrandisement and hero worship of the visionary rajarshi. Rather, the purpose is the greater good of society in seeking to end oppression, domination, injustices, and inequalities based on gender, race, ethnicity, social class, religion, caste, and the like. In practice, there could be several challenges to feminist leadership such as lack of broad support for feminist principles, burnout and exhaustion because of lack of self-care, mentoring support and the need to act authoritatively and decisively on occasion without using a collective approach. Despite these challenges, I argue that feminist leadership offers a significant alternative to traditional hypermasculine notions of leadership that promises to be more inclusive, participatory and transformative.

References

Aviolo, B.J. 1994. 'The Alliance of Total Quality and the Full Range of Leadership', in B.M. Bass and B.J. Aviolo (eds.), *Improving Organizational Effectiveness through Transformational Leadership*, pp. 121–45. Thousand Oaks, CA: Sage.

Bem, S.L. 1993. *The Lenses of Gender: Transforming the Debate on Sexual Inequality*. New Haven, CT: Yale University Press.

Bhat, N. and R. Sisodia. 2016. *Shakti Leadership: Embracing Feminine and Masculine Power in Business*. San Francisco, CA: Berrett-Koehler Publishers.

Blackmore, J. 2013. 'A Feminist Critical Perspective on Educational Leadership', *International Journal of Leadership in Education*, 16(2): 139–54.

Blackmore, J. and J. Sachs. 2012. *Performing and Reforming Leaders: Gender, Educational Restructuring, and Organizational Change*. Albany, NY: SUNY Press.

Burchett, P. 2009. 'Bhakti Rhetoric in the Hagiography of "Untouchable" Saints: Discerning Bhakti's Ambivalence on Caste and Brahminhood', *International Journal of Hindu Studies*, 13(2): 115–41.

Chackalackal, S. 2004. 'Modern Saints of Bhakti Tradition' (Editorial), *Journal of Dharma*, 29(3): 273–8.

Chin, J.L. 2004. '2003 Division 35 Presidential Address: Feminist Leadership: Feminist Visions and Diverse Voices', *Psychology of Women Quarterly*, 28(1): 1–8.

Jones, J. 2009. *Performing the Sacred: Song, Genre, and Aesthetics in Bhakti*. Ann Arbor, MI: Proquest UMI Dissertation Publishing.

Kark, R. 2004. 'The Transformational Leader: Who Is (S)He? A Feminist Perspective', *Journal of Organizational Change Management*, 17(2): 160–76.

Mokashi-Punekar, R. and S. Ramanathan. 2005. *On the Threshold: Songs of Chokhamela*. Lanham, MD: Rowman Altamira.

Omvedt, G. and B. Patankar. 2003. 'Says Tuka', *Critical Asian Studies*, 35(2): 277–86.

Pintchman, T. and R.D. Sherma (eds.). 2011. *Woman and Goddess in Hinduism: Reinterpretations and Re-Envisionings*. New York: Palgrave Macmillan.

Raghavan, V. 1966. *The Great Integrators: The Saint-singers of India* (Vol. 9). New Delhi: Publications Division, Ministry of Information and Broadcasting.

Ramasubramanian, S. 2014. 'Media and Spirituality', in M.B. Oliver and A. Raney (eds.), *Media and Social Life*, pp. 46–62. New York: Routledge.

Rao, A. and D. Kelleher. 2000. 'Leadership for Social Transformation: Some Ideas and Questions on Institutions and Feminist Leadership', *Gender & Development*, 8(3): 74–9.

Tichy, N. and M.A. Devanna. 1986. *The Transformational Leader*. New York: Wiley.

Venkatesan, A. 2010. *The Secret Garland: Āṇṭāls Tiruppāvai and Nācciyār Tirumoli*. Oxford: Oxford University Press.

10

INCLUSIVE LEADERSHIP

A technology perspective

Tilak Agerwala[1]

Introduction

In his description of the Fourth Industrial Revolution, Klaus Schwab makes an important observation and also identifies the breadth of its impact: 'We stand on the brink of a technological revolution that will fundamentally alter the way we live, work, and relate to one another'. He characterises this revolution as evolving at an exponential rate, 'disrupting almost every industry in every country'. He concludes emphasising the importance of using the technology that is emerging during this revolution to 'shape a future that works for all of us by putting people first and empowering them' (Schwab, 2015).

At the core of this fourth revolution is the rapid digitalisation or digital transformation of our world, resulting from the conversion of almost everything in our physical world (including documents, images, sound, and analog signals) into a digital form that can be processed by a computer for various purposes. New data, associated with enterprises, individuals, and the environment in which they operate, is doubling every two years. Our 'digital universe' will have 40 Zettabytes (40 followed by 21 zeroes) of data by 2020. This rapid growth of data does not compromise our ability to utilise them. We are making tremendous progress in advanced computing technologies such as modeling, simulation, analysis, and machine learning—computers that 'learn'—that allow us to analyse and gain insights from the vast amount of data to which we have access. The growth of data and our ability to interpret meaningful trends and extract relevant information will transform industry and all levels of government and will affect individuals—consumers, citizens, professionals—in many ways. Therefore, it is imperative that leaders, managers and individuals understand the data revolution underway and adapt rapidly.

Lange and Tapia (2016) aptly state that 'the 21st-century leader is, by definition, an inclusive leader'. Given the data revolution, it is important to understand the synergies between data and inclusion. We provide an overview of big data and the relevant computing technologies of modeling, simulation, analytics, and machine learning—tools that can be applied to gain insights from the data—and provide examples of how these technologies are being applied to transform public policymaking, business decision-making and talent management. We define 'data inclusion' as including data and the relevant computing technologies as a core element of decision-making at all levels of an organisation. We posit that pursuing a data-inclusion strategy will lead to more participation, greater inclusiveness and substantially improving the quality of decision-making, resulting in better business outcomes. Fostering a fact-based decision-making culture can face many barriers. We discuss how leaders can overcome this challenge and highlight the ethical issues that can arise with a data-inclusion strategy.

Next, we go beyond using computers as a tool to enhance the decision-making capabilities and speculate that the 'inclusive leader of the future' will be a system of humans and computers that interact in natural ways—through speech, text, and vision—learn from one another, and collectively are more effective than either humans or computers acting alone. Computers handle the tasks of sifting through massive amounts of data, analysing it, finding patterns, predicting outcomes based on complex models of the world, and make recommendations to humans. The humans set the values, vision, goals, and context and bring creativity, out-of-the-box thinking and compassion to the decision-making. Dialog between humans and computers refines insights and results in better decisions.

Technology overview

We give here an overview of the computing technologies being used today: big data, computational science, modeling, simulation, and supercomputing, analytics, machine learning, and artificial and augmented intelligence.

Big Data: IBM characterises big data along four dimensions—the 4Vs (IBM, 2012):

- *Volume* refers to the scale of data. According to International Data Corporation, the digital universe consisted of 2.7 zettabytes (2.7 followed by 21 zeros) of data in 2012 and is doubling every two years (IDC, 2012) (Gantz and Reinsel, 2012). Based on this projection, the digital universe is over 10 zettabytes today and will soon be at 100 zettabytes. (A zettabyte would fill 20 billion Blu-ray disks.) These data come from everywhere. To name a few sources: enterprise data, social media posts, digital pictures and videos, Amazon transactions, and sensors.
- *Variety* refers to the diversity (the different forms) of data. Today we are mostly exposed to unstructured data, consisting of text, video, image, and sensor data in many different formats, which do not fit neatly in rows and columns as in the past. Unstructured data are growing ten

times faster than structured data (Inside Big Data, 2017). Some examples of unstructured data and their size are:

The global size of data in healthcare, including all the different varieties of unstructured data, was estimated to be 153 exabytes (153 followed by 18 zeros) in 2013 (Corbin, 2014). As projected, such growth rates will swell to 2,314 exabytes by 2020. On Facebook, 510,000 comments are posted and 136,000 photos are uploaded every 60 seconds and 4.75 billion pieces of content are shared daily—a 94 percent increase from August 2012 to May 2013 (Zephoria Digital Marketing, 2017); and 500 million tweets are sent by 100 million active users daily on Twitter (as of January 2017) (Omnicore, 2017).

- *Velocity* refers to the speed of data (the rate at which data are created, stored and analysed). Examples of high velocity data are explained here. The New York stock exchange captures one terabyte (TB, 1 followed by 12 zeros) of trade information during each trading session. Pratt & Whitney's Geared Turbo Fan engine, fitted with 5,000 sensors, generates up to 10 gigabytes (1 followed by 9 zeros) of data per second. A single twin-engine aircraft with an average 12-hour flight time can produce up to 844 TB of data per day (Rapolu, 2016).

- *Veracity* refers to the certainty (and quality) of data. Having a large volume of data coming in at high speed is worthless if those data are incorrect. Poor-quality data can lead to very wrong conclusions ('garbage in, garbage out') and can cause many problems for governments, citizens and business. Bad data costs the US economy more than $3 trillion per year—more than twice the amount of the 2011 US Federal Deficit—which raises the cost of healthcare by $314 billion and may cost businesses as much as 10–25 percent of the organisation's revenue (Software AG, 2017).

With high volume data of different varieties arriving at high velocities, assurance of data veracity has become a significant challenge. Fast and dependable solutions to detect and repair erroneous data are required. In a good tutorial, Saha and Srivastava (2014) present results on big data quality management and identify a range of open problems for the community.

There are many definitions of big data (NIST, 2015; Mauro et al., 2014). We like the description given by Mayer-Schönberger and Cukiern who focus on value capture: 'the ability of society to harness information in novel ways to produce useful insights or goods and services of significant value' and 'things one can do at a large scale that cannot be done at a smaller one, to extract new insights or create new forms of value' (Press, 2014). Thus, the challenge is to gain insights that produce value quickly from large volumes of unstructured data arriving at high velocity. This is accomplished by using the computing technologies described here.

Computational Science: The study of any complex system in science, engineering, or business, which consists of many components that interact with each other, requires the construction of a model to represent the system. Modeling is the process of collecting data on the system being studied to create an abstract, approximate description of the system. Simulation is the process of exercising the mathematical model on computers, to predict how the system will behave over time. Simulation can be used to inform management or for technical decision-making. Computational science is the field of mathematical modeling and simulation that uses advanced computing capabilities to solve complex problems that cannot be replicated in the laboratory.

The 2005 US President's Information Technology Advisory Committee report reaffirmed that 'computational science has become the third pillar of the scientific enterprise, a peer alongside theory and physical experiment' (2005: 13) and that 'computational science is now indispensable to the solution of complex problems in every sector, from traditional science and engineering domains to such key areas as national security, public health, and economic innovation' (ibid.: 2).

The most demanding simulations are performed by supercomputers—the highest performing computers at any point in time, currently executing at a peak rate of 100 peta (1 followed by 17 zeros) floating point operations per second—the combined performance of approximately 4 million personal computers.

Supercomputers have been used with great success to simulate phenomena in astrophysics, biophysics, material science, combustion, climate modelling, weather forecasting, finance, oil exploration, and a host of other fields. Examples of supercomputers applied to public policymaking are described later.

Analytics: Rouse (2018) defines big data analytics as 'the process of examining large and varied data sets—that is, big data—to uncover hidden patterns, unknown correlations, market trends, customer preferences, and other useful information that can help organizations make more informed business decisions' (para. 1, page 1). There are many different kinds of analytics and Mike Wu, chief scientist at Lithium, makes the case that the analytics landscape can be simplified by examining the underlying computation of different kinds of analytics: 'under this view, there are only three kinds of analytics' (Wu, 2016):

> *Descriptive Analytics*: It answers questions such as 'what happened?' 'How many, how often, where?' 'What exactly is the problem?' They summarise the data for decision makers and inform them of what happened in the past. The computations being performed here are usually straightforward summary statistics.
>
> *Predictive Analytics*: It answers questions such as 'what could happen?' 'What if these trends continue?' 'What will happen next if. . . . ?'

They forecast future scenarios. Existing data are used to create a mathematical model from which data can be extrapolated to make predictions.

Prescriptive Analytics: It answers questions such as 'how can we achieve the best outcome?' 'How can we achieve the best outcome including the effects of variability?' They are used to guide decision-makers to a desired outcome. The computation being performed here is an optimisation of some objective function whose variables are constrained.

Through seven annual surveys of 6,000 organisations, IBM found a 'mind-boggling' rate of adoption of analytics: 'in 2010, the focus was on educating executives about how analytics could create value; most still relied on gut instincts and limited descriptive data. By 2012, a majority of organisations had matured to the use of analytics' (IBM, 2016). A graph in this report indicates that from 2010 through 2015, predictive analytics adoption went up from 40 percent to 70 percent and prescriptive analytics from 10 percent to 60 percent.

Analytics on big data are being deployed pervasively and many real examples can be found in the literature (Castro and Korte, 2013; Morgan, 2015). We give examples of analytics applied to public policy making and business decision-making in subsequent sections.

Machine learning: Machine learning refers to computers with 'the ability to automatically learn and improve from experience without being explicitly programmed' (Expert System, 2017). Machine learning is not a new field and goes back to the 1950s. Machine learning programs can be categorised as being supervised or unsupervised. In supervised learning, the user trains the program with input that is labelled with the correct answer. In unsupervised machine learning, the program is trained on data without any labels. Castle (2017) uses the animal identification example to illustrate the difference. To identify animals correctly, the supervised learning program would be 'trained on a dataset of images that are properly labelled with the species of the animal and some identifying characteristics', whereas an unsupervised learning program 'will look at inherent similarities between the images and separate them into groups accordingly, assigning its own new label to each group'. In both cases, well-known statistical analysis methods are utilised.

In deep learning, a powerful form of machine learning, which can be supervised or unsupervised, the program 'discovers intricate structure in large data sets' and uses 'computational models that are composed of multiple processing layers to learn representations of data with multiple levels of abstraction' (LeCun et al., 2015). Deep learning does particularly well in complex environments, where the right decision depends on many variables. This has led to significant advances in speech recognition, visual object recognition, object detection, and many other domains such as the life sciences.

The logic by which a deep learning program arrives at its conclusions cannot be explained in human understandable terms and this has clear ethical implications as we will see later. Nevertheless, enabled by the availability of cheap computing power, application of deep learning is growing because it provides the core technologies to make sense of our most valuable resource today—unstructured Big Data.

A deep learning system, trained with 12,000 retinal images, automatically identified the condition of diabetic retinopathy, a leading cause of blindness among adults, as consistently as ophthalmologists and exceeded the National Institutes of Health's recommended standard of at least 80 per cent accuracy and precision for diabetic retinopathy screens (Peng and Gulshan, 2016).

Castro and New (2016) describe 30 applications based on machine learning in every sector, including helping people understand sign language, learning as soon as a plant gets sick, learning how to keep customers happy, reducing gender bias in the office, understanding a crisis with social media, predicting which students will drop out, predicting renewable energy availability, preventing vision loss in diabetes patients, streamlining drug discovery, preventing (equipment) breakdowns before they happen, and predicting crime hotspots. We give examples of machine learning applied to decision-making and talent management in government and business in later sections.

Artificial and augmented intelligence: Artificial intelligence (AI) was originally defined in the 1950s as the simulation of human intelligence processes by machines, especially computer systems (Rouse and Laskowski, 2016), and is referred to as artificial general intelligence.

Today, most real examples are based on augmented intelligence, 'an alternative conceptualisation of artificial intelligence that focuses on AI's assistive role, emphasising the fact that it is designed to enhance human intelligence rather than replace it' (Rouse and Wigmore, 2017). IBM uses the term cognitive computing instead of augmented intelligence to describe computing systems 'that learn at scale, reason with purpose and interact with humans naturally. It is a mixture of computer science and cognitive science—that is, the understanding of the human brain and how it works. By means of self-teaching algorithms that use data mining, visual recognition, and natural language processing, the computer is able to solve problems and thereby optimize human processes.' (IBM, 2017a). We will refer to these concepts in Section 5, on Human–Computer Collaboration. It is important to note that statistical analysis is the foundation of analytics, deep learning, natural language processing, speech recognition, and machine vision.

Evidence-based decision-making: examples

In this section, we describe challenges in public policy making, business decision-making and talent management, and provide examples of the use of modeling, simulation, analytics, and machine learning to address these challenges. Our focus is on augmenting decision-making capabilities of leaders using evidence-based approaches in public policy making and business decision-making, and specifically, talent management (because people are the core asset of every organisation).

Evidence-based decision-making is a process for making decisions about a program, practice or policy that is grounded in the best available research evidence and informed by experiential evidence from the field and relevant contextual evidence (Centers for Disease Control, 2017). It is an approach to decision-making and action that is driven by hard fact. A good evidence-based methodology requires an analytic approach that allows for a proper consideration of the nature of the issue or problem and of different options, good data, transparency, and independence from influence—all of which are enabled by data, modelling, simulation, analytics, and machine-learning technologies.

Public policy making: Simply put, public policymaking is about 'deciding who gets what, when and how' (Lasswell, 1936). Public policy issues are extremely complex, occur in rapidly changing uncertain environments and involve conflicts between different interests. Evidence-based policy is public policy informed by rigorously established objective evidence and is necessary to move away from ideology-based decision-making.

To illustrate the impact of computational sciences on national policy and the importance of leadership and vision, the Science Based Stockpile Stewardship (SBSS) program is outlined, drawing from the historical account by Larzelere II (2009). In September 1996, President Bill Clinton formally announced his decision to seek a Comprehensive Nuclear Test-Ban Treaty and directed the US Department of Energy to take the required actions for sustaining confidence in the stockpile without nuclear testing. The goal of the SBSS program was to maintain the safety, security and reliability of the US nuclear deterrent without full-scale testing. The Advanced Simulation and Computing Program—formerly known as the Accelerated Strategic Computing Initiative (ASCI)—was launched in the 1990s to address this need. An early calculation done at Lawrence Livermore National Laboratory (LLNL) concluded that more than 100 teraflops (100 trillion floating-point operations per second) would be required to execute the simulations to sufficient accuracy. LLNL's most powerful computer at the start of SBSS provided only 13.7 gigaflops (13.7 thousand million floating-point operations per second) and computing power at LLNL would have to increase by over 7,000-fold in a decade. In 2005, IBM installed two supercomputers totaling 460 teraflops, the 100-teraflops Purple system and the 360-teraflops BlueGene/L. Together, these two supercomputers far exceeded the original ASCI target. Lazerelle II writes, 'by 2005, ASCI had fulfilled the goals set out a decade earlier. The applications had been created, allowing nuclear weapons scientists and engineers to gain a better understanding of how the weapons work. Indeed, these applications allowed users to see things that were previously unknown – unrecognised in experiments and not imagined in theories' (2009: 4) and 'The factors in ASCI's success generally fell into four categories: vision, leadership, endurance, and partnership' (ibid.: 5). These and subsequent computers have been applied with great success to modeling and simulation phenomena in astrophysics, biophysics, material science, combustion, climate modeling, weather forecasting, finance, oil exploration, and a host of other fields (Secretary of Energy Advisory Board [SEAB], 2014).

Water resource management, natural disaster prediction and response, and urban, energy and environmental planning are a few examples in which computers can be used effectively for policy making. We present two examples here.

Simulations can be used throughout the policy making process to support decision-making. A workshop organised by RAND Corporation and LLNL simulated five different water management portfolios for the Colorado River Basin. These were tested against thousands of scenarios reflecting uncertainty about future climate change and development patterns, something that would be impossible without using supercomputers. The workshop showed how supercomputing 'can accelerate decision and policymaking on one of the critical issues of our time–water management' (RAND, 2016; Groves et al., 2014).

Climate modelling has been a traditional focus area for supercomputing. Today, supercomputers are helping researchers vigorously test climate models to ensure accuracy before applying them to predict future trends, gain a better understanding of historical climate conditions and revise their findings on the future effects of large climate changes like global warming (Mannel, 2017). Climate modelling and simulation can certainly influence public policy but, as was stated earlier, this requires a receptive policy environment.

Over the past several years, researchers have gained new insights into important applications and the capabilities needed to run them effectively, especially their data-handling capabilities (Agerwala, 2014a, 2014b). Recognising this need, SEAB (2014) underscored the importance of building supercomputers in the future that could handle computational and data-centric problems.

In an excellent overview of analytic methods (called Policy Analytics) to support public policy problem-solving and decision processes, Daniell et al. (2015) suggests that all roles of policy analysts can be matched with specific policy analytic methods, for example, text mining in the agenda-setting phase, simulation and optimisation modelling in the analysis phase, resource allocation modelling, and real-time operations optimisation in the policy implementation phase. Analytical methods are being applied successfully to the problem of organising emergency medical services in Milan, Italy, the evaluation of policies to mitigate the effects of excessive alcohol consumption, and the problem of allocating resources after humanitarian disasters.

Business decision-making: According to their landmark 2006 book *Business Wire* (2006), Pfeffer and Sutton argue that business decisions are frequently based on hope or fear, the past experience of senior leaders, intuition, beliefs, and ideology. They show how companies can improve performance and competitiveness through evidence-based management.

Examples of the use of analytics to support better decision-making in organisations abound today. The ones presented here are from an excellent presentation by Doug Laney, Gartner Distinguished Analyst (Laney, 2015).

Preventive Maintenance: Pemex monitors water level, pressure, temperature, flow, PH, conductivity, and turbidity, conducts chemical analysis to calculate cooling tower efficiency, monitors vibration motors and pumps, and runs predictive analytics to reduce refinery issues and unplanned maintenance. As a result, refinery downtime was reduced and 960 hours per year were saved in manual monitoring per refinery.

Program Management: Lockheed Martin correlated and analysed hundreds of metrics for thousands of programs to identify leading indicators of program performance, including specific words from a program manager's comments that were predictors of program downgrade, enabling program managers to apply course correction in advance. This approach allowed earlier program assessments, increased program foresight by three times and saved estimated losses of hundreds of millions of dollars from program delays.

Operations: Passur Aerospace uses publicly available data about weather, flight schedules, and other factors, plus proprietary data, including feeds from a network of passive radar stations installed near airports, to gather data about every plane in the local sky, and maintains an immense body of information over time. This allows Passur to improve on pilot-provided estimates times of arrival, by matching the current 'sky scenario' to prior scenarios, enabling improved efficiency of ground personnel scheduling and throughput of aircraft, which can yield several million dollars a year of savings per airport. One major airline is now avoiding two to three diversions per week.

Beverage Consistency: Variations in orange crops, sourcing and seasonality can create inconsistencies in orange juice. Coca Cola analyses data from up to one quintillion data points—including satellite images, weather, expected crop yields, cost pressures, regional preferences, and detailed data about the 600 flavours that comprise an orange, plus variables such as acidity and sweetness—and uses a precise dynamic formula to blend orange juice for consistent taste, including pulp content, for its $2B orange juice business. After a hurricane or freeze, it can re-plan the business in 5 to 10 minutes.

Law Enforcement: To increase Los Angeles police presence where it is most likely needed, the Los Angeles Police Department uses predictive

analytics on historical crime data and other factors. The software pre-
dicted twice as many crimes as experienced crime analysts in controlled trials and resulted in 33 percent reduction in burglaries and
21 percent reduction in violent crimes in a test region of Los Angeles,
compared to a slight increase in the rest of the city.

Deep learning makes predictions and does particularly well in complex environments, where the right decision depends on many variables (for example,
in an online retail environment with many customers and lots of information about every customer). Examples of such predictions are personalised
recommendations for customers based on forecasts of their preferences,
long-term customer loyalty and credit risk ratings of loan applicants. These
personal forecasts are useful even though the deep learning software doesn't
explain why people like the things they do and how to change what they
like (Yeomans, 2015).

Finance: In Europe, more than a dozen banks have replaced older statistical modelling approaches with machine learning techniques and,
in some cases, experienced 10 percent increases in sales of new products, 20 percent savings in capital expenditures, 20 percent increases
in cash collections, and 20 percent declines in churn. The banks have
achieved these gains by devising new recommendation engines for
clients in retailing and in small and medium-sized companies. They
have also built models that more accurately forecast who will cancel
service or default on their loans, and how best to intervene (Pyle and
Jose, 2015).

Retail: Walmart Labs helps online users find what they're looking for
more quickly. Product and category popularity scores are generated
from social media feeds using text mining with the use of machine
learning-based semantic search capability from the click stream of
45 million online shoppers per month. The Project 'Polaris' search
engine results in a 10 to 15 percent reduction in cart abandonment
(Laney, 2015).

Insurance: Machine learning is saving automobile insurers time and
resources, making assessment of external vehicle damage 'more standardised and objective, reducing the potential for human claims adjusters on the scene to be influenced by the parties involved in the
accident'. Alibaba, a subsidiary of Chinese e-commerce conglomerate
Alibaba Group, and Ant Financial recently staged a demonstration of
a machine learning tool that can assess collision damage. A photo of
the accident taken with a smartphone is sent to the insurer. The Ant
tool enables the insurance company to assess the extent of the damage, estimate the cost of repair and list nearby repair shops and their
prices to fix the vehicle. The tool took 6 seconds, compared with six

156

experienced human claims adjusters, who took six minutes and 48 seconds in 12 separate cases. Both machine and humans judged that one of the 12 cases required further investigation (Body Shop Business, 2017).

Talent Management: Talent management is becoming mission-critical in our rapidly changing environment. 'Know-how, innovation and experience constitute the main advantages that organisations can have over their competitors. The most talented employees drive these advantages. Attracting, developing and retaining talent is fundamental to a company remaining ahead of its competition' (Serendi, 2017). For this reason, companies are investing heavily in data-inclusion programs for all aspects of talent management. People analytics, also known as talent analytics, workforce analytics and HR analytics, is an evidence-based approach to making smarter decisions about employees that result in better outcomes for the organisation. People analytics and deep learning are transforming recruiting, retention, diversity and engagement. We present examples of recruiting here.

Recruiting is perhaps the most important application for machine learning today. Machine learning is being used to better match skills to openings, streamline the entire recruiting and hiring process, and improve candidate experience. Arya, a new recruiting platform, finds both hard skills and soft skills and learns who the ideal candidate is through a combination of machine learning, big data and behavioral pattern recognition. According to HR Technical Analyst Biro (2018), 'the myth that AI-powered recruiting is impersonal and inaccurate is just that: a misassumption about the power of AI. With the ability to greatly increase searches to radically cut down on searching time, as well as a way to reach out and develop a talent pipeline, AI enables recruiters to get back to what they know how to do best: spend time getting to know promising candidates, and find the best fit for each job. And for candidates, AI enables frequent contact and a faster process that improves their experience—and may just affect their decision to join your organization'. Because there can always be bad predictions, human oversight over HR decisions is a must. Though data-based recruiting was considered to be a way of removing biases, there is debate over whether machine learning helps remove human biases or not (Biswas, 2018).

Jenkins (2018) describes several tools, including Pymetrics, HireVue and Textio, that talent acquisition professionals must be equipped with to meet the expectations of Generation Z. Modern talent acquisition platforms use advanced technologies like gamification, on-demand video interviews, real-time online coding interviews, and predictive analytics to cut recruiting costs, reduce screening time, and increase the pool of qualified applicants. Textio is an augmented writing platform that is fueled by massive quantities of data, contributed by companies across industries and around the world, and a predictive engine that uses these data to create highly effective job listings and provides real-time guidance on how to improve them (by removing bias and gender discrimination). Broadridge Financial Solutions, a company that regularly appears on Fortune's World's Most Admired Companies list and boasts a $9 billion market capitalisation, doubled their number of qualified applicants using Textio, enabling the company to hire the best and most diverse candidates possible (Coughlin, 2017).

Data inclusion, inclusive leadership and culture

Lange and Tapia (2016) state, 'the 21st century leader is, by definition, an inclusive leader'; 'if diversity is "the mix," then inclusion is making the mix work by leveraging the wealth of knowledge, insights, and perspectives in an open, trusting, and diverse workplace'; and 'greater diversity and inclusion spark innovation and advances in product development'. The evidence supporting diversity and inclusion is clear (Suzuno, 2017): 67 percent of candidates want to join a diverse team; 57 percent of employees want to prioritise diversity; inclusive companies enjoy 2.3 times higher cash flow; 35 percent of diverse companies outperform homogeneous ones; inclusive companies are 1.7 times more likely to be innovation leaders; and diverse companies are 70 percent more likely to capture new markets.

Today we have access to vast amounts of relevant data and the computing technologies to make good, timely, decisions. Adopting a data-inclusion strategy at all levels of the organisation should empower employees and improve participation in decision-making and engagement, resulting in the outcomes listed above.

- *Employee Participation*: Tennant (2015) writes, 'but if you really want employee buy-in and loyalty, give them something that will enable them to feel a sense of ownership and participation in the company's business strategy: put analytics in the hands of every employee. That piece of advice was my key takeaway from a recent interview with Arijit Sengupta, CEO of BeyondCore, a data analytics company in San Mateo, California'. Though we haven't seen real evidence to support this statement, it makes sense. In our rapidly changing world, a centralised command and control structure will not work because of the speed at which decisions have to be made. One way to improve responsiveness is to enable, data-based decisions using analytics at every level of the organisation, down to the individual. This decentralisation may also make employees feel part of the decision-making process, resulting in improved employee engagement.
- *Engagement*: Companies are using machine learning and natural language processing software to get continual insights into how their employees feel about their workplace and how engaged they are by including

158

insights from seemingly unimportant statements that were previously considered to be too vague or emotion-based to be analysable in any realistic way (Flagella, 2017).

- *Empowerment*: Cisco's Talent Cloud provides employees with the tools and insights to take more control and initiative in their career development. Employees can create their own personal profile, add their skills and competencies, and assess these skills against roles. This helps employees determine suitable career paths within Cisco and highlights learning opportunities that will help them meet their career goals. Managers can also assess the skills of their team members and identify development opportunities for individual employees to explore (Larsen, 2016).

- *Continuous Development*: Workday builds personalised training recommendations for employees based on a company's needs, market trends, and employee specifics (Workday, 2016). The Workday Learning application offers a personalised, meaningful learning experience for organisations to encourage career development at every stage of the employee life-cycle. Using rich context the service 'allows organisations to create data-driven learning experiences that can predictively steer employees toward content that helps them grow. For the learner this means continuous development and enrichment, and for the business, the evolution of workplace learning from a cost center to a growth engine' (Workday, 2016). In the not-too-distant future, machine-learning systems could analyse a user's learning patterns and provide tailored coaching to best fit these patterns.

Though a data-inclusion strategy holds tremendous potential, its effectiveness will depend on fostering the right organisational culture and raising awareness of novel ethical issues that can arise.

Organisational Culture: Through a survey of 600 businesses and IT executives from 70 countries, Balboni et al. (2013) determined that it takes the right alignment of strategy, technology and organisational structure to enable, create and amplify value from big data and analytics. They found that the critical levers for moving an organisation from discovery to value creation were: establishing a fact-based decision-making culture; creating confidence in data through governance and security; and, surprisingly, creating trustworthy relationships (trust between people in the organisation, not trust in the quality of data, the reliability of the analysis, or the veracity of data). Pitney (2018) identified five cultural facets that must be addressed to realise the full potential of data inclusion: understand and embrace the value of analytics; establish the tone from the top; encourage a culture of continuous experimentation, evaluation and improvement; establish a collaborative environment; and schedule continued education and learning designed to empower decision-makers to harness data-based insights. Based on these findings, we can conclude that culture is a big hurdle, but one that can be overcome through data inclusion and executive commitment.

Organisational culture is cultivated from the top down. Starting from the top, leaders at every level must demonstrate their commitment to adopt a fact-based approach to decision-making; be a visible role model; create a receptive environment; set realistic goals, metrics, expectations, and priorities; communicate; and facilitate.

Leaders must adopt a data-inclusion strategy that is fully aligned with the business strategy and invest in the required technical capabilities to enable value capture. Two key elements are: rigorous system of enterprise-level standards and data-management best practices to ensure the timeliness, quality, security, and privacy of data and create confidence in them, and a platform capable of handling high volume, high velocity and structured and unstructured data and of incorporating the required modelling, simulation, analytics, and machine-learning tools that can evolve with technology and changing business needs.

To foster a culture of continuous improvement, leaders must encourage experimentation and agile development, introduce data inclusion incrementally, and expand its scope iteratively and continuously and must recognise and reward people who are willing to try the new data-inclusion approach, who demonstrate its value to their work, generate unbiased metrics and make evidence-based decisions.

Data inclusion is most effective when applied across the entire enterprise. Leaders must foster a collaborative environment and can use the data-inclusion strategy to break traditional silos by encouraging business units to assess the value of the data available from other business units, share data and analytics across the organisation and empower employees to access analytic results that can improve the quality of their work.

Finally, in an environment of rapid change and disruption, continuous learning is critical. All employees (including managers and executives) must be aware of the rapid changes in technology and its application and possible ethical issues that may arise (see the following).

Ethical Issues: Though there are more questions than answers at this stage, this section describes the ethical issues that can arise with a pervasive use of data inclusion. Our goal is to increase the awareness of managers, leaders and individuals.

Duhigg (2012) gives one example. A retail chain identified about 25 products that, when analyzed together, allowed the prediction of a woman's pregnancy with high levels of confidence and also provided an estimated due date that accurately fell within a narrow window. To increase sales, the retailer sent out coupons to pregnant customers with the mailings of the coupons correlated with very specific stages of their pregnancy. This strategy resulted in alerting the father of a pregnant teenager—who, prior to seeing the coupons, was unaware that his daughter was pregnant. The coupon program had the unanticipated consequence of violating the privacy of customers.

Since digital data can easily be repurposed for new, previously unantici-pated analyses and researchers are increasingly using material posted on social media, gaining informed consent in big data research on humans is challenging.

A classic example of the controversy around informed consent is the study on emotional contagion (Kramer et al., 2014) in which the authors state, 'the experiment manipulated the extent to which people (N = 689,003) were exposed to emotional expressions in their News Feed. This tested whether exposure to emotions led people to change their own posting behaviors' (2014: 1). The study found that the content presented affected what those users posted on Facebook. More negative newsfeeds led to more negative posts and more positive ones led to positive posts. The study concluded 'that emotional states can be transferred to others via emotional contagion, leading people to experience the same emotions without their awareness' (ibid.). The paper resulted in a big public controversy about big data research ethics, with experts criticising and defending the work. Jouhki et al. (2016) found:

> The experiment caused ethical concerns within and outside academia mainly for two intertwined reasons, the first revolving around the idea of research as manipulation, and the second focusing on the problematic definition of informed consent. The article concurs with recent research that the era of social media and Big Data research are posing a significant challenge to research ethics, the practice and views of which are grounded in the pre social media era, and reflect the classical ethical stances of utilitarianism and deontology.

Metcalf et al. (2016) argue that big data stretches our concepts of ethical research and that 'there is a substantial disjunction between the familiar infrastructures and conceptual frameworks of research ethics and the emerg-ing epistemic conditions of big data'. The report raises important questions that need to be addressed. For example, should human data science be regarded as human-subjects research? How is big data redefining public benefits from research? How can these benefits be assessed more precisely? How should data privacy and security scientists approach illicitly gained, publicly available data? What are the options for self-regulation in data science?

Clark et al. (2015) provide an excellent overview of the ethics of research and the large impact that digitalisation has on ethics and concludes that digi-tal data requires rethinking the adequacy of past practices to ensure ethical research and provides guidelines that can help investigators, institutes, and ethics review committees.

Though we have not discussed cyber security in this chapter, it should be noted that data security affects privacy more than ever in a world of massive digitalisation. Data from different sources are correlated and have different levels of security increasing the likelihood of security breaches and the resulting loss of privacy and misuse for unethical activities.

As deep learning gains acceptance and leads to increased levels of automated decision-making, new ethical issues arise, since the logic by which deep learning algorithms arrive at certain decisions often cannot be explained in human-understandable terms. One can imagine numerous scenarios, not far from reality, in which machine learning systems can actually introduce biases, because the data used to train machine learning systems has built-in bias. For example, if a university uses historic admissions data to create an automated machine learning admissions system, biases in the old admissions process will be reflected in the new, automated system. It may be nearly impossible to understand why, or even how, an automated mortgage algorithm judges applicants based on their race.

There are real examples as well. Computer scientists at Carnegie Mellon University found that significantly fewer women than men were shown online ads promising them help getting jobs that paid more than $200,000 per year (Spice, 2015). ProPublica found that software used across the country to predict future criminals is biased against black people. The algorithm is particularly likely to falsely flag black defendants as future criminals, wrongly labelling them this way at almost twice the rate of white defendants. Courts rely on the software in different ways but, since the software is proprietary, the logic behind the predictions is unknown (Crawford, 2016).

In an excellent piece, Bostrom and Yudkowsky address these issues of

> Responsibility, transparency, auditability, incorruptibility, predictability, and a tendency to not make innocent victims scream with helpless frustration: all criteria that apply to humans performing social functions; all criteria that must be considered in an algorithm intended to replace human judgement of social functions; all criteria that may not appear in a journal of machine learning considering how an algorithm scales up to more computers.
>
> (2011: 3)

Though there are more questions than answers at this stage, it is important for managers, leaders and individuals to be aware of the new ethical issues associated with big data, analytics and machine learning.

Human–computer collaboration

We have established that data inclusion can be an effective tool to substantially improve decision-making and implement a strategy of diversity and inclusion, resulting in improved business outcomes, provided organisational culture and ethics are properly addressed. In this section, we go beyond using computers as a tool and speculate on the nature of future interactions between humans and computers and the benefits that can accrue to society as a whole.

Game-Playing Computers: It is instructive to consider the history of computers and humans pitting themselves against each other in games of increasing complexity. The history of chess-playing computers illustrates that computers and humans working together represent the winning combination in chess. Computers are required to rapidly evaluate board positions and ingenious humans are required to program the computers and teach them essential strategies.

Two decades ago, in 1997, an IBM computer, Deep Blue, beat the then–world chess champion Gary Kasparov, having lost the previous year. The computer did not play chess intuitively or creatively like the world champion it beat. The number of legal chess positions is $10**40$ and the number of different possible games is $10**120$; brute-force computing was not feasible. The computer won based on ingenious programming and the ability to evaluate 200 million possible moves per second. A state-of-the art PC in 1995 could play very decent chess and a form of chess known as 'freestyle chess' became popular. That year the online site Playchess.com hosted a 'freestyle' chess tournament in which anyone could compete in teams with other players or computers. Kasparov (2010) states (page 5), 'the surprise came at the conclusion of the event. The winner was revealed to be not a grandmaster with a state-of-the-art PC but a pair of amateur American chess players using three computers at the same time. Their skill at manipulating and "coaching" their computers to look very deeply into positions effectively counteracted the superior chess understanding of their grandmaster opponents and the greater computational power of other participants. Weak human + machine + better process was superior to a strong computer alone and, more remarkably, superior to a strong human + machine + inferior process'.

IBM's Watson gained the world's attention in 2011 when it defeated two champions, by a wide margin, at the game of Jeopardy! on live TV. Since 2011, Watson has been used in several industries, especially healthcare. IBM and its collaborators recently demonstrated the clinical utility of Watson in oncology and for clinical trial matching (IBM, 2017b). Watson exemplifies how humans and computers can collaborate to make decisions. At its core, Watson is an open-domain question answering system that can answer questions posed by humans in a natural language about nearly anything in close to real time.

Watson accepts questions posed by the user in natural language and provides the user with a response (or a set of responses) by generating and evaluating various hypotheses around different interpretations of the question and possible answers to it. Unlike keyword-based search engines, which simply retrieve relevant documents, Watson gleans context from the question to provide the user with precise and relevant answers, along with confidence ratings and supporting evidence.

(Deloitte, 2015: 9)

Watson combines three transformational technologies: it understands natural language and human communication, generates and evaluates evidence-based hypotheses, and adapts and learns from user selections and responses. The process for decision-making involves the following: the decision-maker asks a question in natural language; Watson understands the question and produces possible answers and evidence (considers large amounts of data—Electronic Medical Records, literature), analyses evidence and computes confidence (without bias) and then delivers the response, evidence and confidence to the decision maker while identifying any missing information; and the decision-maker considers the answer and the evidence and makes a decision or provides more information to make a better decision (Kohn, 2012). Thus, Watson can learn from very large volumes of unstructured data dynamically and decision-makers can get evidence-based advice from Watson on complex issues and improve the confidence level in Watson's advice interactively. (The downside is that teaching Watson the 'language' of each domain, e.g., oncology, is time-consuming.)

Coming back to board games, Google's AlphaGo program uses deep learning to excel at Go, a complex board game that is much harder for machines than chess. The experience of champions defeated by AlphaGo indicates they can improve their Go skills by playing against AlphaGo. In 2016, AlphaGo defeated Lee Sedol, one of the best Go players in the world. Mr. Sedol was surprised to lose the match four games to one and admitted that AlphaGo had given him new insights into the game: 'the typical, traditional, classical beliefs of how to play—I've come to question them a bit' (Economist, 2016). Interestingly, Fan Hui, the European champion and de facto trainer of AlphaGo, lost five matches to the program earlier in 2016 when he was ranked 633 in the world. Studying AlphaGo's game inspired Fan Hui to change his own game and his ranking jumped to 300 (Zeiler, 2016). AlphaGo was training Mr. Hui. Ke Jie, the reigning top-ranked Go player, who was skeptical of AlphaGo's capabilities in 2016, acknowledges that human beings are no match for computers in Go and that, 'Go players should now start to learn from computers to improve their skills' (Huang, 2017).

The chess examples illustrate that computers are required for computationally intense tasks and humans for ingenious programming. AlphaGo illustrates that computers can excel at very complex strategy games like

Go, can help improve players' skills, and require supervised training. Watson illustrates that humans and computers working together can be a very powerful combination, not just to win at games, but to arrive at better evidence-based decisions. They can learn from each other and thus establish a virtuous cycle.

The Inclusive Leader of the Future: Generalising what we have learned from game-playing computers and the other examples presented in this chapter, we speculate that the most effective and inclusive leader, in a future of rapid digitalisation and change, must necessarily be a collaborative human-computer system:

- Humans describe the vision and goals, set the context, think out of the box, continue to reinforce the organisation's vision and goals, live the values, communicate effectively, exercise emotional control, manage uncertainty and chaos, and create a receptive environment for evidence-based decision-making.
- Powerful supercomputers and cognitive computers find solutions to very complex problems; identify trends in high-volume, high-variety and high-velocity data from many different sources; and predict future outcomes, specifying their level of confidence and explaining their reasoning.
- Collaboration that occurs across an intuitive, usable interface through speech and natural language produces new insights, better decisions and novel solutions.

This inclusive evidence-based system can discourage unethical decisions by making the decision-making process transparent and visible to all stakeholders but will be challenged when dealing with ideologues and inherently unethical players.

There is an ongoing debate on whether computers with artificial general intelligence will take over the world or whether we should focus on the assistive role of artificial intelligence, emphasising the fact that it is designed to enhance human intelligence rather than replace it. Notable personalities have expressed strong fears about the future of general artificial intelligence and its impact, fueling a human versus computer debate. Elon Musk, founder of Tesla Motors and aerospace manufacturer SpaceX, claimed that humans would become nothing more than pets for the superintelligent computers that we helped create (Wakefield, 2015). Steven Hawking told the BBC, 'the primitive forms of artificial intelligence we already have, have proved very useful. But I think the development of full artificial intelligence could spell the end of the human race' (Ingham and Mollard, 2014). The debate is beyond the scope of this chapter, but we point out the following: big data and supercomputers can cost-effectively solve complex problems through simulation. Humans cannot deal with this complexity but have complementary characteristics: thinking, creativity, spontaneity, adaptability, and improvisation.

Humans are needed where computers cannot explain the logic behind their decisions. Since machine-learning computers provide reliable answers only when the data is complete and representative of the context in which they are deployed, there will be many scenarios where a human must be in the loop. For example, if a driverless car ends up in a unique situation that was not encountered during training, human judgement will be required.

Jankel (2015) argues that computers will never create disruptive innovations because breakthroughs are unpredictable: 'countless ground-breaking artists—from multiple Booker Prizewinner Hilary to Mantel to Isabel Allende; from Ludwig Van Beethoven to John Lennon—have made it abundantly clear that they have never been able to predict what creations will emerge next; and indeed, know where they really come from'.

Mamodia (2014) writes,

> We must be able to set the appropriate context to ask real questions if any of this massive quantity of data is to inform change that truly matters. . . . So what is it that can make data useful by setting an appropriate context? It may be surprising to some that the real game changer is . . . human beings armed with the right thoughtful questions and some game changing technology of course.

Using baseball general manager Billy Beane as an example, Florian Zettelmeyer (2014), professor of Marketing at the Kellogg School of Management at Northwestern University, argues that 'Big Data is a leadership problem'. Driven by a very small budget, Beane relied on statistics and analytics to predict high-run scorers undervalued by baseball scouts and in 2002 built a world-class team using this approach. Zettelmeyer states, 'what was new in 2002 was that a leader, Billy Beane, had the courage to use the insight gleaned from data analytics to drive the way he ran his business. It took courage both because what the analytics said went against the conventional wisdom of how to run a successful baseball team and because Beane had to overcome a lot of reluctance inside the organization to changing its approach'. Marina Gorbis conjectures, 'we'll come to understand ourselves at a new level as we build machines that can do different human tasks. We'll enter into a new kind of partnership with these machines—one that will shine light on the unique comparative advantages of humans: thinking, creativity, spontaneity, adaptability, and improvisation' (2011: para. 1, page 6).

Though the debate will and should continue, we believe that that the community must focus on augmented intelligence and explore the enormous potential to amplify human intelligence, pursuing incremental and continuous improvement through prototyping real systems, focusing on the human–computer interface, incorporating multidisciplinary perspectives and addressing the issue of trust in computers.

Conclusions and future research

This chapter provided an overview of big data and the relevant computing technologies of modeling, simulation, analytics, and machine learning that can be applied to gain insights from the data, with examples of how these technologies are being applied to transform public policymaking, business decision-making and talent management. We define data inclusion as including data and the relevant computing technologies as a core element of decision-making at all levels of an organisation. We argued that pursuing a data-inclusion strategy will lead to more participation, greater inclusiveness and substantially improve the quality of decision-making, resulting in better business outcomes. Fostering a fact-based decision-making culture is an important barrier. We discussed how leaders can overcome this challenge and highlighted the ethical issues that can arise with a data-inclusion strategy. We suggest that 'data inclusion' be introduced incrementally and evolved continuously, following the guidelines for establishing a fact-based decision-making culture. We note that there are many more questions than answers on ethical issues and more consciousness-raising is required.

We speculate that the 'inclusive leader of the future' will be a system of humans and computers that interact in natural ways, through speech, text and vision; learn from each other; and collectively are more effective than either humans or computers acting alone. Computers handle the tasks of sifting through massive amounts of data, analysing it, finding patterns, predicting outcomes based on complex models of the world, and making recommendations to humans. The humans set the values, vision, goals, and context and bring creativity, out-of-the-box thinking, and compassion, to the decision-making. Dialogue between the humans and computers refines insights and results in better decisions. Much more work is needed to establish this speculation.

A key barrier to overcome is trust among humans and computers. The benefits of augmented intelligence will not be fully realised until humans learn to trust computers and not fear them. The inclusive leadership model presented above will not gain traction either, for the same reason. On the other hand, if humans trust computers and have a commitment to improve and seek the truth, perhaps technology can help improve intellectual honesty (using evidence-based processes); decision-making (by tracking motivations, expected results and actual outcomes); and emotional intelligence by providing feedback on one's emotional state (as detected through speech, text and body language analysis).

Everett et al. (2017) determined that it may not be enough for us that machines make the right judgements—even the ideal judgements. We want those judgements to be made as a result of the same psychological processes that cause us to make them: namely, the emotional reactions and intuitive responses that have evolved to make us distinctly moral creatures. Until technology is capable of this feat, any attempts at making ethically autonomous machines will likely be met with suspicion.

Research shows that evidence-based algorithms more accurately predict the future than do human forecasters. Yet, when forecasters are deciding whether to use a human forecaster or a statistical algorithm, they often choose the human forecaster. People are especially averse to algorithmic forecasters after seeing them perform, even when they see them outperform a human forecaster. This is because people more quickly lose confidence in algorithmic than human forecasters after seeing them make the same mistake. 'People don't lose confidence in themselves when they are wrong but they do in computers' (Dietvorst et al., 2014). Contrast this with the experiment on emergency procedures to determine whether human participants would evacuate on their own or follow a robot's guidance. People overwhelmingly trusted the robot, even in a case where the robot clearly broke down as it was leading an evacuation. 'It is concerning that participants are so willing to follow a robot in a potentially dangerous situation even when it has recently made mistakes', wrote researchers (LaFrance, 2016).

McAfee (2013) is convinced that 'we should turn many of our decisions, predictions, diagnoses, and judgements—both the trivial and the consequential–over to the algorithms. There's just no controversy any more about whether doing so will give us better results'. He observes that this shift will take 'transparency, time, and consequences: transparency to make clear how much worse "expert" judgement is, time to let this news diffuse and sink in, and consequences so that we care enough about bad decisions to go through the wrenching change needed to make better ones'.

Psychological projection is a theory in psychology in which unwanted thoughts, motivations, desires, and feelings are displaced onto another person—where they can then appear as a threat from the external world (Freud, 1988). Do we fear computers because we are apathetic, dishonorable and unethical and we project these qualities onto computers? Or is this because 'the mind is a machine for jumping to conclusions' as Nobel Prize winner Kahneman argues? (Winerman, 2012)

Trust in computers is a complex issue that will require cross-disciplinary, experimental research across several disciplines: human–computer interface technologies, cognitive sciences, ethics, psychology, and social sciences.

Note

1 Acknowledgement: I would like to thank Professor Manmohan D. Chaubey, School of Business, Robert Morris University; Professor William Knack, SUNY Old Westbury; Nita Narayan, social justice lawyer and advocate; Mr. Atma Ram; Dr. Satish Gambhir, independent IT consultant; and Geeta Agerwala, whose reviews and comments significantly improved the quality of this chapter.

References

Agerwala, T. 2014a. 'Data Centric Systems: The Next Paradigm in Computing', Keynote, 43rd International Conference on Parallel Processing, Minneapolis, MN, September, http://icpp.cs.umn.edu/agerwala.pdf (accessed on 29 January 2019).

Agerwala, T. 2014b. 'A New Paradigm for Computing: Data-Centric Systems', *Wired Magazine*, www.wired.com/insights/2014/12/data-centric-systems/

Balboni, F., G. Finch, C.R. Reese and R. Shockley. 2013. 'Analytics: A Blueprint for Value', IBM Institute for Business Value. https://mdi.missouristate.edu/assets/mdi/Analytics-A_Blueprint_for_Value.PDF

Biro, M. 2018. 'How AI Makes Hiring More Accurate and More Personal', https://goarya.com/blog/ai-makes-hiring-accurate-personal/

Biswas, S. 2018. 'Can Artificial Intelligence Eliminate Bias in Hiring?', www.hrtechnologist.com/articles/recruitment-onboarding/can-artificial-intelligence-eliminate-bias-in-hiring/

Body Shop Business. 2017. 'Artificial Intelligence System Can Assess Collision Damage in Six Seconds: Alibaba' (July), www.bodyshopbusiness.com/artificial-intelligence-system-can-assess-collision-damage-six-seconds-alibaba/

Bostrom, N. and E. Yudkowsky. 2011. 'The Ethics of Artificial Intelligence', in W. Ramsey and K. Frankish (eds.), *Draft for Cambridge Handbook of Artificial Intelligence*. Cambridge CB2 8BS, UK: Cambridge University Press, https://nickbostrom.com/ethics/artificial-intelligence.pdf

Business Wire. 2006. 'Corporate Management Based on Facts', in J. Pfeffer and R.I. Sutton (eds.), *Hard Facts, Dangerous Half-Truths, and Total Nonsense: Profiting from Evidence-Based Management*. Cambridge: Harvard Business School Press, www.gsb.stanford.edu/faculty-research/books/hard-facts-dangerous-half-truths

Castle, N. 2017. 'Supervised vs. Unsupervised Machine Learning', DataScience.com, www.datascience.com/blog/supervised-and-unsupervised-machine-learning-algorithms

Castro, D. and J. New. 2016. 'The Promise of Artificial Intelligence', Center for Data Innovation, www2.datainnovation.org/2016-promise-of-ai.pdf

Castro, T. and T. Korte. 2013. 'Data Innovation 101: An Introduction to the Technologies and Policies Supporting Data-Driven Innovation', Center for Data Innovation, www2.datainnovation.org/2013-data-innovation-101.pdf

Center for Disease Control (CDC). 2017. 'Understanding Evidence: Evidence Based Decision-Making Summary', Division of Violence Prevention, https://vetoviolence.cdc.gov/apps/evidence/docs/EBDM_82412.pdf

Clark, K., M. Duckham, M. Guillemin, A. Hunter, J. McVernon, C. O'Keefe, C. Pitkin, S. Prawer, R. Sinnott, D. Warr and J. Waycott. 2015. *Guidelines for the Ethical Use of Digital Data in Human Research.* Melbourne: The University of Melbourne, https://publications.csiro.au/rpr/pub?pid=csiro:EP152562

Corbin, K. 2014. 'How CIOs Can Prepare for Healthcare "Data Tsunami"', www.cio.com/article/2860072/healthcare/how-cios-can-prepare-for-healthcare-data-tsunami.html

Coughlin, M. 2017. 'How Broadridge Doubled Qualified Applicants', https://textio.ai/how-broadridge-doubled-qualified-applicants-d9d9c638c007

Crawford, K. 2016. 'Artificial Intelligence's White Guy Problem', *The New York Times Sunday Review*, www.nytimes.com/2016/06/26/opinion/sunday/artificial-intelligences-white-guy-problem.html

Daniell, K., A. Morton and D. Rios. 2015. 'Policy Analysis and Policy Analytics' [Abstract], Annals of Operations Research, www.researchgate.net/publication/279243943_Policy_analysis_and_policy_analytics

Deloitte. 2015. 'Disruption Ahead: Deloitte's Point of View on IBM Watson', www2.deloitte.com/content/dam/Deloitte/us/Documents/about-deloitte/us-ibm-watson-client.pdf

Dietvorst, B.J., J.P. Simmons and C. Massey. 2014. 'Algorithm Aversion: People Erroneously Avoid Algorithms after Seeing Them Err' (forthcoming), *Journal of Experimental Psychology: General*, https://ssrn.com/abstract=2466040 or http://dx.doi.org/10.2139/ssrn.2466040

Duhigg, C. 2012. 'How Companies Steal Your Secrets', *The New York Times Magazine*, www.nytimes.com/2012/02/19/magazine/shopping-habits.html?mcubz=0

Economist. 2016. 'Artificial Intelligence and Go: A Game-Changing Result', Science and Technology, www.economist.com/news/science-and-technology/21694883-alphagos-masters-taught-it-game-electrifying-match-shows-what

Everett, J., D. Pizarro and M. Crockett. 2017. 'Why Are We Reluctant to Trust Robots?', Psychology Headquarters, www.theguardian.com/science/head-quarters/2017/apr/24/why-are-we-reluctant-to-trust-robots

Expert System. 2017. 'What Is Machine Learning? A Definition', www.expertsystem.com/machine-learning-definition/

Flagella, D. 2017. 'Machine Learning in Human Resources: Applications and Trends', Techemergence, https://emerj.com/ai-sector-overviews/machine-learning-in-human-resources/

Freud, S. 1988. 'Case Histories 2', Angela Richards (ed.), Penguin Freud Library. Published 1990 by Penguin (first published 1895) Original Title Case Histories: Vol. 2, 'Rat Man', Schreber, 'Wolf Man', Female Homosexuality ISBN 0140137998 (ISBN13: 9780140137996).

Gantz, J. and D. Reinsel. 2012. 'The Digital Universe in 2020: Big Data, Bigger Digital Shadows, and Biggest Growth in the Far East', www.emc.com/collateral/analyst-reports/idc-the-digital-universe-in-2020.pdf

Gorbis, M. 2011. 'Human Plus Machine', Institute for the Future, Technology Horizons Program, www.iftf.org/uploads/media/Human_Plus_Machine_MG_sm.pdf

Groves, D., R.L. Lempert, D.W. May, J.R. Leek and J. Syme. 2014. 'Using High-Performance Computing to Support Water Resource Planning: A Workshop Demonstration of Real-Time Analytic Facilitation for the Colorado River Basin', www.rand.org/content/dam/rand/pubs/conf_proceedings/CF300/CF339/RAND_CF339.pdf

Huang, Z. 2017. 'AlphaGo AI Secretively Won More Than 50 Straight Games against the World's Top Go Players', https://qz.com/877721/the-ai-master-bested-the-worlds-top-go-players-and-then-revealed-itself-as-googles-alphago-in-disguise/

Ingham, R. and P. Mollard. 2014. 'Experts Are Divided on Stephen Hawking's Claim That Artificial Intelligence Could End Humanity', *Business Insider*, www.businessinsider.com/afp-artificial-intelligence-hawkings-fears-stir-debate-2014-12

Inside Big Data. 2017. 'The Exponential Growth of Data' (Editorial Team), https://insidebigdata.com/2017/02/16/the-exponential-growth-of-data/

International Business Machines Corporation (IBM). 2012. 'Extracting Business Value from the 4 Vs of Big Data', 4Vs_Infographic_final, www.ibmbigdatahub.com/sites/default/files/infographic_file/4Vs_Infographic_final.pdf

International Business Machines Corporation (IBM). 2016. 'Analytics: Dawn of the Cognitive Era', www-01.ibm.com/common/ssi/cgi-bin/ssialias?htmlfid=GBE03773USEN

International Business Machines Corporation (IBM). 2017a. 'Artificial Intelligence, Machine Learning and Cognitive Computing', www.ibm.com/blogs/nordic-msp/artificial-intelligence-machine-learning-cognitive-computing/

International Business Machines Corporation (IBM). 2017b. 'At ASCO 2017 Clinicians Present New Evidence about Watson Cognitive Technology and Cancer Care', Press Release, www-03.ibm.com/press/us/en/pressrelease/52502.wss

International Data Corporation (IDC). 2012. 'IDC Worldwide Big Data Technology and Services 2012–2015 Forecast', http://ec.europa.eu/information_society/newsroom/cf/dae/document.cfm?doc_id=6242

Jankel, N.S. 2015. 'AI vs. Human Intelligence: Why Computers Will Never Create Disruptive Innovations', *Huffpost*, www.huffingtonpost.com/nick-seneca-jankel/ai-vs-human-intelligence-_b_6741814.html

Jenkins, R. 2018. 'Recruiting Generation Z? You'll Want to Use These', www.inc.com/ryan-jenkins/8-generation-z-recruiting-tools-you-need-to-know.html

Jouhki, J., E. Lauk, M. Penttinen, N. Sormanen and T. Uskali. 2016. 'Facebook's Emotional Contagion Experiment as a Challenge to Research Ethics', *Media and Communication* 4(4): 75–85, www.cogitatiopress.com/mediaandcommunication/article/download/579/579

Kasparov, G. 2010. 'The Chess Master and the Computer', in D. Rasskin-Gutman (ed.), *Chess Metaphors: Artificial Intelligence and the Human Mind*, translated from the Spanish by Deborah Klosky, *New York Times Book Review*, p. 205. Cambridge, MA: MIT Press, https://marom.net.technion.ac.il/files/2016/07/Kasparov-2010.pdf

Kohn, M.S. 2012. 'Putting IBM Watson to Work in Healthcare', IBM Corp., www.slideshare.net/AndersQuitzauIbm/ibm-watson-in-healthcare

Kramer, A.D.I., J.E. Guillory and J.T. Hancock. 2014. 'Experimental Evidence of Massive-Scale Emotional Contagion through Social Networks', *Proceedings of the National Academy of Sciences of the United States of America*, 111(24), www. pnas.org/content/111/24/8788.full

LaFrance, A. 2016. 'The Human-Robot Trust Paradox', *The Atlantic*, www.theatlan tic.com/technology/archive/2016/03/humans-robots-future/472749/

Laney, D. 2015. 'Innovating with Analytics: 40 Real Examples in 40 mins', Gartner Business Intelligence & Analytics Summit, 30 March–1 April, Las Vegas, New York, www.gartner.com/webinar/3163318

Lange, D. and A. Tapia. 2016. 'The Inclusive Leader', Korn Ferry Research, www. kornferry.com/institute/the-inclusive-leader

Larsen, J. 2016. 'How Cisco Is Getting to Know Each of Its 70,000 Employees', TLNT Talent Management and HR, www.tlnt.com/how-cisco-is-getting-to-know-each-of-its-70000-employees/

Larzelere II, A.R. 2009. 'Delivering Insight: The History of the Accelerated Strategic Computing Initiative (ASCI)', Lawrence Livermore National Laboratory, https:// asc.llnl.gov/asc_history/

Lasswell, H.D. 1936. *Who Gets What, When and How*. New York: Whittlesey House, www.policysciences.org/classics/politics.pdf

LeCun, Y., Y. Bengio and G. Hinton. 2015. 'Deep Learning', *Nature*, 521: 436–44, www.nature.com/nature/journal/v521/n7553/full/nature14539.html?foxtrotcall back=true

Mamodia, R. 2014. 'It's Not Just the Data: It's the Questions: On the Business Power of Human Thoughtfulness Meets Cognitive Computing', Brillio, www.brillio.com/ insights/post/just-data-questions-business-power-human-thoughtfulness-meets-cognitive-computing

Mannel, B. 2017. 'Supercomputers Helping Researchers Predict Climate Change', www.hpcwire.com/solution_content/hpe/weather-climate/supercomputers-helping-researchers-predict-climate-change/

Mauro, A.D., M. Greco, M. Grimaldi. 2014. 'What Is Big Data?', A Consensual Defi-nition and a Review of Key Research Topics, 4th International Conference on Inte-grated Information, September, doi:10.13140/2.1.2341.5048, www.researchgate. net/publication/265775800_What_is_Big_Data_A_Consensual_Definition_ and_a_Review_of_Key_Research_Topics

McAfee, A. 2013. 'Big Data's Biggest Challenge? Convincing People NOT to Trust Their Judgment', *Harvard Business Review*, https://hbr.org/2013/12/big-datas-biggest-challenge-convincing-people-not-to-trust-their-judgment

Metcalf, J., E.F. Keller and D. Boyd. 2016. 'Perspectives on Big Data, Ethics, and Soci-ety', Council for Big Data, Ethics, and Society, http://bdes.datasociety.net/council-output/perspectives-on-big-data-ethics-and-society/

Morgan, L. 2015. 'Big Data: 6 Real-Life Business Cases', Information Week, www. informationweek.com/software/enterprise-applications/big-data-6-real-life-business-cases/d/d-id/1320590?image_number=7

National Institute of Science and Technology (NIST). 2015. *NIST Big Data Interop-erability Framework: Volume 1*, http://dx.doi.org/10.6028/NIST.SP.1500-1

Omnicore. 2017. 'Twitter by the Numbers: Stats, Demographics & Fun Facts', www. omnicoreagency.com/twitter-statistics/

Peng, L. and V. Gulshan. 2016. 'Deep Learning for Detection of Diabetic Eye Disease', https://research.googleblog.com/2016/11/deep-learning-for-detection-of-diabetic. html

Pitney, R. 2018. 'Developing an Analytics Strategy: The Role of Culture', www.elderresearch.com/blog/analytics-strategy-and-the-role-of-culture

President's Information Technology Advisory Committee (PITAC). 2005. 'Computational Science: Ensuring America's Competitiveness', Report to the President, www.nitrd.gov/pitac/reports/20050609_computational/computational.pdf

Press, G. 2014. '12 Big Data Definitions: What's Yours', www.forbes.com/sites/gilpress/2014/09/03/12-big-data-definitions-whats-yours/#285c212113ae

Pyle, D. and C.S. Jose. 2015. 'An Executive's Guide to Machine Learning', *McKinsey Quarterly*, June, www.mckinsey.com/industries/high-tech/our-insights/an-executives-guide-to-machine-learning

RAND Corp. 2016. 'RAND and Lawrence Livermore National Lab Combine High-Performance Computing and Public Policy Analysis for Demonstration of Water Resource Management', www.rand.org/news/press/2016/08/25.html

Rapolu, B. 2016. 'Internet of Aircraft Things: An Industry Set To Be Transformed', http://aviationweek.com/connected-aerospace/internet-aircraft-things-industry-set-be-transformed

Rouse, M. 2018. 'Big Data Analytics', https://searchbusinessanalytics.techtarget.com/definition/big-data-analytics

Rouse, M. and N. Laskowski. 2016. 'AI (Artificial Intelligence) Definition', TechTarget, http://searchcio.techtarget.com/definition/AI

Rouse, M. and I. Wigmore. 2017. 'Augmented Intelligence Definition', TechTarget, http://whatis.techtarget.com/definition/augmented-intelligence

Saha, B. and S. Srivastava. 2014. 'The Other Face of Big Data', 2014 IEEE 30th International Conference on Data Engineering (ICDE), 31 March–4 April, Chicago, IL, USA.

Schwab, K. 2015. 'The Fourth Industrial Revolution: What It Means and How to Respond', *Foreign Affairs*, www.foreignaffairs.com/articles/2015-12-12/fourth-industrial-revolution

Secretary of Energy Advisory Board (SEAB). 2014. 'Report of the Task Force on High Performance Computing', https://energy.gov/sites/prod/files/2014/08/f18/SEAB%20HPC%20Task%20Force%20Final%20Report%2008-10-2014_1.pdf

Serendi. 2017. 'Talent Management: Why Is Talent Management Fundamental?', www.serendi.com/en/talent-management-definition/how-important-is-talent-management.html

Software, A.G. 2017. 'The True Cost of Bad Data', Software AG Infographic, https://lemonly.com/work/the-cost-of-bad-data

Spice, B. 2015. 'Questioning the Fairness of Targeting Ads Online: CMU Probes Online Ad Ecosystem', www.cmu.edu/news/stories/archives/2015/july/online-ads-research.html

Suzuno, M. 2017. '6 Statistics That Will Convince You to Prioritize Diversity & Inclusion', https://blog.teamable.com/6-statistics-that-will-convince-you-to-prioritize-diversity-inclusion

Tennant, D. 2015. 'How to Motivate, Empower Employees: Give Them Access to Analytics: IT BusinessEdge', www.itbusinessedge.com/blogs/from-under-the-rug/how-to-motivate-empower-employees-give-them-access-to-analytics.html

Wakefield, J. 2015. 'Intelligent Machines: Do We Really Need to Fear AI?', BBC Technology Section, www.bbc.com/news/technology-32334568

Winerman, L. 2012. 'A Machine for Jumping to Conclusions', Interview with Daniel Kahneman, *American Psychological Association*, 43(2), www.apa.org/monitor/2012/02/conclusions.aspx

Workday. 2016. 'Workday Delivers a Personalized, Immersive Learning Experience with Workday Learning', www.workday.com/en-us/company/newsroom/press-releases/press-release-details.html?id=2098063

Wu, M. 2016. 'What Is Prescriptive Analytics Really?', https://community.lithium.com/t5/Science-of-Social-Blog/What-is-Prescriptive-Analytics-Really/bc-p/253213#M1480

Yeomans, M. 2015. 'What Every Manager Should Know about Machine Learning', *Harvard Business Review*, https://hbr.org/2015/07/what-every-manager-should-know-about-machine-learning

Zeiler, M. 2016. 'Some Artificial Intelligence Applications Are Making Humans Better People', www.recode.net/2016/3/23/11587194/some-artificial-intelligence-applications-are-making-humans-better

Zephoria Digital Marketing. 2017. 'The Top 20 Valuable Facebook Statistics' (updated August), https://zephoria.com/top-15-valuable-facebook-statistics/

Zettelmeyer, F. 2014. 'Billy Beane Shows Why Leaders Can't Leave Data Science to the Data Scientists', Forbes Leadership Forum, www.forbes.com/sites/forbesleadershipforum/2014/09/23/billy-beane-shows-why-leaders-cant-leave-data-science-to-the-data-scientists/#9730d0c4c7c6

11

THE FRAMEWORK FOR TRANSCENDENTAL LEADERSHIP THROUGH ACTIVE AND TRANSFORMATIVE ENGAGEMENT

Sangeetha Menon

Theorists and scholars of leadership studies continue to analyse one of the greatest of the psycho-philosophical ideas, which is understanding leadership, percolating to different facets of the sociocultural world, the art and science of effective leadership itself have seen several experiments in public administration, military and defence forces, and more specifically in business and corporate establishments. That which makes the epistemology of leadership a tough one is the inalienable relation between the agent and act of leadership. Both the person- and behaviour-oriented facets of leadership gain meaning and relevance only in the unique contexts that are perhaps outlined by culture, community and the nation. Swami Bodhananda places his philosophy of leadership with this background of individual psychology infused with organisational and group dynamics.

What the present world lacks is wise leadership in all areas of human activity to lead us out of a pervasive meaninglessness, crass materialism and paralysing moral relativism. One unchanging truth about the world and the human condition is that there are no perfect answers to problems. There can be only optimal answers. It is a compromise involving tradeoffs. To win something is to lose something else. Economists nickname this phenomenon 'opportunity cost'. Every solution is a package, a mixed bag of good and bad. You get a package—take or leave it. Strategic thinkers call it 'win–win solutions', a situation in which both you and your enemy win. The great challenge today is optimising human satisfaction with minimal resources for maximum people. It is a situation of the winner playing a positive-sum game versus a zero-sum game and sharing his/her victory with the loser (Swami Bodhananda, 2015: 107–8).

From Charisma to capabilities approach to happiness experience

Is leader an individual, a force, a vision, or a tool for enforcing decisions and power? Commencing from Weber to Amartya Sen, the fundamental human trait that is studied is what is that which inspires one to lead. All human actions, we can say, are intended by a desire. The desire to exist, which precedes the Cartesian desire to think, is frilled by the need to connect, relate, and be together in multiple ways. Weber identified the facet of authority as part of being a leader, and he classified the exercise of authority in three ways: traditional, bureacratic and charismatic. According to Weber, the charismatic leader will be one who will be able to impart a moral purpose and mission to the individual who is otherwise influenced by bureaucratic and rational ways of social relations (Weber, 1947). But then, in time, the Weberian charismatic leader also evolves into either the bureaucratic or the traditional type.

Another important discussion is on the nature of visionary leadership which relates to strategy management. Frances Westley and Henry Mintzberg give a typology of visionary leadership such as 'the creator, the proselytizer, the idealist, the bricoleur, and the diviner' (Westley and Mintzberg, 1989: 17–32). Envisioning primarily involves an imagining and representation of the image in terms of the work environment. To envision the individual it is necessary to delineate the structures of his/her possibilities, responses to given challenges, ability to think creatively, and so on. Howard Gardner's theory on multiple intelligences suggests that what we have traditionally considered methods and behaviour because of intelligent thinking are primarily rationality driven.

The tension that persists in perceiving human nature to be free, rational and in optimal relation with the environment is seen from Aristotle to Weber, to Freud and to Amartya Sen. The nature of such a tension is to relate and hold the psychology of the individual along with a group psychology to explain the interrelations and the individual nature. Leadership connotes a very complex set of functions which occur in every group and involve a combination of personal, environmental and situational variables (Scheidlinger, 1980: 6). In the more recent version of the capability approach correlating doings and freedoms with well-being, Sen proposes the complex relationship of human action with the environment on one side and his own sense of freedom and desire for well-being on the other. The capability approach gives a better account of the freedoms actually enjoyed by different people than can be obtained from looking merely at the holdings of primary goods. Primary goods are means to freedoms, whereas capabilities are expressions of freedoms themselves. The claim is that the functionings are constitutive of a person's being and an evaluation of a person's well-being has to take the form of an assessment of these constituent elements (Sen, 2003: 44, 48).

Sabina Alkire summarises the capability approach of Sen in the following words: "furthermore, subjective data reflect relationships, achievements and environmental factors, as well as material means" (Alkire, 2015: 8). Also, even if capabilities or freedoms were the focal objective, it might be hoped that happiness would follow from their achievement, at least in some cases: 'it is natural to take pleasure in our success in achieving what we are trying to achieve. Similarly, on the negative side, our failure to get what we value can be a source of disappointment'(Alkire, March 2015).

The irony in the analysis of the deeper human ontology is the shortage in concepts that are true to its category and method. Human happiness and the pleasure that is received from the fulfilment of a single effort are fundamentally different, both by dimension and cause. To perceive eudaimonia along with the life purpose that bestows a causal happiness is necessarily beyond one's sense and experience of freedom in exercising choices in a world of material objects and menial goals. The idea and experience of leadership along with common good can be placed only if the markers of the person that is beyond the immediate sense-and-object gratification are identified in exploring a deeper, stronger and more inclusive identity.

Is the freedom and well-being experienced by a leader different from that of any other individual? Or, in other words, is there a personal influence too along with the style of leadership exercised by the leader for his or her followers and community or organisation? Can the leader be immune to the influence of his or her own ways and means of leading the rest? In much of the current discussion on human nature and agency, the power of human action is seen in the context of the totality of the person; specifically, his or her world of experiences that contain, emotions, values, attitudes, states of mind, and a vision of life purpose. Perhaps because of the disenchantment of post-Enlightenment philosophy that has also affected a country like India and its thinkers, the rich classical philosophy of India, which considers the person and his or her experiential world as significantly connected with his or her yearnings for transcorporeal identity, is not explored enough. Thus, often the theories of leadership, models and exercises that are framed are linear in nature, unknowingly bringing in a Cartesian divide between knowing and being, leading and following, thinking and doing. The whole person is missing along with his or her intimate and ultimate goal of life and living.

It is in the context of this background of the need for a framework of an inclusive and transformative style of leadership that the theory of transcendental leadership (Swami Bodhananda, 1994b) as developed by Swami Bodhananda gains importance. He writes: 'when you accommodate, you transcend. Then you grow and you move on. If you resist you are stuck. You have to get going, and that ability to get going is possible when you can accommodate' (Swami Bodhananda, 2013b: 63). A study of his philosophy and management of leadership brings in his argument that well-being concerns and the fundamental urge for higher life purposes are not to be disconnected from any human action. Unless well-being concerns and efforts are correlated with higher life purposes, the leader cannot experience deeper satisfaction and contentment. Such a view is different from the capabilities approach in which happiness or subjective well-being is seen in the context of exercising freedom or consuming material objects.

The theory of happiness which is neither based on object (the other)–driven pleasures or the experiential world proposes that the inner self is the source of happiness. Hence, one cannot obtain happiness, but can only 'be' happy. The nature of happiness is either ontological, psychological or causal.

> *Sukham* or happiness means a state of being where you accommodate and integrate all the experiences into wisdom and purposeful action. You don't get displaced or displeased by any experience. Sometimes success goes to your head, sometimes failure depresses you, but a leader cannot be influenced by these fleeting successes and failures. He has to think of the ultimate goal.
>
> (Swami Bodhananda, 2013b: 62)

As a matter of fact satisfaction does not lie in the object, but in the nature of self. Objects give you the feeling of satiation which is actually reflected from the self. Different cultures attribute values to different things. Whatever brings you to your natural self has instrumental value; it can be a material object or a state of mind. When you are in a balanced state of mind, you are with yourself. So when you say I have a value for something, what you mean is that you value that something because it makes you comfortable with yourself and abide in yourself. That is your end value. Anything that can take you to the end value, you have value for that too, because that is an instrument, a means to realize an end. When you say I am honest, the honesty is a means to abide in yourself, to be yourself. When you are with yourself, you have total satisfaction. When you are not honest, you create a split and conflict in yourself; then you suppress thoughts and feelings and develop an unconscious, the underworld of phantoms, a thick miasmic cloud of unaccounted and undigested thoughts, because of which you are not able to abide in yourself. You ask your conscience to shut up and not to bring up inconvenient thoughts; thus, the shadow personality is formed. It is this shadowy, cloudy, swampy personality that disallows you to abide in your true, happy self. Therefore, by being honest you are not favouring or serving anybody. By being honest you are serving yourself. Not the limited ego self, but the limitless transcendental pure self. That is why rishis say that the value holder must have a personal value for values. You must be personally involved by knowing that you will be directly benefitted by practicing those values (2013b: 133–4)

The framework of transcendental leadership as proposed by Swami Bodhananda is best explained with the help of the epistemology that he uses to understand human action and agency, along with the tools of ontology that he brings in to emphasise happiness as the essential nature of the leader's being.

Epistemology of transcendental leadership

Various styles of leadership, whether leader-centered or team-centered, adopt a knowledge system that creates and uses a certain amount of psychological manipulation which could be participative or authoritative in nature. At the same time, there is an intersubjective element even in an autocratic method of leadership. The self–other binary is pervasive in all relations whether it is transactional or transformative in character. Is there a way to go beyond the self–other binary? 'Transcendental leadership' as proposed by Swami Bodhananda responds to the self–other epistemological structure by offering a first-person method which has transcendence as its focus. He writes:

> The most radical theory of karma says that the individual's freedom of choice is unconditional and unaffected by the past. Being conscious, the agent enjoys freedom to submit or transcend the conditionings of the past and make fresh beginnings. The past is fully transformed by reflective action into the luminous present. The boundaries of agency and conditioning collapse and the future reveals in the here and now.
>
> (Swami Bodhananda, 2013a: 29)

> Moral and spiritual authority do not come by simply showing physical prowess, they come from depth of character. Ultimately leader is a spiritual person.
>
> (2013b: 68)

The self–other binary is influenced by the autobiographical self (Damasio, 1999) carving an identity and imposing action with the conditionings of perceptions and judgements. The singular way in which the narrative of the self-identity that is continuously stitched by the self–other divide can move away from the fundamental existential divide is by employing self-reflection that is neither self-centered nor other-centered. Self-reflection according to Swami Bodhananda is not an isolated psychological process, but a spiritual tool that is connected on the other side with action through imagination and thinking. This tool is described as the 'way of the rishi—thinking, reflecting and imagining a new future' (Swami Bodhananda, 2015: 56), and imagination as the 'connecting link that leads to action, creation and recreation' (Swami Bodhananda, 2015: 46). Such a concept of self-reflection that is tied up with both imagination and thinking tends to be action-oriented, with the capability to give an organic view of the challenge and the environment in which one is situated. Further, such a tool offers foresight into the possible outcomes of action, and 'radical changes occur in our consciousness when we self-reflect' (2013a: 29), one of the great secrets of success is the willingness and ability to adapt to the changing nature of challenges (2015: 157).

> When Arjuna became self-reflective, he paused for a minute between the impending action and his present status. And when he paused he suddenly realised that the war he was going to start is not going to solve any of his problems. War and violence is no solution to human problem. There are conflicts in our daily lives, in our minds, at our homes, in the family, in the government. . . . There are conflicts because we are all individuals. We have our own personalities and individualities, and we want full expression. When you try to express your individuality, to discover yourself, to unfold your potential, there is going to be strife, struggle and conflict. But war is not the mechanism for solving conflicts. The two super powers had tried that for the last 50 years. They misdirected the resources of the world for accumulating nuclear stockpile and created a balance of terror. Finally they discovered the foolishness they have been practising. Arjuna discovers in the battlefield that war is no solution: 'I may win the war, I may get my kingdom back but I have to kill a lot of people—innocent people, innocent children, youth, women and all of them—for my own glory'. Arjuna thinks about this situation, the consequences of his actions. This is the meaning of reflection—to think about the consequences of your action.
>
> (Swami Bodhananda, 1994a)

There is much excitement in interdisciplinary studies discussing the nature of the self. One of the dominant views is to consider the self as fleeting (Ledoux, 2002), caused by neural origins (Koch and Greenfield, 2007) and having cultural origins (Churchland and Sejnowski, 1997). If we have to analyse a self that cannot hold substantiality and existence as its core, then to discuss the identity of the leader and the individual becomes an exercise that could be accurate in a superficial plane without deeper implications. Hence, the epistemology that is adequate and focused for understanding leadership styles have to conceptualise the self that is acausal but is the source and ground of change. It is also interesting that much of the theorising on the neural self or no-self relegates the existential and fundamental urges of the individual which are not possible otherwise without a core self. Thus: 'even while you say there is no self, you need food when you feel hungry; you need respect; you need love. Our intellectual beliefs and experiences seem to be different. The spirit in the human to survive and live happily cannot be suppressed by anyone. The self that is revised or destroyed is our idea of the self; only our concepts of the self are revised or destroyed'(Swami Bodhananda, 2005). We are responsible for what we are today and shall be tomorrow. What we are today cannot be changed, but what we will be tomorrow depends on what we do with what we are today. A tree that clings on the edge of a rock hanging on the cliff was a seed that refused to roll down to the abyss (2017: 46).

With a deep vision of the imaginative eye, integrating the inevitability of change, adapting to that which changes, and the possibility of transformation that arises from imaginative vision of the inner eye Swami Bodhananda writes: "Change is the only constant in this ever-changing world. And the rate of change accelerates as days pass by. It is dizzying. To see the future while glued to the present, to dream with eyes wide open, to cut through the mess and reach the heart of a situation, to shoot the target looking at its shadow, to swim against the current, to keep the spirit high while all is seemingly lost, to set people's heart raising just by a look or touch, to communicate profound ideas in simple metaphors, lead change and make things happen is the calling of a leader" (Swami Bodhananda, 2008: 2). What is the nature of the knowledge that ensues from the imaginative vision, and how it relates and inspires human action is a discussion that requires the analysis of the concept of karma along with pramana. Is imagination an epistemological tool to reach and express the inner self?

Knowing as per the epistemology of Indian wisdom traditions is of six types (Datta, 1960). These six *pramana*s or means of knowledge and the validity of verbal knowledge relate to different modes of sense perception, inference and verbal testimony. The overt attention on reasoned knowledge as the benchmark for understanding is primarily an outcome of the continental philosophy commencing with Rene Descartes. Indian philosophical thinking conceives understanding as not just a product of knowledge but also doing and being, conveying and listening; for instance, the Upanishadic concept of *sravana* or reflective listening.

> Listening capacity is a rare gift. Our tradition emphasise on the importance of 'sravana' that is listening. When I listen to you fully, I understand you well, and when I understand you well, I communicate with you better. Sometimes you need someone listen you sympathetically. For example, subordinate comes with a complaint. What he wants is compassionate listener. He may even know that there is no solution for his problem, that there is no redress. But he wants the boss to listen. Listen with quality attention, not that boss is busy and just tolerates you. The boss listens to your version of the story and assures you that he will look into your grievance and you feel wanted and cared for. But if the boss shows impatience you feel neglected and unwanted. Ability to listen and empathise is impor-

tant skills for successful leadership. A leader must know the mind of his interlocutor, as they say, before a whisper becomes a scream!

(Swami Bodhananda, 2011c: 112)

The fundamental questions on knowledge and knowing process and their answers may not have any immediate practical value, but have existential value, and they frame our other questions in sciences and humanities (Swami Bodhananda, 2015: 5). Swami Bodhananda enlists five epistemological tools for understanding, such as: 'Knowledge, Imagination, Creativity, Optimal Solution and Total Success', and qualifies such a five-fold epistemology as 'that which builds the foundations of leadership excellence' (Swami Bodhananda, 2015) along with five psychological spaces for operating these tools, such as: 'Relationship, Happiness, Joy of Doing, Nurturing Values, and Caring and Sharing' (2013b). These arise from the space of the spirit, the inner dimension of the individual. The spirit is an intangible value and expresses itself as self-confidence, love, compassion, understanding, faith, a feeling and care for the other, and belief or insight into your own inner potential (1994a: 44). Success in management and leadership depends upon how imaginatively you plan and execute tasks (2015: 59) using these tools which have an ontological power inbuilt in them.

These ten sublime and subtle tools and spaces belong to a dimension which is beyond the material and the mental and is infused with the unitary nature of consciousness connecting and correlating the diverse forms of existence and experiences. Such a dimension is identified as 'the spiritual space' by Swami Bodhananda. According to his analysis,

"The spirit is something which cannot be measured, but still the existence can be felt in a different way. As you prepare yourself for it, at unexpected moments, when you feel everything is at sixes and sevens and the world is in a mess around you, and you feel you cannot go further ahead, then you experience a shower from beyond. And your whole life gains a new spring. And you start seeing flowers blooming everywhere and there is a new message, a new energy welling up from within you. That is the dimension of the spirit. You may not be able to quantify it. You may not be able to convince somebody of the existence of the spirit unless that somebody is ready to learn, watch you with a different eye, not with a suspicious eye".

(Swami Bodhananda, 1994b)

One of the accepted trends in creating knowledge is sense perception inspired by external object sources. Following Bacon, Descartes and the lineage of rational thinking, the West successfully created a subject–object divide, and such a division and embrace of the source of object was perhaps a relevant strategy in the times of scientific revolution. Though the focus on external reality and empirical means favouring logical positivism was indeed a successful plan to create scientific advancement, the postmodern trend showed that the expulsion of the subject led to disenchantment and disillusionment of the person. Existential philosophy and the phenomenological method succeeded in bringing back the importance of subject and the agent in defining and designing human experiences. In India, to begin with, the classical traditions favoured a person- and subject-centred enquiry.

> The Indian knowledge system insisted that the 'I', It and the 'Thou' are one, or constitute a whole. Their separation is ego and ignorance and the cause of suffering. For the western binary thinkers this 'non-separation' is childish fantasy and stunted growth. The Indian Rishi insisted that knowledge is not complete without self -knowledge. For the western scientist all knowledge is knowledge of the other. For the Rishi, the 'I-It' dialectic is the object of knowledge. You will not understand the other (not-self) without understanding the I (self) and vice versa. That is called the holistic knowledge. On this fundamental issue, the East and West disagree and depart. The West still has not developed any tool for the inner, first person investigation.
>
> (Swami Bodhananda, 2015: 24)

We live in a complex world. But then we also live with a deeper system of the inner world. In spite of the authority of the mind, personality, attitudes, emotions, and values on our ways of developing judgements and making decisions, we seldom ignore the fact that in a public world of knowledge transaction and public transference, such a deeper system of the inner world of the individual is not considered. William James said that our identity is not only the material objects we possess, but also the various sentiments and ownerships we hold in our minds and in the inner world. James remarked:

> In its widest possible sense, however, a man's Self is the sum total of all that he *can* call his, not only his body and his psychic powers, but his clothes and his house, his wife and children, his ancestors and friends, his reputation and works, his lands and horses, and yacht and bank-account. All these things give him the same emotions. If they wax and prosper, he feels triumphant; if they dwindle and die away, he feels cast down, not necessarily in the same degree for each [p. 292] thing, but in much the same way for all.
>
> (James, 1890)

There is an explicit division of the material, mental and spiritual self in the psychology of William James, which also is perhaps the resultant of the dominant divide that West believed in terms of the subject and the object. Yet, James postulates a 'greater Self' which cures the mind, 'giving your private convulsive self at rest', and keeps the discussion open on a core non-reducible self. Such a cure for the mind, according to James, might undermine the scientific method, however, its successes can be verified experimentally (Menon, 2014: 97).

The theory of envisioning the individual as a complex combination of 'guna' as exemplified in the system of Samkhya, Yoga and Ayurveda, has been elaborated in the context of understanding the dynamics of leadership and team building by Swami Bodhananda, based on his insightful analysis of the classical sources (Swami Bodhananda, 1994b: 64). Consolidating the Yogasutra philosophy and psychology, he suggests that 'there are three fundamental factors in our life experiences', which consists of 'the sensate world of objects made of gunas; the quality of mind that you bring to bear upon the objective world determining the nature of your subjective experiences; and the fundamental individual in you (the person), the one who owns and operates the body–mind complex interacting with the environment', which is also 'the ultimate goal, and not instrumental to anything beyond'(1994b: 64–5).

According to Swami Bodhananda, communication has to be directed to address the inner mind subliminally. According to his outlook on motivation, 'the Indian guna theory gives insights on the analysis of the deeper structure and motivations of human mind in thought and action—its individual orientation, group dynamics and the nature of human satisfaction and flourishing' (Swami Bodhananda, 1994b, 2012). A reviewer on 'Indian Management and Leadership' (Swami Bodhananda, 2007b: 37–52), writes that the focus of guna analysis by Swami Bodhananda gives a good insight into the power and working of the human mind, which is essential for rational personnel management. In brief, the guna theory analysis is the following: The guna theory categorises people into three types according to their attributes: namely, sattvic, rajasic and tamasic. Although rajasic types display qualities of love, caring, wisdom and inner peace, the rajasic type love power, domination, ambition, valour, personal courage, and manipulative skills. On the contrary, the tamasic type is usually dull, indifferent, stubborn, and pays little attention to work and responsibilities. This theory can be applied to the workplace in order to identify the right person for the right job. This chapter gives a good insight into the power and working of the human mind so essential for rational personnel management (Mathur, 2011: 132–5).

Desire, freedom and the moral responsibility of the agent

Human action and agency are major cognitive and management concepts used today to analyse one's behaviour, decision-making process and the ethical normative. Traditionally, the discussion on karma extends to the retributions to be received in a future life based on actions in the present life. Perhaps because of the overemphasis on the idea of karma as a system to explain the illogical and unequal ways people prosper or perish in spite of the presence or absence of good or bad actions, the idea of change agency and the central place of the doer has not been discussed enough. One instance of the theoretical explanation for karma concept in a classical style is given by Deutsch arguing that the pramana theory cannot substantiate the presence of karma in Advaita Vedanta. Remarking on karma as a 'convenient fiction' in the Advaita Vedanta, Deutsch says:

> Karma is not the only possible supposition to account for the good and bad luck of persons (i.e., the differences in their moral, intellectual, spiritual capacities), as indeed many others (e.g., divine predestination or naturalistic hereditary factors) have been put forward and have been capable of generating strong belief. Karma is thus not established by arthapatti: it is not the only way by which inequalities can be made intelligible.
>
> (Deutsch, 1965: 8)

It is important to reckon that along with the pramana theory another significant theory employed in Vedantic tradition is that of maya, a highly complex notion of change and causality. Does the concept of maya say something that is more significant than the metaphysical status of the experiential world?
  According to Swami Bodhananda:

> Change is the law of life. By trying to arrest change, you only come under the juggernaut of change. Change cannot be stopped. We have a wonderful idea in Indian wisdom tradition—that of 'maya', or 'samsara'. Samsara means constant change. Maya means that which appears and disappears. Life is like a river. Not only life, even an organisation is like a river. When you fly up you can see meandering rivers. Or on a cruise you see the crooked changing course of river. Rivers are in constant motion. The water constantly flows. A Greek philosopher said that you cannot step into the same river twice. If the river encounters obstacle, either it overflows the hurdle, or flanks, divides on both sides of the obstacle and join again or it goes under and re-emerges or it changes its course altogether. If nothing works, the river will patiently wait gathering strength and when strong enough it will blast the hurdle and move ahead.
>
> (Swami Bodhananda, 2008: 93–4)

The persisting philosophical question is about the nature of the change that happens to the external world and the inner world. Are these two different types of change, and do they influence each other so as to impact upon the individual and his/her leadership acumen? One response is:

There are two dimensions of change: one outer and other inner. Outer change happens due advancement in technology, emergence of new ideas and demographic shifts. Those changes are beyond our control. When such changes occur we go out of control. But to remain in harmony with change outside we have to change ourselves—our beliefs and attitudes. Inner change is within our control. We are basically concerned with inner change. The question is how do you change internally—as individuals and as organisations? First step is change in belief about oneself and in the attitude thereof. The weak-hearted will cry, 'I can't do anything', 'nothing can be done'. But for a leader the phrase, 'I can't' is anathema. A true leader is always ready to learn and change with the times.

(Swami Bodhananda, 2008: 103)

The dynamics of the outer and inner change, and the perception that everything changes bring in the crucial subject matter of understanding moral responsibility, particularly since the ways in which we act are not always guided by the principles of valid knowledge but by passion, beliefs and attitudes. The study by Fischer argues for not a control-based but a 'guidance-based' approach to understand moral responsibility. John Martin Fischer writes:

Moral responsibility requires (among other things) control of one's behaviour. But there are different kinds of control. One sort of control entails the existence of genuinely accessible alternative possibilities; I call this sort of control, 'regulative control'. The presence of regulative control is typically signalled by the use of the preposition, 'over'. So, when an individual has control over his behaviour, he has more than one path available to him; he (say) performs an action, but he could have done otherwise (in the sense of 'could' that expresses the distinctive sort of ability involved in free will). I believe that an agent can control his behaviour, and be in control of it, without having control over it.

(Fischer, 1999: 277–8)

According to Fischer, it is self-expression which is entailed in freedom and which gives the guidance control for moral responsibility.

Although change is inevitable, the paradigms of change, such as change leadership and other competencies based on change, are receiving new attention. One of the prominent expositions on change leadership capability is given by Higgs and Rowland who have identified eight overall change management competency clusters: change initiation, change impact, change facilitation, change leadership, change learning, change execution, change presence, and change technology. According to this work:

> What is important is that the leadership is built to diagnose, understand, confront and reshape the reality as people see it. Change cannot be predicted, yet the ability to harness it can be developed. It is only by learning new things about ourselves, our relationships with others and discovering new ways of seeing reality that we can start to implement new business practices, which ultimately will lead to new business results.
>
> (Higgs and Rowland, 2000: 123)

In order to understand and reshape change, the power of the 'inner self' is needed. Otherwise the change management competency can in due course be relegated to a process similar to object manipulation which is bereft of the sensitivity for the other. Change thus is founded on a self that has a quality of interiority to it. Indian philosophy is particularly interested in discussing the relation between action, change and the inner self.

The analysis of human action cannot be completed without the context of the nature of the self. The self has been variously interpreted as a historical entity that develops in time, an essential core, a process, or as a narrative. It is only in recent times that the narrative account of the self has gained attention in neuropsychiatry and neuroscience in general (Kircher and David, 2003). Swami Bodhananda's theory of human action is intricately tied up with a narrative notion of the self which also carries an essentiality which is dynamic and not ahistorical. He proposes three laws that operate under the theory of karma:

> The first law of karma is that it is a process with a beginning and an end. Karma is not just action, but action and its consequence—the karmaphala, or the fruit of action. The cause and consequence are together called karma. The second law is that the result, karmaphala, is a modification of the cause, karma. The third law is that all choices are intentional whether you are conscious or unconscious of your intentions; and further, the results of karma come back to the doer—the choose who performs the karma.
>
> (Swami Bodhananda, 2011b: 136)

This above approach to karma theory, with the help of three laws, extends the scope of the popular interpretation and connects the past, present and future of human action. He writes:

> Though the basis of karma is individuality, freedom, and the moral responsibility of the agent, often karma is mistaken for

predestination. That is the belief that the destiny of the individual has been already determined by some unknown power or by the first act of the individual. Both are absurd. If used as a pawn by some unknown power, the agent will no longer be morally responsible for its actions or be the recipient of results. So too it is illogical to assume that one single action produces an endless series of results. . . . The most radical theory of karma says that the individual's freedom of choice is unconditional and unaffected by the past.

(Swami Bodhananda, 2013a: 26)

Therefore, the freedom of the individual lies not in succumbing to the perceived effects of the past actions but using the environment and the presentness of the given to make a fresh move. The common understanding of karma is that right actions produce good results for the agent and wrong actions produce bad results which leads to sukha (enjoyment) or dukha (suffering) in life, and the agent takes birth after birth to reap the fruits of actions, which mature in different time periods. The samsara cakra (cycle of birth and death) thus is *ananta* (goes on endlessly). This cycle, according to the interpretation of the classical sources by Swami Bodhananda,

Can be ended by four types of interventions: jnana (self knowledge), *iswarabhakti* (surrender to God), karma yoga (nonreaction to the fruits of action), and *citta vrtti nirodha* (mind control by watching), and as a result, the agent discards all limitations and immerses in supreme consciousness, putting a final end to suffering. It is up to the agent to choose this path.

(2013a: 28)

Will the exercise of choice leave us with redemption from the desired project? All human actions are initiated by desire, whether in the form of the Husserlian objectivating intentionality (Hopkins, 1993: 44) or cognitive focus derived from a sociocultural evolutionary history (Heyes, 2012) or, as Taittiriya Upanishad states, to be *kamayata bahusyam prajayeyeti* (urge to become more than one). In a recent article, Temple and Gall make a reference to the interrelation between desire and freedom. Freedom is not preestablished but is changing and is in a process of development, which can enhance one's life or can cause one to regress and retreat. Values such as love, honesty and courage spring forth from the value of being free. Values are diminished if the individual is not free to choose to exhibit and live by them. Freedom, therefore, is fundamental to the capability to value and the possibility of valuing (Temple and Gall, 2016: 177).

The idea of value which runs through the experience of freedom in desiring is connected ontologically with the deep experience of satisfaction according to Swami Bodhananda. He writes:

When you say that you have value for 'something' it means that that 'something' gives you an intangible called 'satisfaction', which is the value that you see in that 'something'. 'Satisfaction' is the end value and money is only an instrumental value. The satisfaction can be gained in association with an object, or a person or a place. When I am satisfied I feel relaxed, abiding in myself and in a state of perfect balance (samadhi). For example, when you desire a cup of coffee, you are ready to do anything to possess that cup of coffee, ready to pay, ready to walk to the shop in rain or shine. Finally when you drink and taste coffee, and as the caffeine rushes through your bloodstream, and the dopamine floods the brain, you get the 'aha' feeling and you are in temporary Samadhi, a state of transient bliss. This is because psychologically you are free from a given desire, and whenever you are free from a particular desire, and no new desire has taken its place, you abide in your inner self (*tada dhristu-svarupe-avasthanam*: Yogasutra:1.3).

(Swami Bodhananda, 2013b: 131)

From his outlook on value and satisfaction, the theory of happiness is presented not as the necessary consequence of entertaining and pursuing a desire. 'Happiness is an innate value. You choose to be happy. Happiness is what you invoke and what you discover. You can choose to be happy regardless of where you are, who you are and what you have' (Swami Bodhananda, 2013b: 131). He explains: 'You can desire, not for happiness, but desire as a happy person. So a desire which spring from a happy mind is a creative desire. A desire which comes from an unhappy mind is a destructive desire, because as an unhappy person you want to exploit, control, dominate and eat up all. Where you are a happy person, you want to network, support, share, be transparent, want to know and understand—an entirely different quality of mind' (2013b: 68). The tools of self-expression such as 'creativity arise in the individual human mind and not in a collection of minds. A collective mind can create only a resolution, the lowest common denominator. It cannot scale or discover the highest peak of human intelligence. Creativity cannot be a collective product' (1994b: 78).

A leader has to be self-sufficient and happy and his or her happiness does not depend on what happens outside. When you are secure in yourself, you are able to understand what is going on inside and outside and to develop moral and spiritual capabilities and the authority to offer solutions. Otherwise you become part of the problem and not the solution, because you are the problem. When you yourself are the problem, when a duster itself is dusty, how can it clean the board? When the physician himself is sick, how can he cure others? (2013b: 68).

The leader–manager has to be flexible, accommodating and learn from all bitter and sweet experiences. This ability to accommodate is called 'sukham'. When you have large enough space to accommodate differences, contradictions, paradoxes and unexpected experiences in life, that is the state of mind in which your natural happiness manifests. One of the central teaching of Indian wisdom tradition is that your happiness is within you. You are the source of all happiness there is. Your happiness is within you. It is a matter of expressing and experiencing it. Happiness is something that is to be expressed. When you express it you have it, when you don't, you miss it. Express your happiness, be happy. Don't try to find explanations and reasons for your unhappiness. It is futile exercise. Your whole life is wasted in giving reasons and explanations for your unhappiness. In the process you may write books, you may create philosophies, set up political parties, give discourses, but only get further entrenched in your unhappiness. Throughout all these feverish activities you forget to sit still for a while and reflect on the experience of unhappiness. Reflecting on the experience of unhappiness is going beyond it to the source of happiness.

(2013b: 63–4)

The self-discovery of happiness as pre-existent, and that which is to be invoked in actions and initiatives is further founded on the value of the unity, in spite of 'the differences which are in the natural order of things and beings. But human evolution is inexorably towards realisation of the unity of existence. This is a consciousness of Unity in Diversity and not a forced Uniformity. That being the case, conversation, sharing, and consensus rather than conversion, force, or domination become the most civilised way of human interaction and discourse' (Swami Bodhananda, 2013a: 60).

The interconnected theory of desire, human action, freedom, and happiness is the basis for understanding an individual, being sensitive to the team members, and thus reflecting on the markers of a transcendental leader.

Success and motivation in self-discovery

There is a larger philosophical question about how or whether success can lead to happiness and life contentment. And the existential predicament is the following:

Nobody in this world wants to be a failure. All want to be winners, and successful. But what is success, who is successful—the powerful, the rich, the strongest, the most beautiful? Based on a profit and loss analysis, we find that sometimes the early loser has the last laugh and that all the winners are not savouring their victories. Success like health seems to have material, mental, ethical, and spiritual dimensions. Success also has long-term and short-term implications and cost factors.

(Swami Bodhananda, 2012)

Perhaps one challenge that is seen in happiness studies is that the review and analysis of happiness is done in a post-facto experiential manner; that is, happiness as a utilitarian value, consequent to an action or attitude. The happiness theory promulgated by Swami Bodhananda in his philosophical analysis takes a different angle and brings in the ontological context of the person's true self. Happiness is identified as the nature of an individual, and not a subsequent addition, or changing experience. Which means 'a successful leader or manager has to be a happy person to begin with. Everyone looks up to him but he has no one to look up to for inspiration or solace. He is on his own, is the salt of the organisation. By looking for happiness outside the leader forfeits right to leadership' (Swami Bodhananda, 2011c).

The leader who is happy exudes a natural ability to motivate people and help them by facilitating a space to express their hidden potential. Motivating people to work for organisational goals is the greatest management challenge for a leader. The team as a whole and every member of it has to 'enjoy work and know and feel that work is a means of self actualisation' (Swami Bodhananda, 1994b). The act and technique of motivation is a subject of being sensitive to the inner mind and the way it works out for each individual.

In the Bhagavad Gita, the focal method that is given for motivation is self-motivation. In the beginning of the battle, as described in the Gita, we see that there are attempts to motivate Arjuna by resorting to invoke his feelings about belonging to a well-known family, tradition, achievements, success, and so on. These are the techniques that are employed in usual practice by appealing to our national pride, family pride, various glories, names, and the recognition that we have in society. When the material motivation methods fail, we come to the spiritual and visionary methods of motivating people (2013b: 79). After the failure of these external tools of motivation, Krishna gives Arjuna finally a new self-identity, a new sense of himself, that his true nature is happiness and he doesn't have to do anything to be a happy person (Swami Bodhananda, 1994b: 47). In modern management what is more important is to manage oneself than manage others. Indeed, managing others is equally important when relationships are involved. But you will not be able to manage others unless you learn how to manage yourself (Swami Bodhananda, 2010b: 4).

The transcendental state of one's self is disclosed through one discovering one's identity. Engaging with the identity can happen only through activity and challenges that karma bring in. Karma and yoga thus are the key concepts in the Gita. Karma has a phenomenological and transcendental nature about it that it becomes expressed in either way according to one's constitutional make-up, guna prakrti. Karma can bind the individual or can liberate the individual by being a means to self-discovery.

Acausal transformative happiness

The epistemology for both knowledge and the ontological well-being is a detached mind, which, according to Swami Bodhananda, helps to understand and respond to situations both objectively and creatively (2007b: 98). *Sukha prapti,* or seeking happiness, is the ultimate goal in life. But from where can one get happiness? The Gita says your happiness is not in people, not in situations, not in things, not in success, not in money, nor in fame. Your happiness is the quality of yourself. Your happiness is your nature. If you seek happiness outside, you will indeed miss it. So stop seeking happiness and start leading a happy life. Be happy all by yourself . . . seek your happiness within yourself (2007a: 98–9). Swami Bodhananda believes that 'it is very important to live in constant awareness of oneself so that one has power over one's thoughts, and can choose responses to the world as per one's values' (Adhia et al., 2010).

The transcendence of karma is experiential, and the phenomenology of karma is transcendental. This is evidenced by the four definitions given to yoga, according to the Bhagavad Gita. The first definition is that yoga is the pursuit of excellence (*yoga karmasu kausalam*). It means that whatever you do has to be done perfectly, even if it is the just the routine of fixing a breakfast. Excellence is integration of multiple skills: 'the ability to manage, channelise and coordinate emotions and feelings into productive team work. We need excellent leaders who pursue excellence in life and work. . . . Excellence is a relentless, ongoing pursuit. You cannot say I have reached excellence. There is no end in the pursuit of excellence' (Swami Bodhananda, 2013b: 3).

The second definition of yoga is balancing of mind equanimity and contemplation, cutting off thoughts and observing the situation in a detached manner. The third definition is that yoga is the capacity to remain rooted in yourself while you interact with the world. This means that you are not upset, but calm and cool under all circumstances. A person who stays rooted in yoga never feels any tiredness and is able to bring new energies— doing things in his or her own innovative way. The more he or she works, the more he or she is inspired; that is, he or she can inspire energy within him- or herself (Swami Bodhananda, 1994b: 61).

Swami Bodhananda describes these three definitions as 'the three stages of yoga':

> The concentration powers are developed, then the detachment powers are developed, and you are able to concentrate with detachment.

New dimensions of consciousness open up in yourself, and you are able to concentrate with contemplative detachment, you strike roots into your own inner self. Which is the source of infinite energy. A yogi therefore does not look for inspiration from the outside world, on the contrary he inspires the world around him.

(1994b: 62)

He further details two more definitions of yoga from the Bhagavad Gita: Yoga as the means to attain freedom from misery. A yogi is one who can be naturally, effortlessly happy, who does not become unhappy owing to a situation. The state of natural happiness is the final achievement of the yogi (1994b: 62).

Indian management framework and its philosophy

The study of leadership incorporates several key traits of leaders and the interactions between leaders and followers based on social and organisational psychology. The challenge which persists is to contextualise and integrate the dimensions that are closely connected but not amenable to tools of social psychology, such as effectiveness in human action, and the relation with common good with a discussion on plurality in ethical norms and cultural diversity.

Although it has at present no global answers to the essence of leadership, social psychology literature does contain many useful, limited-domain theories and research observations with direct relevance to people-helping groups. What is especially noteworthy is the uncontestable finding that contrary to folklore and human wishes, leadership connotes a very complex set of functions which occur in every group and involves a combination of personal, environmental and situational variables (Scheidlinger, 1980: 6). These variables present to oneself through values and choice making. Traditionally, we have seen the highest plane of values as an alienated enterprise discussed in isolation from practical life. In the West, although Plato, Kant and a few others have given importance to the highest planes of ideals and values that are of the nature of categorical imperative, in the classical Eastern traditions, values are one of the key components of life goals. But are the *purushar-tha* (life purposes) discussed in Indian tradition integrated in contemporary leadership studies in a dynamic fashion or more as a disconnected mystical plane? The latter is a common trend. In contrast, Swami Bodhananda proposes that the value planes are all equally important whether they relate to material or spiritual pursuits. He suggests the concept of 'self management' in the following approach to integrating reason and passion:

There is passion on one side made up of feelings of insecurity—fear, anxieties, need for space around you, etc.—and reason on the other side, exercising a modest control over your passion. It is difficult to

193

win over passion completely. There is therefore a tug of war going on in between these two energies in you and self management is managing this conflict between your selfish interest which is defined by your passions, and your altruistic interest which is your concern for others encompassed in your reason.

(Swami Bodhananda, 1996: 23)

How easy is it to balance the interests of passion and reason—the egoistic and altruistic desire-centric actions? Swami Bodhananda explains the balancing act through the exposition of four contending values that bring in the dynamics between individual and group interactions and decide effective leadership:

One is that this life and this body alone are real, enjoyment in this life and in this body is practical and the rest are only empty words. The second is that accumulation of wealth is the basis of a good life and the third that ethics is the harbinger of quality life. And finally you have the spiritual idea that our ultimate purpose is 'moksha'— freedom or liberation. So there are four contending values that are vying for our attention. All those values have their place in a debate. They all contribute in creating a dynamic balance in a given situation in the society. If you don't create the dynamic balance and give overwhelming importance to one value, the society will fall apart. That is what had been happening in India. We gave overwhelming value to 'moksha' and ignored other values in the dynamics.

(Swami Bodhananda, 2011c: 5)

How does one choose and follow one of the four contending values, is a matter to be understood and reflected upon on the basis of the 'rishi vision' (Swami Bodhananda, 1992) and 'seven Hindu spiritual laws for success' (Swami Bodhananda, 2004). The Indian philosophical tradition is described through the idea of who is a 'rishi'. Swami Bodhananda defines the classical tradition with the concept of the vision of the rishi: 'Rishi is not an individual or a group of individual. They constitute a tradition, an institution, a way, a paradigm. They are known as *mantra dristas*—seers of mantra or mystic meanings, connections and interactions. They were a parampara—an unbroken flow of wisdom, insight, values, and beliefs' (Swami Bodhananda, 1992: 5). With this fundamental outlook on Indian classical philosophy, he describes in detail how Indian wisdom tradition can be explained through seven fundamental principles of brahman, maya, dharma, karma, yajna, yoga, and *leela*. Freedom is that ability to make use of your environment. Whatever it may be, explore your potential and express that infinite potential while interacting with the world. This is the true meaning of moksha, not to achieve something in an afterlife or in some future lifetime (Swami Bodhananda, 2004).

There have been misinterpretations on Indian philosophical thinking, qualifying it to be 'otherworldly', highly metaphysical, and the like. In contrast to such popular perception, the classical approaches have given utmost importance to the experiential world. The concepts of dharma, ideal living, living in harmony with the environment, and more are imbued with the philosophy of the common good.

> The foundation of spirituality and ethics is holistic view of life and concern for common good—'do unto others as they would do unto you'. The ethical standpoint changes your mindset. You will start looking at things differently. You start experiencing life differently. Some people may consider you foolish when you give up some of your comforts for the sake of others and that your martyrdom is fruitless. But some others will indeed say that you have acted rightly. When we set our minds on those lines of thinking, our acts become altruistic which gives you more joy than selfish acts.
>
> (Swami Bodhananda, 2010b: 15)

According to Swami Bodhananda, philosophy in the West develops by critiquing and contradicting past thinkers and their thoughts, whereas in the East it develops by adding new meaning to old concepts and expanding their interpretive scope to address emerging challenges. Indian thought grows organically, branch by branch, and has continuity, whereas Western thought grows mechanically, block by block, and undergoes discontinuities. India believes in unity in diversity, whereas the West wants to extract unity from diversity (Swami Bodhananda, 2011a: 27). A central feature of the organic approach in Indian philosophy is the concept of 'dharma'.

Dharma is a central principle that guides both Indian philosophy and Indian management methods. According to Swami Bodhananda, the best definition of dharma is that which good people practise. He engages with the concept of dharma in the Mahabharata to illumine how the idea of common good can be juxtaposed with what is ideally good for the individual. In another work on the five spiritual questions of Arjuna, he gives a philosophical anaylsis of existence and healthy living so as to both transcend and encompass life's dilemmas and personal struggles (Swami Bodhananda, 2007a: 1).

The approach to understanding what is common good is undertaken by Swami Bodhananda in the context of the contemporary cultural plurality and societal complexity of India, and perhaps the global world itself. He remarks that it is circular to say that good is that which good people practice but the question is 'what is good' before we settle on 'who is good'. He argues that the concept of dharma cannot be understood if distilled from the complexities of actual life. A life lived is the foundation of dharma.

> Mahabharata presents dharma inalienable from its context. Dharma is meaningful and recognisable only in contexts. What is brought into the foreground is *svadharma*, individual action in the community, with *sanatana*, *varnasrama* and *apat dharma* kept in the background. . . . Individual fulfilment and the highest common good are not seen as contradictory values. The Mahabharata discusses three values in the context of dharma. They are *prabhava*—prosperity, *dharana*—sustainability and ahimsa— nonviolence. The practice of dharma should lead to material prosperity, sustainable environment and protection from violence. Chanakya says that right conduct and social harmony flows from material prosperity. Social harmony and peace without equitable prosperity will neither be sustainable nor justifiable. Mahabharata prescribes the pursuit of Purusharthas— creature needs, wealth/security and freedom/happiness/knowledge within the framework of dharma. The heart of dharma is balance between conflicting interests. It is the philosophy of rational, prudent pursuit of self-interest in an interdependent world. Adherence to dharma secures self-interest optimally.
>
> (Swami Bodhananda, 2010a)

According to Swami Bodhananda, one of the main challenges of modern business and the professional career is the difficulty of being good and ethical. Lust for easy and quick profit has replaced all other considerations, which has led to the present economic crisis. Business leaders are now talking about value-based and ethical business. The nonnegotiable interests of all stakeholders are to be synergistically incorporated in envisioning sustainable solutions to conflicts that arise among individuals, departments and communities. Decision-making is prioritising and balancing those interests for positive and organised action to create acceptable outcomes. The character and empathy of the leader matter a lot in this area. The Vedic ideal of dharma gives us valuable insights in this complex matter. A great leader strategises organisational interest with concern for public good, especially in the present post-capitalist global business context. The ideal of nishkama–karma, or self-giving work to promote public good, offers valuable lessons for the modern leader who wants to do well by doing good. The primary duty of a leader is to make decisions that affect people's thinking and choices and eventually the quality of their lives. In this ever-changing, complex world, no leader has the time and leisure to ponder eternally and process all the information effectively to arrive at optimal decisions. The leader has to tap into his/her guts or intuitive faculties to make effective and innovative decisions. Principles and ethics give conviction and direction in times of confusion and ambiguity. The rajarshi model of leadership discussed in Ramayana and Mahabharata is a treasure chest of insights on ethical leadership in times of crisis (Swami Bodhananda, 2010a). And why crisis is to be taken seriously in transforming a person is because 'a crisis is an opportunity to do things differently, because, when we are in a crisis, we cannot act from our memory. We are forced to act from a higher level, from our spiritual core, and the Spirit's creations are always new' (Swami Bodhananda, 2011a: 9).

Conclusion

The transcendental framework for leadership suggested by Swami Bodhananda develops an epistemology of enactive well-being with the five limbs of knowledge, total success, imagination, optimal solution, and creativity; seven spiritual laws for success; the three phenomenological characteristics of karma theory; and four existential approaches to the experience of yoga, through an interpretative analysis of classical Indian literature described as 'rishi vision'. Understanding the multifaceted features of the self, managing those aspects with balance, and expressing the same in the spirit of integrating the individual good along with the common good, is considered by him as the goal of management studies. Interpreting the Bhagavad Gita and the Yogasutra, Swami Bodhananda suggests that the framework for successful leadership consists in mastery of mind, being efficient in doing what one does, being equanimous irrespective of the binaries around, to stay established in the inner self, and to be happy acausally. Such a psychological principle is suggested by him in the foreground of the definitions from Bhagavad Gita and stages of Yoga, and the three fundamental factors of life experiences according to Patanjali's Yogasutra (1994b: 64). The excellence of human expression lies in creativity, efficiency and innovativeness, and these spring from one's inner self (1994b: 78). It is noteworthy that in India, when management and leadership studies were striving hard to gain a unique vision and perspective during the pre-liberalisation period, Swami Bodhananda through his book *The Gita and Management* (1994b) made a call by 'appeal[ing] to the leadership impulses in a few people, people who care for excellence, quality, initiative, and competitiveness' (1994b: 87). An extensive discussion is engaged on the economic and geopolitical space of India in the 90s distinguishing from a Western mode and presenting an Indian framework of management based on transcendental leadership. Such a framework is presented to offer the style of Indian management which focuses on analysing agency and responsibility through 'inaction in action', contextualising dharma and leadership values. According to the transcendental leadership framework, 'Embodied enlightenment is exploring and expressing the infinite bliss and power of the self through self-giving altruistic work in an interactive world' (Swami Bodhananda, 2010a: 9). The transcendental leadership framework suggested by Swami Bodhananda helps connect and move forward from social psychology and group psychology to practical management excellence and effective leadership.

References

Adhia, H., H.R. Nagendra and B. Mahadevan. 2010. 'Impact of Adoption of Yoga Way of Life on the Emotional Intelligence of Managers', *IIMB Management Review*, 22(1–2) (March–June): 32–41, https://doi.org/10.1016/j.iimb.2010.03.003

Alkire, S. 2015. *The Capability Approach and Well-Being Measurement for Public Policy*. Ophi Working Paper No. 94, March.

Churchland, P.S. and T. Sejnowski. 1997. *The Computational Brain*. Cambridge: MIT Press.

Damasio, A. 1999. *Feeling of What Happens: Body and Emotion in the Making of Consciousness*. London: Heinemann.

Datta, D.M. 1960. *The Six Ways of Knowing: A Critical Study of the Vedanta Theory of Knowledge* (2nd revised edition). Calcutta: University of Calcutta.

Deutsch, E.S. 1965. 'Karma as a "Convenient Fiction" in the Advaita Vedānta', *Philosophy East and West*, 15(1) (January): 3–12.

Fischer, J.M. 1999. 'Responsibility and Self-Expression', *The Journal of Ethics, the Contributions of Harry G. Frankfurt to Moral Responsibility Theory*, 3(4): 277–97.

Heyes, C. 2012. 'New Thinking: The Evolution of Human Cognition', *Philosophical Transactions of the Royal Society B: Biological Sciences*, 367(1599)(August 5): 2091–6.

Higgs, M. and D. Rowland. 2000. 'From: Building Change Leadership Capability: The Quest for Change Competence', *Journal of Change Management*, 1(2): 116–30.

Hopkins, B. 1993. *Intentionality in Husserl and Heidegger: The Problem of the Original Method and Phenomenon of Phenomenology*. Dordrecht: Springer Netherlands. doi:10.1007/978-94-015-8145-5

James, W. 1890. *The Principles of Psychology*. Retrieved January 25, 2018, from Classics in the History of Psychology, http://psychclassics.yorku.ca/James/Principles/prin10.htm (accessed on 12 May 2019).

Kircher, T. and A. David (eds.). 2003. *The Self in Neuroscience and Psychiatry*. Cambridge: Cambridge University Press.

Koch, C. and S. Greenfield. 2007. 'How Does Consciousness Happen? Scientific American', *Scientific American*, 297: 76–83.

Ledoux, J. 2002. *Synaptic Self: How Our Brains become Who We Are*. New York: Penguin Books.

Mathur, J. 2011. 'Review of the Book "Indian Management and Leadership by Swami Bodhananda"', *Indian Jorunal of Public Administration*, 57(1): 132–5. doi:10.1177/0019556120110112

Menon, S. 2014. *Brain, Self and Consciousness: Explaining the Conspiracy of Experience*. New Delhi: Springer India.

Scheidlinger, S. 1980. 'Psychology of Leadership', *Group*, 4(1): 5–17.

Sen, A. 2003. 'Development as Capability Expansion', in S. Fukuda-Parr and A.S. Kumar (eds.), *Readings in Human Development* (Vols. originally appeared in *Journal of Development Planning*, 19: 41–58), pp. 3–16, 41–54. Oxford: Oxford University Press.

Swami Bodhananda. 1992. *Rishi Vision*. New Delhi: Sambodh Foundation.

Swami Bodhananda. 1994a. *Bhagavad Gita: Ch.15*. Retrieved January 23, 2018, from Sambodh Foundation, India, www.sambodh.org/B/message/gita-ch15.pdf (accessed on 12 May 2019).

Swami Bodhananda. 1994b. *The Gita and Management*. New Delhi: Sambodh Foundation.

Swami Bodhananda. 1996. 'Managing Self', in *Management in Daily Life*. Ahmedabad: Ahmedabad Management Association (AMA).

Swami Bodhananda. 2004. *Seven Hindu Spritual Laws for Success*. New Delhi: Blue Jay Books.

Swami Bodhananda. 2005. *Self and Consciousness*. S. Menon, Interviewer. New Delhi: Sambodh Foundation.

Swami Bodhananda. 2007a. *A Conversation with Lord Krishna: Five Spiritual Questions of Arjuna*. Kalamazoo: The Sambodh Society, Inc.

Swami Bodhananda. 2007b. *Indian Management and Leadership: Spiritual and Ethical Values for Corporate and Personal Success*. New Delhi: Blue Jay Books.

Swami Bodhananda. 2008. *Spirituality and Ethics in Management*. Ahmedabad: Ahmedabad Management Association (AMA).

Swami Bodhananda. 2010a. 'Dharma in the Mahabharata: Values for Management and Leadership (S. Menon and S. Sharma, eds.)', *IBA Journal of Management and Leadership*, 2(1) (July–December): 7–13, http://iba.ac.in/wp-content/uploads/2013/12/july_dec_2010Sangeethamenon.pdf (accessed on 12 May 2019).

Swami Bodhananda. 2010b. *Yoga and Management*. Ahmedabad: Ahmedabad Management Association (AMA).

Swami Bodhananda. 2011a. *From Crisis to Confidence*. Kalamazoo: The Sambodh Society, Inc.

Swami Bodhananda. 2011b. *Happiness Unlimited: Self-Unfoldment in an Interactive World*. New Delhi: Srishti Publishers.

Swami Bodhananda. 2011c. *Leadership and Tradition*. Ahmedabad: Ahmedabad Management Association (AMA).

Swami Bodhananda. 2011d. *Lectures by Swami Bodhananda*. Retrieved January 28, 2018, from Sambodh India, http://sambodh.org/B/lecture.html (accessed on 12 May 2019).

Swami Bodhananda. 2012. *Lectures by Swami Bodhananda*. Retrieved January 28, 2018, from Sambodh Foundation India, http://sambodh.org/B/lecture.html (accessed on 12 May 2019).

Swami Bodhananda. 2013a. *Hindu Dharma*. Kalamazoo: The Sambodh Society, Inc.

Swami Bodhananda. 2013b. *Leadership Excellence and Power of Soft Skills*. Ahmedabad: Ahmedabad Management Association (AMA).

Swami Bodhananda. 2015. *Foundations of Leadership Excellence*. Ahmedabad: Ahmedabad Management Association (AMA).

Swami Bodhananda. 2017. '365 Mystic Meditations', *Ganesam*, www.sambodh.org/B/Ganesam-Sambodh-Bangalore-2017-Souvenir.pdf (accessed on 12 May 2019).

Temple, M. and T.L. Gall. 2016. 'Working through Existential Anxiety toward Authenticity: A Spiritual Journey of Meaning Making', *Journal of Humanistic Psychology*, 58(2): 168–193. doi:10.1177%2F0022167816629968

Weber, M. 1947. *Max Weber: The Theory of Social and Economic Organization.* A.M. Parsons (trans.). New York: The Free Press.

Westley, F. and H. Mintzberg. 1989. 'Visionary Leadership and Stratgeic Management', *Strategic Management Journal*, 10(Special issue): 17–32.

INDEX

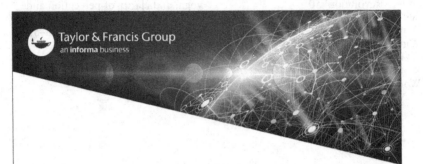

Printed in the United States
by Baker & Taylor Publisher Services